Set Adrift

Set Adrift

Capitalist Transformations and Community Politics along Mumbai's Shore

GAYATRI NAIR

OXFORD
UNIVERSITY PRESS

OXFORD
UNIVERSITY PRESS

Oxford University Press is a department of the University of Oxford.
It furthers the University's objective of excellence in research, scholarship,
and education by publishing worldwide. Oxford is a registered trademark of
Oxford University Press in the UK and in certain other countries.

Published in India by
Oxford University Press
22 Workspace, 2nd Floor, 1/22 Asaf Ali Road, New Delhi 110 002, India

ISBN-13 (print edition): 978-0-19-013024-4
ISBN-10 (print edition): 0-19-013024-5

ISBN-13 (eBook): 978-0-19-099293-4
ISBN-10 (eBook): 0-19-099293-X

Typeset in Scala Pro 10/13
by Tranistics Data Technologies, Kolkata 700 091
Printed in India at Rakmo Press Pvt. Ltd.

For Appuappan and Sharmila

Contents

Acknowledgements

A project that began as a doctoral research, this book has been a work in progress for quite a while; there is much in the way of gratitude and love that I have incurred along the way, which has allowed this book to be realized.

The biggest debt of gratitude I owe is to the fishers of Mumbai, particularly the fisherwomen who, so kindly and graciously, allowed me to peek and step inside their world. The patience and generosity with which they shared their histories, struggles, pain, and victories makes me wish to do justice to them in this work. There are also many fishermen whom I am thankful to, who always took the time and effort to reveal not just the bare bones of their world of work but also the many intricacies of it. For all those who answered the many questions, tolerated my presence, and explained their point of view even in the face of trouble for them—thank you with all my heart. In order to protect their identities, especially in cases where there have been histories of legal trouble, I have used pseudonyms.

As a doctoral student interested in the fisheries, my early visits to Mumbai played a significant role in shaping this research. I am especially grateful to my early meeting with N.D. Koli in 2012—his recollection of the early history of fisher struggles and shared interest on the gender aspect of it has been invaluable. His passing has left a void that will be hard to fill. Before he passed, Mr Koli introduced me to two important interlocutors, Purnima tai and Ujwala tai, who agreed to let me accompany them on the political journey of organizing fisherwomen that they were setting out on. They have both gone above and beyond to provide me an insight into their lives and work.

Without them, this book would not have happened. I am also thankful to the Maharashtra Machimar Kruti Samiti (MMKS) and the National Fishworkers' Forum (NFF) for opening up their political spaces to me. I met Rambhau Patil at one of these meetings and I am immensely thankful to him, not only for taking the time and effort to speak to me on several occasions but also for engaging with the research and easing my entry into many *koliwadas* by pushing the case for why this research was needed. My early entry into the field was made possible not only by these leaders from the NFF and the MMKS but also with help from unexpected quarters. Kailash Tandel familiarized me with the koliwadas and hosted me many times, which helped me get a sense of the life within them. I am also thankful to Shuddawati Peke and Vijayan for being essential to the life of this research.

The wonderful staff at the State Archives, Elphinstone College, Mumbai, helped me navigate the archives. The ready aid and warm friendships forged over chai are something that I will cherish. Thanks are also due to the staff at the International Collective in Support of Fishworkers, Chennai, whose archives I made much use of.

I would also like to thank the many people who were kind enough to comment on and guide this work. Primary among them is my doctoral supervisor Maitrayee Chaudhuri. Thanks are also due to Valerian Rodrigues, Divya Vaid, and late Prof. Dhanagare, who gave valuable insights in the course of this work. This work has benefitted from many workshops and conferences along the way, but most significantly from the Yale Modern South Asia workshop held at Yale University, New Haven, Connecticut, USA, in 2014 and the Association for Indian Labour Historians Conference held at V.V. Giri National Labour Institute, Noida, Uttar Pradesh, India, in 2014. Comments, questions, and insights from Rana Behal and the participants at the Yale workshop have played an important role in shaping this book.

It is hard to accurately describe the gratitude I feel towards my family and friends who have nurtured this project alongside me. First, I would like to thank Rachna and Rajiv Gedam for opening their loving home to me and treating me as one of their own. I am ever grateful to them for their hospitality and kindness, and for providing me with the comfort of a home during the arduous months of fieldwork. My dear friends Raina, Gargi, and Alison have been in the thick of this and have always, with great warmth, shared the experience of this work with all its highs and lows.

The many years that have gone into the making of this book have seen the support and encouragement of many friends. Aardra Surendran has been with me from the very beginning, when we started out in the same cohort, and has read many drafts, given invaluable comments and insights, and been the voice of calm over the years. Conversations with Dipti over the years have shaped this work and have been the source of both intellectual stimulation and emotional nourishment. Gratitude can never be enough for Khaliq Parkar, Divya Kannan, and Suchismita Chattopadhyay for their comments, questions, laughs, and encouragement. Dhiren Bhorisa patiently taught me to work with quantitative data for which I am forever in debt, and Paritosh fielded my many questions on accessing data. Aditya Verma methodically read and copyedited my early drafts, and this work has benefited immensely from his patient endeavours.

I have been fortunate in the last few years to have worked in universities and benefited from the friendships and relations forged there. At the Tata Institute for Social Sciences (TISS), where I was when the process of converting this dissertation to a book began and ended, Amit Upadhayay, Amit Sadhukhan, and Ekta Singh were a team of unparalleled support. Swati Sharma, Nikhil Thorat, Nikhil Narkar, and Ananya Parikh at the Symbiosis School for Liberal Arts, where I was prior to TISS, doused me in cheer and love throughout. Lastly, many thanks to Anindita for a friendship rekindled over the last few years that I will always treasure. Without her, this book would have never taken off. I would like to include a note of thanks to the team at Oxford University Press—Chandrima Chatterjee, Moutushi Mukherjee, Vandana Menon, and Rekha.

The gratitude I owe to my parents Asha and Venu is incalculable. Their support and faith in this work has been unwavering. I am particularly thankful to my mother for taking time out to copyedit the early chapters, when she very well could have spent her retirement years engaged in more enjoyable tasks. I am thankful to my brother Prashant and sister-in-law Gowri for their support and for my niece Swara, whose smile has lit up many a dark day. My parents-in-law Rukmini Menon and Venu Menon have been thoroughly invested in this work and have been its most cheerful supporters.

Finally, to Rahul Menon, who has nurtured and dreamed this work with more love and attention than I have. He has endured long conversations and suffered through editing many drafts. His sharp insights, gentle provocations, and careful edits have informed this work. But most of all, I am thankful for the deep love, kindness, and meaning that he brings to our shared lives.

There are a few people who I wish were alive to see this book come to fruition. My grandparents would have enjoyed this, but my grandfather in particular, who had witnessed a lot of the early period of this work and infected me with his curious spirit, would, I believe, have derived much joy from seeing this. Sharmila Rege, my teacher and mentor, shaped that curiosity, gave it direction, and inspired in me a deep passion for the discipline. Her commitments to rationality and justice, I hope, will always serve as the ethical compass of my life. To them, I dedicate this book.

Abbreviations

BSE	Bombay Stock Exchange
CITU	Centre of Indian Trade Unions
CRZ	Coastal Regulation Zone
FAO	Food and Agriculture Organization
FRA	Forest Rights Act, 2006
ICSF	International Collective in Support of Fishworkers
MMKS	Maharashtra Machhimar Kruti Samiti
MMMS	Maharashtra Machimaar Masivikreta Sangh
NCDC	National Cooperative Development Corporation
NFF	National Fishworkers' Forum
NSSO	National Sample Survey Office
PPP	public–private partnership
PTI	Press Trust of India

Introduction

The landlocked city of Delhi is not a likely place to find a collective of fishers—yet this is precisely where the year-long local meetings and agitations of fishers from the coastal states of India eventually coalesce. In the first week of March 2013 (and in the years following) at Jantar Mantar, the official protest site in New Delhi, the National Fishworkers' Forum (NFF), an umbrella body comprised of fisher organizations of coastal states, were agitating. The protest sought to draw the union government's attention towards the state of India's seas and the people who depend on them. Among the demands raised was the issue of securing exclusive rights of fishing for traditional fishing communities, most of whom are classified as backward classes.

This book explores and analyses the ways in which this demand has shaped strategies for organizing the fisher community of Kolis in Mumbai. Through a focus on the demand for exclusive fishing rights, this book will elaborate upon the complex relations that have emerged around the presence of a common property (the seas) in the city of Mumbai and the caste community of Kolis, whose livelihood of fishing is dependent on the seas. The changes introduced by a transition to capitalist production in the fisheries forms the backdrop of this exploration. In other words, this book looks at the complex history that ties together large narratives of capitalism and the city, with smaller ones of a fisherwoman struggling to survive in fishing and a fisherman increasingly distancing himself from it. In thinking about capital and the city, this work foregrounds the existence of livelihoods that draw from the commons[1] in a city that, in popular imagination, remains linked primarily to finance. In doing so, it seeks to highlight how such livelihoods are integral parts of global production networks, as well as how a process of capital accumulation is transforming the nature of work and social relations in fishing communities. The outcomes of such a scenario are text-book-like when examined at a macro level—accumulation dispossessing individuals in small-scale and artisanal fishing, the creation of labour reserves through such dispossession, and the emergence of a distinct capitalist and labouring class with the employment of technology that has dramatically altered the nature of skills required of labour. But the macro perspective alone can flatten the nuances that inform everyday social and political practices. With a closer eye on the local, the ramifications of these changes on emerging political formations in the fisheries become more apparent. Aside from national organizations, such as the NFF, that work to safeguard the interests of small-scale fishers, unions and cooperatives backed by local parties too have been a feature of the fisheries. With early interventions by the Shiv Sena, many of these organizations have come to acquire a strong local flavour in addition to their larger challenge to global capitalism. But in order to consider livelihoods and the right to work, it is important to explore who the key figures in this charged context are.

The Kolis, around whose political discourse this work is built, are an integral part of the history of Mumbai. Regarded as being among the earliest inhabitants (Census of India 1901; GoI 1909) of the seven islands that make up Mumbai, they have been identified as traditional fish workers, even as other Koli castes were agriculturalists. The caste of fishers, the Son Koli—officially classified as a backward caste—continues to live in the city, often in settlements referred to

---

[1] Commons or common property resources lie outside the capitalist norm of private ownership. These are natural resources, such as forests, seas, and so on, that are used in common by members of a community or across communities for livelihood and other purposes.

as *koliwadas* and most of them continue to engage in fishing or ancillary activities as occupations. There is, however, a transition at work, and while this is in part because of the shift towards capitalist production in fishing, much of it can also be traced to the urban growth that Mumbai has witnessed, which has exerted pressures on a community that has been relegated to the margins of social and economic development.

Mumbai—Bombay as it was known earlier—emerged as a city under the auspices of colonial rule turning what were once quiet islands into a major port city. The city soon came to be a site of manufacturing with textile mills dotting the city landscape. It has since transitioned into the finance capital of India with the BSE (formerly known as the Bombay Stock Exchange) being the largest stock exchange in the country. The accumulation of capital has underscored the rise and growth of Mumbai.

This has translated into wide-scale changes for the city dwellers, Kolis included. The concentration of capital in Mumbai has meant that urban development is a dominant part of the discourse of the city. Land has come to be a scarce and valuable commodity contributing to a speculative real estate market that has developed around it. The impact of this is unsurprisingly borne by the working classes, whose occupation of land is viewed through prisms of legality and concerns of sanitation and pressures on urban infrastructure (Bhowmik 2010). The weak control these classes have over the land they live on proves to be useful in evicting them over claims of rehabilitation, thus providing a potential space for capital to be invested in, always a profitable venture in Mumbai. The Kolis, who occupy what is an extremely valuable asset in the land-starved city—the coasts—are especially susceptible to moves to wrest control of land away from them. The most glaring instance of this concerned the Sion Koliwada, which, having been categorized as a slum, was earmarked for redevelopment. Protesting Kolis were told they would be rehabilitated, but such moves did little to take into consideration how the use of coastal land was integrally tied to the livelihood practices of Kolis. Other pressures such as a high cost of living in the city, where rents and prices of goods and services are high, weigh heavy on the inhabitants of the city. Processes such as these have contributed to a mounting pressure on many Kolis in Mumbai.

Additionally, the advent of capitalist production in fishing has made small-scale and artisanal fishing increasingly unviable, not only due to increasing scales of production but also owing to the technology employed, which plays a critical role in determining access to the marine resources. This capital-intensive technology introduced by the state has led to increased production in the fisheries (catering primarily to an export market), generating profit for private investors and a revenue stream for the state. This has changed the pattern of usage of the commons. While fishing was earlier practiced almost exclusively by the Kolis in Mumbai, it has now expanded from a caste-based livelihood practice to a profitable venture, drawing investors from outside the community. This has taken place at the cost of a gradual displacement of the artisanal and small-scale fishing sector that finds it difficult to sustain itself in a market now accustomed to a changed scale of production. But in the emerging contestation that takes place, the Kolis, who feel dispossessed of their rights over their livelihood, close their ranks and identify 'outsiders' as trawler owners from other castes, as well as migrant labourers as one of the sources of their troubles. Migrant workers, who are economically and politically much weaker than the Kolis, are thus rendered especially vulnerable. Unable to exercise claims over the city or the livelihood as the Kolis do, they remain marginalized even as their labour is critical to the fisheries. Migrants, often themselves dispossessed through processes of accumulation, are thus considered as threats and not allies in the larger struggle against capitalist development.

The focus on the demand by the NFF for exclusive access to fishing is based on the changes in the nature of production and the social relations that inform production. The NFF argues that access to fishing and the seas is increasingly mediated by capital-intensive technology, which lies in the hands of an elite class that is not traditionally fishing oriented. Therefore, fishing is no longer seen as a livelihood with close links to a sensitive ecosystem but rather as an avenue of profit generation. Access, thus, becomes the foundation on which the critique of capitalist production for the NFF rests.

But in the context of Mumbai seeking to re-establish fishing as a livelihood and not an industry, it has meant limiting who can work rather than how work is done. Even as the Kolis are increasingly being dispossessed, it raises questions of how we understand dispossession. Dispossession with regard to the commons is usually understood as an event or process that causes those with previous rights over the commons to lose them. This could be the case when the commons are opened for privatization or where access is opened through use of capital-intensive technology or even where the state does not permit any use of the commons—usually associated with calls for conservation. In the case of fisheries in India, access to the commons was restricted to caste groups that possessed the customary knowledge of fishing. But should fishing remain a caste-based occupation? And are migrants, who come from the agrarian interiors or the coasts seeking work in the informal economy of the fisheries, not part of the dispossessed too?

In light of what has been discussed earlier, this book focuses on the traditional Koli fishing community in Mumbai to understand how claims to commons and labour organization unfold. This has been done with two aims: first, because Mumbai is a site where fisherwomen have been at the fore to demand a recognition of their traditional rights to fishing; and second, because the urban commons in Mumbai and in particular, Mumbai's fisheries, have received scant academic attention. This book situates the occupation of fishing as caught in the throes of global capital as well as its more local iterations seen through city-based politics. Local fisher organizations in alliance with the NFF are seeking to challenge the path of capitalist development but, brewed in a climate of nativist politics that has dominated Mumbai for the last five decades, this takes place through localized concerns such as questioning the role of migrant workers in the fisheries and the city. It is this complex interaction between the city, the commons, and the community that is mapped through a focus on the demand of traditional fisher communities being granted an exclusive right to fishing. A multi-sited ethnography, interviews, and a survey were conducted as part of the research for this work. Fishworkers (both men and women), trawler owners, labourers on boats, and most significantly activists of the Maharashtra Machhimar Kruti Samiti (MKKS; the local affiliate of the NFF) and the NFF have all contributed towards making sense of the national and local iterations of demands. I owe a debt to the works of Harvey (2003, 2010) and Bonacich (1972) in framing questions of dispossession that have been central to understanding the context in Mumbai. The central argument of the book is that a blunting of the class question within the movement has led to a dissonance between the NFF's demand and its local interpretation, and that community identity must be understood as historically constructed and anchored in a political economy. In other words, struggles against capitalism and those rooted in ecological concerns operate on multiple registers—both the immediacy of the local context and a larger regional/national/global context. The ability of movements to be able to build broader solidarities often rests on its ability to navigate these multiple registers.

Conceptual Keys of the Argument

Three keys emerge as significant for understanding the nature of change that has taken place in the fisheries in Mumbai. These are the community, the commons, and the city, each of which impinge on the other, leading to a complex web of interactions between them. The first three chapters will focus on each of these elements separately, and, through a political economy framework, highlight how urbanity exerts a pressure on the community owing to processes of development as well as capital accumulation in the fisheries itself. A consideration of such claims, deconstructing the terms of community and identity, and evoking history, demands a study of the political economy. In a variation from studies in political ecology that explore cultural identities and community representation as significant in struggles around livelihood deprivation, this work begins by exploring the grounds of identity formation itself (Baviskar 2008: 6–7). This work will seek to complicate the 'Koli' and migrant identity, where both have emerged through a social and political process that has defined Mumbai and left an indelible mark, especially on the Kolis for whom their links to the city of Mumbai are of political and social import.

The City and the Community in Sociology

Each of these elements has been the subject of academic attention, particularly in sociology. The city and especially the community have often been considered together, with the urban often defined in consonance with a particular kind of culture it embodied, and the community with the space it inhabits.

Much work has sought to relate the two because of a belief that the nature of the community changed with the emergence of cities. Within sociology, the term 'community' has acquired a distinct sense. It has commonly been associated with a small group of people who exhibit among them dense social relations. It was precisely this meaning that was understood as changing in the context of industrialization and the emergence of cities as spaces that brought together a large number of people at the same place for the first time. These cities were marked by the anonymity they offered to individuals (Wirth 1938), which was considered unlikely in pre-industrial social formations. Modernity is an important paradigm that emerges in this relation between communities and cities, as a process linked to the emergence of industrialism and capitalism. Since the rise of cities was seen as tied to capitalism and the generation of surplus production, cities were seen as emblematic of modernity. It was owing to this that cities as modern spaces were treated as sites which emphasized the retreat of the community and the ascendance of the individual, and thus engendered a transition from communities to voluntary associations.

This argument underscored the work of prominent sociologist Ferdinand Tönnies who claimed that social groups move from what he termed as *Gemeinschaft* (community) to *Gesellschaft* (society). Tönnies asserted that cities bring together a large number of people, and consequently interaction and social relations between these individuals emerge not from familial or social compulsions but are born of perhaps more utilitarian motives. However, the presence of a large number of caste and regional associations that play important roles in educational and cultural spheres of their urban members, along with caste and linguistic segregation, demonstrates that familial and communal motives can thrive in urban spaces (Vidyathil and Singh 2012).

However, what is important to note is that the notion of the community is not a simplistic one. It is an identity that evolves in a complex manner. Not all communities have an immediate common cultural resource of language, ethnicity, or region, which helps define themselves. Often, constructions of a community take place over a period of time and draw from history and/or myths. They do so while rooted in a particular social and political context. It is precisely this process of giving shape to the community identity that is highlighted here. The emotive and political strength that the Kolis gain by describing themselves as the original inhabitants of Mumbai is of immense value in a political culture that celebrates, even valourizes, nativism.

A tendency to valorize communities is particularly prevalent in studies that explore communities and their use of resources. Baviskar (2008: 5) cautions against this, asserting how such a position is one that is marked by the categories of 'virtuous peasants' versus 'vicious state' or by an assumption of identities assumed by communities. Kumar and Vasan (1997) also argue against the adoption of such a position, which according to them results in external actors—such as the state or the entry of capital—being considered responsible for corrupting the virtuous community. They add that doing so blinds one to the presence of hierarchies and differences within communities which always play a role in how resources come to be used. A shift away from this has characterized the works of Jean-Phillipe Platteau (2008), Tania Murray Li (2008), Agrawal and Sivaramakrishnan (2000), Brara (2006), Cederlof and Sivaramakrishnan (2006), Jeffery and Sundar (1999), and Sivaramakrishnan (1999), who have unpacked both the notion of the community and its interest and links to resource use.

The City Space

Cities, as an embodiment of modernity, enjoyed considerable attention within sociology. In spite of this, scholars such as Castells (cited in Susser 2002) argue that there remains considerable confusion regarding what the urban constitutes. Instead of a clear definition, Castells points out that the 'urban' is often defined in opposition to the rural, in demographic terms or as representative of a particular culture. The absence of clarity on what the urban means has lent itself to hazy and incorrect theorization, a subject that is taken up for detailed discussion in Chapter 1.

It was under the aegis of the Chicago School that a theory of the city and its ecology (Burgess 1925) and urbanism as a process (Wirth 1938) were conceived. The city as a theme emerged in the works of several thinkers including Weber (1958) and Marx who analysed the difference between the country and the town. Urban sociology has developed as a significant field of study and has been recognized not only as a theorization of a space but also of the social relations that constitute it. Following from these, this research will draw on the work of David Harvey (1985), whose theoretical contribution has been on the production of urban space under capitalism. Drawing on Marx's notion of accumulation, Harvey conceptualizes the city as a site that enables circuits of accumulation. Critical to this is his intervention on modes of accumulation, otherwise identified as 'primitive accumulation' and restricted to an early stage of the development of capitalism. Harvey (2003), who categorizes such a form of accumulation as emerging from a problem of surplus production and not under-consumption as Luxemburg (1913b) did, identified it primarily as a process of dispossession through which common resources, public services, and older modes of production can be opened to allow for the profitable investment of capital. The process that Harvey (2003) terms as 'accumulation by dispossession' is a useful framework through which the changes introduced in the fisheries can be examined. As the subsequent chapters will demonstrate, this process is responsible for the diminishing size of the small-scale and artisanal fishing sector, and has also allowed for the creation of labour reserves, evident not only through the large numbers of migrant workers (from agrarian economies) entering cities to seek work but also through the number of Kolis—men and women—who are forsaking fishing to seek wage labour elsewhere. A focus on the process of accumulation by dispossession engenders not only an analysis on the specific outcome for the fisheries in Mumbai, but also focuses attention on a macro analysis of the development of capitalism.

The process of uneven development that has become characteristic of capitalism is critical to processes of accumulation. The use of migrant labour—a prominent feature in cities, as Castells (cited in Susser 2002) points out—is of particular significance to this work. Migrant labour's entry into the fisheries produces a work force that comes to be divided on the lines of ethnicity, the repercussions of which can be seen in the political mobilization of Kolis. An ethnically divided labour force and its impact on the labour market has been analysed previously by sociologist Edna Bonacich. In her insightful work addressing the split labour market theory Bonacich (1972), explores the racial divide in the American labour force between whites and blacks from the antebellum period, examining the reasons for the conflict to emerge around questions of ethnicity.

She argues that what appears as a conflict centered on race is in fact a product of both racism as well as class inequities and is driven by capitalism's need for a cheap and docile workforce. Pointing to the particular social and economic conditions that gave rise to this ethnic antagonism, she details how economic conditions at a site can not only spur migration but may also contribute to depressing wages at the migrant's destination, leading to hostility towards them. The split labour market theory is particularly useful in understanding the situation in the fisheries in Mumbai today, especially so in identifying the causes of why migrant entry in one sector of the fisheries alone has shaped into ethnic antagonism in Mumbai, as discussed in Chapters 2–4 of this work.

Urban Commons

The commons is now a subject of study that is firmly embedded at the heart of several disciplines. Within academia, a debate on the commons has usually revolved around issues of governance and/or management of the commons. Over the years this academic debate has grown more vociferous with an extremity of positions gaining significant weight.

On one end of the spectrum lies Hardin's well-known position advocating for privatization or state control of the commons discussed in his popular paper 'Tragedy of the Commons' (Hardin 1968).[2] On the other end, Elinor Ostrom's (1990) widely accepted position has been one which highlights the role of communities in developing a variety of strategies for a sustainable use of the commons. This is not to say that these two positions exhaust our possibilities on the commons. The book's aim is to look at a materialist methodology rooted in empirical research in order to understand the contestation around commons by examining earlier regimes of use and older state interventions in these regimes, and particularly focuses on social relations among the Kolis and their ties to the city of Mumbai. A crucial part of this work, thus, is to understand the particular ramifications that are brought into effect with the presence of the coastal commons within the city, here Mumbai.

[2] Hardin's argument relies on the belief that rational individuals always act out of self-interest and this results in the over-exploitation of the commons.

In an important intervention, Parthasarathy (2011) draws attention to the myriad forms of labour that inform Mumbai's economy, including livelihood practices that are built on common resources as well as those based on foraging and collecting. Much of the work done on the commons, such as forests and common village land or even fisheries, conjures an image of it as lying away both spatially and materially from the arrangements of capital. In other words, the natural home of such resources is seen to be the city but pristine nature where communities develop close ties of relation and dependency on these resources. While much of this is true, it is even more important in the context to then look at what happens to the commons that lie within our cities. As Parthasarathy (2011) points out, especially in the case of urban commons, there is a tendency to see such livelihoods as unrelated to networks of capitalism, which is often not the case.

It is, therefore, crucial that a study of the coastal commons also incorporates a political economy framework to analyse the city in order to understand the impact it may have on the commons. Easier access to new technology and credit present in urban areas leads to the ability to engage in larger scales of production: a process that is likely to proceed at a faster pace in cities compared to other locales.

The State and Communities

Hardin's article, 'Tragedy of the Commons', fits into the dominant capitalist paradigm and the methodology of mainstream economics to demonstrate that rational individuals would always act out of self-interest, thus endangering the commons (Hardin 1968). Contrary views on the subject usually call for community management of resources (such as Ostrom 1990), but hierarchies within and between communities that make use of common resources persist. The state is an important figure in this debate, called on either to seize control of a resource and open it for investment or protection, or to demarcate it as being under the direct governance of the community in question. What is significant is that movements around commons now address their concerns to the state and seek legal resolutions for the conflicts they find themselves in. This is unlike earlier social movements which came to be defined by viewing the state as complicit in their problems, and therefore sought to transform the nature of the state (Hensman 1994). More recent ecological movements, however, do not follow a similar path, adopting a discourse of ecology and conservation over one of class, these 'new social movements' engage with the state differently. With increasing collusion between state and private corporations over resource extraction, questions on the nature of the state become pertinent. The state has played a prominent role in the history of the fisheries. Schemes (such as diesel subsidies) and loans for investing in technologies (such as trawlers) and equipment (such as outboard motors) have resulted in a conscious promotion of a particular model of development. Diesel, for instance (subsidies for which are a sensitive issue with fishing cooperatives), is used in trawlers and mechanized boats, while smaller crafts use of kerosene. Older activists[3] in Mumbai recollected that it was only following agitations on the issue that the government introduced a subsidy in kerosene as well to benefit artisanal fishers. This was indicative, they argued, of the kind of production system the state sought to support.

Outside of organizations such as the MMKS, which work towards mobilization of fishworkers, interactions between the state and Kolis is defined primarily by networks of patronage and influence. Cooperatives that have been the most important institutional bodies in the politics of fishers in Mumbai view themselves largely as a medium between the state and individual fishers. Its members, dominated by men and primarily those who own capital-intensive technology such as trawlers and purse-seine nets, also tend to be members of various political parties. Chapter 2 details this history of state intervention in the fisheries, mapping the transition from the colonial state to the Indian state.

Fishing Communities

In light of the aforementioned details, it is especially relevant to consider the history of the fisheries and fishing communities. The discourse falls into two broad categories: environmental degradation and a changing scale of production introduced through new technology. Both these areas are not exclusive of each other—a change in the

---

[3] Conversations with Rambhau Patil and N.D. Koli, both of whom were activists alongside Bhai Bhandarkar who formed the MMKS.

scale of fisheries along with the use of new technology has contributed to overfishing. Consequently, today, the discourse on fisheries pivots on schemes of regulation, zoning, and management. Work of this kind in India has been largely examined in the case of Kerala (Kurien 1985; Kurien and Achari 1990; Kurien and Vijayan 1998), which witnessed large scale changes with the discovery of a large market for the export of fish, particularly prawns. The period of the Pink Revolution—as Kurien terms it—led to increased state support for mechanization and the introduction of technology such as trawlers. The use of such technology led to problems of overfishing, measured in both economic and biological terms,[4] according to him. The impact of overfishing has been particularly severe on small-scale fishers who find the seas barren in the waters where trawlers and purse-seine nets operate, and whose own nets are often damaged by larger crafts.

While these questions remained crucial, there was little by way of sociological insight over the changes that had occurred. Subramanian (2009), in a seminal work on the Mukkuvar fishing community and their political struggles, locates questions of technology, ecological sustainability, as well as changing scales of production in a social universe, examining the historical background and the social and political consequence of each of these for the Mukkuvars. The Mukkuvars, much like the Kolis, are a caste whose traditional occupation was that of fishing. In rich historical detail, Subramanian (2009) draws on the early colonial interventions that began introducing institutions (cooperatives) and technology to the fishing communities in the hope of improving on the 'primitive' methods they otherwise employed.

4

'Economic overfishing occurs when marginal costs of an additional unit of fishing effort are higher than the marginal revenues. The economy experiences loss (even though total fish catch may increase) because of a misallocation of capital and labour which might have produced higher economic yields in alternative activities. Biological over-fishing occurs when the marginal yield of an additional unit of fishing effort is negative. At such a level of effort the fish population stock is prevented from generating its maximum sustainable yield.' (Kurien and Achari 1990: 2011)

Through her work, Subramanian (2009) seeks to highlight the Mukkuvar's political actions as being distinctly modern and demands a rethink on how struggles around livelihood questions have hitherto been framed.

Books by Subramanian (2009) and Ram (1991) are instances of exceptional academic work on resource-based livelihoods and labour practices which moves beyond what have become typical questions of the field—access and use of commons (Parthasarathy 2011: 55). The keen attention paid to the questions of class and gender, which in the case of Ram's work are examined in the context of capitalist transformation in the fisheries, is particularly relevant at a time when local agitations have now coalesced into a nation-wide struggle by fishers for their rights over their livelihood practice.

Both Ram's and Subramanian's works are based on the Mukkuvar community in Tamil Nadu; Kerala in contrast has the site of many studies on the fisheries including the work of Korakandy (1984), Iyengar (1985), Kumar (1988), Kurien and Achari (1990), Kurien and Vijayan (1998), and Kurien (2008). Maharashtra in this regard has received surprisingly scant attention, Vijaya Punekar's (1959) work on the Son Kolis being the only ethnographic work of the community. The monograph is a thick descriptive account of Koli life with valuable quantitative data on the social indicators of the community, particularly in the field of education. Punekar's ethnography paints a vivid picture of community life but also leaves several important questions undeveloped. Central to these are the beginnings of the state programme of introducing mechanization to expand production, substantive questions of gender and caste, and the role of a rapidly urbanizing space on the livelihood and politics of the community.

This book seeks to bridge the lacunae that emerge in Punekar's (1959) work and incorporate the insights of Ram's (1991) and Subramanian's (2009) works to unpack the impact of the capitalist transition on the Kolis' claim to the commons. It is through a focus on labour, a site at which caste, class, and gender intersect, that the analyses in Chapters 2–4 proceed to understand the contestations that arise as a result of the process of accumulation.

Mumbai is a particularly useful site to study these connections between the local and the global. The research was based on the site of a Koli settlement in southern Mumbai, which I will call Sagar Park (pseudonym). The other koliwada site included is located in a western suburb which I will call Sagar Nagar. Many other locations in the city were also covered through interactions with the NFF and the MMKS activists who organized meetings in various koliwadas.

The koliwada at Sagar Park is markedly different from the area that envelops it. The settlement that lies on the shore is separated only by a narrow street from the up-market residences that dominate the rest of the area, demonstrating at once the urban spatial dynamic of Mumbai. The koliwada marks a departure from its neighbouring area, not merely in style and aesthetics borne of sharp socio-economic differences but also because it marks a distinct lifeworld. Narrow lanes run through the settlement and bring one to the sea front. Houses are cramped together, much like in the rest of the city, with lanes lying parallel to one another. A row of homes at the very end of the settlement, lying perpendicular to the lanes, lies right along the shore, with the walls of many such homes being lashed by sea waves. The area in the front is a small playing yard for children where nets dry alongside, followed by a narrow corridor lying perpendicular to the lanes which houses a daily market. To one side of the settlement lie the offices of the cooperative, a shed where net repairs are undertaken, and the beach where boats are anchored.

This part of the beach, thronged by workers, and the nearby sheds, where boat owners congregate, were similar to another important site of study in koliwada at Sagar Nagar. In addition, the drying yard where Koli women would dry fish and purchase the day's catch came to be an important site. Since women's work in the fisheries takes place primarily in the markets, the Shakti Mandi (pseudonym) market in South Mumbai was another site of study. Another reason behind choosing this market was that it had the presence of a market association that had been tied to the first women's trade union and was also involved in establishing the new women's union. Additionally, it was one of the markets that was earmarked for redevelopment and which had faced the license issue that defined Koli women's early political ventures.

I entered the field through networks of NFF activists in Delhi, who helped me identify and connect with other NFF activists in Mumbai. During an early conversation with a veteran fisher leader, N.D. Koli, the question of fisherwomen's political participation emerged. As he introduced me to two prominent women activists of the NFF, the fisherwomen and their political concerns sharpened in focus. As a female researcher, gaining access to spaces identified as sites of women's work was easy. But to understand the nature of contestations in the fisheries, it was not enough to restrict conversations to fisherwomen alone. Entry into 'male spaces' was not always easy. Most significant among this was the critical space in production—the boats. Social norms that consider fishing as an activity carried out by men, and the inability to form a rapport with workers on boats (reasons for which are elaborated later in the chapter), prevented me from going on a fishing trip to observe the manner in which work proceeds. My gender identity, which had until now granted me relatively easy access into the homes of residents of the Sagar Park koliwada, the fish markets, and drying yards, now proved to be a major impediment. A major part of this problem surfaced when it came to conversing with migrant labourers. As will be elaborated in Chapter 3, most male migrant labourers who worked on the boats in the Sagar Nagar koliwada, as is usually the case, did not have a dwelling. During the fishing season, they live on the boats—going out to sea in the evenings and returning in the day with the catch. On trawlers, they stay out at sea for ten to twelve days, returning for a short time in which the catch is unloaded and taken for auction, only to set out again. This short period spent on land is used for resting and doing odd jobs along the beach front, also occupied by owners of boats. Due to this, the limited time spent with migrant labourers was spent on the beach front as they worked, in spite of the less than adequate environment it presented. However, even these conversations took place with great difficulty. The nature of the workday made it difficult to contact migrant workers, except through their employers. Resultantly, I was often left at the mercy of the owners who were reluctant for this conversation to take place in their absence. Many would therefore invite me to speak to them as they would be sitting alongside the workers or would give me a time when the boat would return only to point out when I landed that the workers had been sent away for some other work. It was after much difficulty that snatches of conversations and interviews were conducted with the workers alone, as they worked on the nets on the jetty and away from their employers.

Similarly, I could not establish contact with male migrant fish vendors who conducted fish vending. Since their mode of operation also involved moving from one area to another in the city, it was hard to establish contact. This work, therefore, suffers from the absence of voices of those who have come to be vilified by and shaped the position taken on rights over the livelihood practice by Koli women. What has been foregrounded instead are perceptions of Koli women which shaped their political interventions. Chapter 5 examines the effect of these perceptions on organizations ranging from local village cooperatives, to the MMKS and the female fishworkers organization that was being established, and how it shapes their demand for exclusive access.

Chapter 6 will examine the process of accumulation in the context of the fisheries in Mumbai. The question of dispossession is set in the context of a city rife with nativist politics, labour that is divided both in terms of hierarchies of class and ethnicity and caste, and the conflicts that emerge from this. This work will examine who, in such a scenario, can be said to be dispossessed and what are the implications of the adoption of a discourse on ecology and a disavowal of class by organizations, such as the NFF and the MMKS, and the Kolis. The impact of this on the form and content of the fisher organizations' struggles as well as what this has meant for addressing ecological sustainability in a fragmented social and political context is explored. This book argues that capital draws on differences and hierarchies within the labouring class in order to aid the process of accumulation. Finally, the book considers the alternatives that lie ahead for the movement on questions of technology, livelihood, and sustainability.

1

Capital and the City

The city has long been an enigmatic presence, even within the social sciences. As we continue to debate its exact definition and meaning, we note a distinctiveness in its spatial forms, culture, and the social relations that embody it. But what the 'urban' is demands closer attention, not just to clarify earlier theoretical assumptions but in particular for the role it plays in our understanding of contemporary political economy.

The expansion of urbanization under capitalism has been well documented alongside the implications of accumulation-fuelled urban growth and its impact on poorer residents of a city. But this has been typically understood in the form of economic outcomes—a shift from manufacturing to service economies, unaffordable housing, rising informalization, and so on. While these remain significant to our understanding of both capitalism and urbanization, the nature of the relationship between the two in times of advanced capitalism requires further consideration. What does the economy of cities really look like—does it entail agriculture, foraging, and hunting/fishing (Parthasarathy 2011)? Is the city merely a space within which political economy unfolds or is there an interaction between the space, culture, history, and ecology of the city and its political economy? These are some of the questions this chapter seeks to explore.

A History of Urban Studies

As noted earlier, early sociologists such as Marx, Weber, Durkheim, and Simmel considered the city in terms of the social processes it embodied. Much of the early work in this regard coalesced around the idea that the spatial organization of population based on its size and density constituted the process of urbanization, and these remain the most definitive markers of what constitutes the urban globally. Manuel Castells (cited in Susser 2002) claimed these were fallacious criteria. He argued that there can be no clear demarcations regarding what the size and density must be in order to constitute the urban, with it ultimately being arbitrarily fixed—it may ease administrative functioning but is not a useful theoretical indicator. Another fundamental way of establishing what constitutes the urban has been by establishing its difference from other social formations, most typically the rural. This is strongly exemplified in the Indian state's definition of the term 'urban' as that which involves over 75 per cent of the male population in non-farm activities, thereby associating agriculture with the rural and marking it in opposition to the urban. This economic criterion too has come under criticism as it does not sufficiently allow us to capture the extent of urbanization in India and, for no strong reason, uses agriculture as the dividing line between the urban and the rural and relies on a patriarchal understanding of work for the same.[1] This does not suggest that there is no difference between the urban and the rural; rather it is their entanglement instead of their opposition, within larger economic and social processes, that seems significant.

Chandavarkar (2009) argues that the early works by Marx, Weber, and Durkheim did not engage with the city as the subject of sociological understanding, but rather with capitalism and industrialization. The city provided the inroad to understanding these larger processes. Attempts, thus, to develop theories on the city as a socio-economic entity of its own have met with failure. In the course of this, however, a larger number of concepts and typologies have been developed. The Chicago School made substantial efforts to document and understand the city on its own terms through its urban ecology, although

---

[1] As Denis et al. (2012) note, very few countries across the world even use these criteria.

that came to be critiqued precisely for delinking the city with the economic and social processes that constituted it. Urban ecological studies remain dominant, however, leading to a profusion of urban typologies. For urban scholars across disciplines, a precise definition of what the urban entails has led to two strands of thinking that gained popularity. The first, as Chandavarkar (2009: 210) points out, is the association of urbanization with 'an index of economic development and social change'. The second is the association of the urban with cultural forms or, as Chandavarkar (2009: 210) claims, 'a state of mind'.

The association of urbanization with development is one which Castells (cited in Susser 2002: 31) believed required further clarification. Development, he argues, is associated with technological and economic advancement, as well as larger qualitative processes involving the transformation of the social structure. This association of urbanization with development produces an 'ideological function', one which makes it appear as though the transition towards urbanization is an inevitable process born of the technological and material development of society.

Cultural associations of modernity with the city emerged, as Chandavarkar (2009) and Castells (cited in Susser 2002) argue, because of the natural relation assumed between the ecological space of the city and social relations within it. But this interrelation was viewed as a myth by Castells (cited in Susser 2002). Its propagation came through the German sociological school with its evolutionist-functional thinking, characterizing the work of Tönnies, Spengler and Simmel. Instead Castells (cited in Susser 2002: 35) argued that the:

> theoretical model of 'urban society' was worked out, above all, in opposition to 'rural society' by analysing the passage of the second to the first, in terms used by Tönnies, as the evolution of a community form to an associative form, characterized above all by a segmentation of roles, a multiplicity of loyalties and a primacy of secondary social relations (through specific associations) over primary social relations (direct personal contact based on affective affinity).

Scholars such as Spengler (1928) built on the idea that urban culture was linked to the city and, in turn, associated urban culture with westernization, which, as Castells (cited in Susser 2002: 36) points out, was true only for some parts of the world. The problem remained that instead of a working definition, what emerged were a series of associations. Urbanization, thus, stood in for urban culture and was seen as synonymous with industrialization, which in turn was seen as identical to modernity.

This manner of theorizing on the urban was given further impetus by the Chicago School. Under the tutelage of Robert Park, the Chicago School was at the forefront of investigating 'new forms of social life' in the city (cited in Susser 2002: 36). Due attention was given to the subject of urbanization by Louis Wirth from the Chicago School. Wirth, in Castells's opinion (cited in Susser 2002: 37), does not merely link the city with an urban culture, but analyses the link to elaborate on specific conditions in the city that give rise to this urban culture. However, later scholars drawing on Wirth often fell into the trap of advocating an evolutionist cultural approach to the study of the city (Castells, cited in Susser 2002: 37).

In South Asia too, theorization around the urban followed similar problems of an evolutionist approach and the association of the form (city) with content (urban/modern culture). In the focus on the form of the city, work revolved around whether the colonial state aided or inhibited the process of urbanization and, by extension, modernization in India. Concern with urban culture is demonstrated in work that draws attention to the uniqueness and specificity of Indian towns. As a part of this, cities and towns were categorized according to 'cultural models'—Hindu, Islamic, and 'Colonial',[2] for instance—and were marked as being distinct from towns and cities of the 'West', thus attributing to Indian urbanization a completely different path from that of the 'West' (Chandavarkar 2009: 213). Chandavarkar (2009) contends that because the conceptual apparatus employed in

---

[2] Chandavarkar (2009: 218) criticized the conceptual weakness present in several urban studies as adding to this problem of mischaracterization of urbanization in India. He argued that often, cities are categorized on the basis of their morphology which is usually understood through the world view of the town. This is similar to the notion that cities give rise to an urban culture. In this case, almost anything could be enveloped by the notion of 'world view'. This typology is based on the flawed periodization of South Asian history.

such studies was derived from the western European experience, it impeded the understanding of the South Asian cities, and their context has remained underdeveloped in such studies.

For Lefebvre (2003), Castells (cited in Susser 2002), and Harvey (1985, 2008), the ability to unearth relations between space and society requires a consideration of the link between the social production of space and the structural transformations in society. In other words, they advocate the use of a materialist approach to urban spaces. In a similar voice, Chandavarkar (2009) argues that it is important to not study cities as generic social entities. He points out that it is imperative to study a city by locating it firmly within a larger framework that does not abstract the city out of the social and political relations at work within society. It is the exclusive focus on social forms alone without investigating the underlying social processes or meanings that leads to confusing conclusions being drawn regarding change and continuity and binaries being constructed between social forms. According to Chandavarkar (2009: 219), if change and continuity are to be actually understood, it is critical to recognize the city as a 'relational category' that is 'constituted by and dependent upon its wider political economy'. Similarly, Castells (cited in Susser 2002: 23) defines the city as follows:

> The cities were the residential form adopted by those members of society whose direct presence at the places of agricultural production was not necessary. That is to say, these cities could exist only on the basis of the surplus produced by working the land. They were religious, administrative and political centres, the spatial expression of a social complexity determined by the process of appropriation and reinvestment of the product of labour. It is thus, then, a new social system but one that is not separate from the rural one, nor posterior to it, for they are both closely linked at the heart of the same process of production of social forms, even if, from the point of view of these forms themselves, we are presented with two different situations.

In keeping with this methodological consideration, this book adopts a political economy approach to understanding the urban. The city features in this work not merely as the backdrop where struggles for rights over commons emerge, but also as a social formation that shapes such conflicts, as it is constituted and representative of wider social, economic, and political processes. The city is also not analysed merely as an abstraction, the site through which capital accumulation flows and expands. Instead, the particular history of Mumbai and its role in shaping accumulation and the nature of social relations among various groups is seen as vital for understanding the relation between local and migrant workers and the relevance of claims of indigeneity. As both Chandavarkar (2009) and Castells (cited in Susser 2002) point out, the link between changes in the social structure and transformations in social relations is central to understanding the role of the city.

The urban commons here provide us a distinct opportunity to understand resource-dependent livelihoods in the city, their links to global capitalism, as well as the ecological, social, and economic conditions within which commons come to be used. In this context, looking at commons in the urban allows us to understand the larger processes of accumulation, migration, as well as demands for 'ownership' of the commons.

The Urban Process under Capitalism

In light of the work previously discussed, it is critical to understand the urban, not merely in terms of its morphology/form or its culture/ ecology but also in relation to its inextricable links with the larger political economy. In order to do so, it is critical to locate the importance of space in the development of capitalism. This in turn helps us understand why the process of urbanization finds an impetus under capitalism. In a vein very similar to Castells (cited in Susser 2002), David Harvey (1985) argues that the contribution of accumulation to the urban process is that the generation of surplus value and its investment and concentration in a particular location leads to the (re) development of cities. Here, Harvey is drawing from Marx (2010a) and his theory of 'primitive accumulation', wherein accumulation is derived from an appropriation of resources with an eye to privatize its claim and use. This, for Marx, is the beginning of the capitalist process, under which communities and individuals engaged in self-sustained production are forced out of and transformed into a new 'free' labouring class. The Enclosure Movement in Britain was a form of such primitive accumulation at work. The shift from small-scale fishing to industrial fishing is another example of this.

Accumulation, however, should not be understood merely as an economic process. Beginning from primitive accumulation, there have always been associated social and political processes at work. The forced breakdown of older forms of livelihood and the privatization of resources also entailed changes in forms of living and in how people relate to their environment and space. The existence of the self-oriented rational individual is far from a natural phenomenon; rather it is a product of a complex social and economic process.

The manner in which accumulation unfolds, however, is not always spatially even. The centralization and concentration of capital in particular spaces ensure that the development of capitalism is never even, and certain places remain at a lower level of development than others. When accumulation is the primary motor of capitalism, then along with the drive to expand capital through accumulation, there also exists a tendency to over-accumulate. According to Harvey (2003: 149), over-accumulation is primarily a problem of a surplus of capital that is lying idle with 'no profitable outlets in sight'. In such a scenario it is not uncommon for capitalism to seek what Harvey terms as a 'spatial fix' for its problem, and it is this 'fix' which drives urban growth. Harvey examines Marx's theory on accumulation and arrives at what he describes as three circuits of capital. In its primary circuit, capital is accumulated through the means of commodity production. Here surplus is accumulated through an investment in the system of production. When a problem of over-accumulation is encountered (such as the over production of goods and a fall in profit level), it necessitates the need for the system to switch to another mode of accumulation—the secondary circuit (Harvey 1985: 2–4).

The secondary circuit of capital requires accumulation to shift into two sectors—the built environments for production and for consumption. It is this aspect that ties in closely with urban growth. The built environment for production refers to large investments in spaces, in a way that aids production. This can take the form of establishing industries, factories, or even something like a transport network, all of which can contribute towards furthering production without operating as raw material (Harvey 1985: 6). Marx (2010b) refers to this form of capital as fixed capital, Harvey (1985) adds to this by distinguishing between fixed capital and the built environment. The former, he claims, is tied into the production process, while the latter acts as a 'physical framework for production'. A similar parallel exists on the consumption side, where one can identify and distinguish between a fund that directly aids consumption, and a built environment, which operates again as a physical framework to facilitate consumption, for example, sidewalks and houses (Harvey 1985: 6). Harvey (1985) points out that certain elements of this built environment, such as the development of a transport network, can be used for both production and consumption. Investments of this nature are not only large but are also often fixed in space. What this results in is the creation of a space that comes with heavy invest-ments in it, which are meant for long-term use. The development of a rail network, housing projects for workers, and industrial sites can contribute to the development of the city, which attracts not only more surplus value but also labour, both of which are crucial to the process of urbanization.

There are constraints as to what can be achieved within each of the circuits. With regard to the secondary circuit, a potential for new investment sometimes comes at the cost of abandoning or destroying the value still embedded in the built environment. A solution to this problem in the secondary circuit is switching accumulation to what Harvey terms as the tertiary circuit of capital. This involves invest-ment in technology in order to increase productivity and thereby generate a higher surplus value, as well as investment in what con-tributes towards the social reproduction of labour. This can be further divided into costs towards a productive labour force, such as invest-ments in health and education, as well as investments towards ensur-ing a plaint labour force in the form of either co-option or coercion of labour.

From the previous discussion, it is clear that even though the forms of accumulation ultimately work to the benefit of capital, these are in fact investments that individual capitalists would not necessarily undertake of their own accord. Therefore, the state plays a central role in these circuits of accumulation. The state can ease accumulation through financing as well as in guaranteeing these long-term investments. And as Harvey (1985) indicates, since the role it plays is critical, it can determine whether the problem of over-accumulation is resolved through a switch to the secondary circuit, as well as determine the volume of capital that is invested in the built environment. The state, through its role in aiding accumulation, also plays a key part in determining the scale and rate of urbanization that takes place. Harvey (2008) cites the cases of the redevelopment of Paris in 1853 under George Eugene Haussmann, as well as the development of the city of New York in the 1940s under Robert Moses. In both cases, massive urban restructuring took place in the form of the development of public works such as parks, canals, rail networks, and ports and harbours. According to Harvey, what guided the programme was a problem of over-accumulation of both surplus capital and labour with no outlet for their profitable use. It was due to this that urban projects of such a scale were carried out, including the redevelopment of entire neighbourhoods and the establishment of suburbs in Paris and New York. This form of urban restructuring ushered in changes in lifestyles and consumption patterns. As Harvey points out, in the United States this change in consumption patterns, especially with respect to home ownership among the middle classes, also contributed to changes in political values that now increasingly focused on protection of property and ownership rights (Harvey 2008: 27)

However, in case of both New York and Paris, these solutions were only temporary. This has not diminished the role of the urban within processes of accumulation, the recent crisis of 2008, perched as it was on the sub-prime mortgage crisis, being proof of this. What is of interest is the fact that this model of accumulation now has a global spread. As opposed to transformations of cities within a country, Harvey (2008: 29–31) argues that multi-national banks and investment firms with easy access to credit have ensured that the urban transformations introduced through accumulation take place in cities across the world. Newer forms of this spatial fix include privately owned cities (Lavasa in India) and transnational tech corporations governing cities in different parts of the world. Even in cases where the switch to the secondary circuit has not come through over-accumulation, states may choose to invest in these built environments to attract capital flows to it. Redevelopment in cities works favourably in such a scenario. Mumbai's stated aim to turn into another 'Shanghai' was rooted in this.

Capital and the Rise of Bombay

Not much was known about the islands of Bombay[3] in recorded history until the sixteenth century, except that it was sparsely inhabited and fishing was of importance. But with the British taking over the islands in the seventeenth century and with the role that trade from the western coast played in the economy, Bombay began to witness large-scale changes. Its modern history is deeply enmeshed in the history of capitalism and the role of colonialism. Its urban growth was fuelled by the infrastructure projects in the nineteenth century, within the city that transformed the terrain of the islands as well as outside; similar changes occurred after the opening of the Suez Canal in 1869. Connections and land reclamation between the islands literally reshaped the city, and its ports along with the railways connected it not only internationally but also to its domestic interiors.

Yet it was not Bombay that was always the favoured site for economic activity; Surat on the western coast was also a prominent economic hub. Chandavarkar (1994) argues that the British began asserting control over western India 1800 onwards. Having defeated the Marathas, Bombay came to be both a political and an administrative centre. Subsequently, Bombay transformed from a small sparsely populated island to a major urban space due to colonial policies that contributed to it becoming a site where the transfer of surpluses from the colonies to the metropolis took place. Surplus was transferred through the export of two main items: raw cotton and opium (exported to China). Chandavarkar (1994: 23) notes that a gradual shift of commercial enterprise from Calcutta (now Kolkata) to Bombay was already underway in the nineteenth century, but what also gave a boost to the rise of Bombay was the American Civil War. Since the cotton supply from the United States was not available anymore, Bombay became one of the prime exporters, handling 92 per cent of India's raw cotton exports (Chandavarkar 1994: 23). And while this boosted the fortunes of the metropolis, the surplus generated was also reinvested in construction projects undertaken in Bombay. However, the end of the

---

[3] Bombay's name was officially changed to Mumbai in 1995. Hence, when referring to a time period before this name change occurred, Mumbai will be referred to as Bombay.

Civil War resultantly saw a crisis unfold in the municipal finances of Bombay (Dossal 1989).

While the beginnings of industrialization in Bombay may have been inaugurated by the British, Indian capital too came to play a significant role in it. Indigenous enterprise was very much a feature of the growth of Bombay and the fact that banking and credit networks were often controlled by Indians testified to their strong presence in the city. This was in addition to the fact that they also controlled real estate. As Farooqui (1996) notes, many local businessmen owned properties in areas such as Malabar Hill and Breach Candy, even though such areas were almost completely occupied by Europeans.

> In 1914, Bombay received over 87 percent of the total value of Indian capital investment while Indian capital accounted for nearly half the total value of private industrial investment centred in the city. In the late nineteenth and twentieth centuries, Bombay remained the bastion of Indian capital. (Chandavarkar 1994: 26)

In this regard, the development of the railways was of critical importance. Although the railways followed old trading routes, it brought about new significant changes. Chandavarkar (1994: 24) argues that goods could now be moved at a much faster pace and it was now considerably cheaper to do so. Cotton was brought in from Gujarat and Malwa for export, and the increasing demand in this growing city and the surplus to be made from exports meant that there was a constant supply of goods coming in. Much like in the movement of goods, the establishment of the railways allowed for the movement of people and, therefore, aided migration. Since colonial policies gave rise to urbanity in many parts of the country, Farooqui (1996) argues that this growth was often uneven and not spread across uniformly. This in turn explains the streams of migration that have historically taken place to Bombay.

Given that the colonial state's primary interest was in appropriating resources and surpluses from the colonies and protecting a key part of the empire (Spodek 2013), they were not enthused by the idea of investing in the city. However, not doing so led to public pressure (Dossal 1989) and also inhibited the accumulation of capital which was integral to the logic of colonialism. It was because of this that capital was primarily invested towards the expansion of commercial infrastructure rather than towards improving the living conditions of the masses.

However, even this form of accumulation could not continue for long. The development of housing in the city, along class lines, led to a deplorable condition of sanitation. This in turn played a part in the break out of the bubonic plague in 1896. The large number of mortalities and the social conflict[4] that emerged as a result of the epidemic forced the colonial state to intervene in developing social infrastructure. The plague gave rise to a spurt in urban planning in Bombay, albeit guided by ruling class interests, and therefore one which Chandavarkar (1994: 43) argues was more effective than ever before in segregating the citizens of the city by class. In addition, before long, the Improvement Trust (established in 1898 in the wake of the plague outbreak), which had been tasked with improving the social infrastructure, lost interest and began once again to develop commercial infrastructure in Bombay. They in fact ended up demolishing more slums, and even koliwadas (*Times of India* 1905), rather than actually developing housing.

Accumulation by Dispossession in Mumbai and the Fisheries

Much of what happened in Bombay with regards to the struggles around social issues linked to urban processes continues even today. It is therefore that scholars such as Harvey, Castells, and Lefebvre argue that the process of urbanization is integral to capitalism. Lefebvre (2003) notes in *The Urban Revolution* that the struggle over the urban would come to be a crucial aspect of class struggles.[5]

[4] Chandavarkar describes the breakout of a riot in 1898, following the plague outbreak, in which Europeans were targeted. The plague he argued led to a 'social moment', disrupting both commerce and the political order. Through the interventions of the colonial state, class identities came to be crystallized (Chandavarkar 1994: 39).

[5] Castells, however, disagrees with Lefebvre because of the latter's assertion that working-class politics is on the decline. For Lefebvre, the focus is on the urban as the space that engenders collective political action, not the industrial. Following from this he argues that it is not working-class politics which will define the urban revolution, but rather a politics arising from the alienation experienced in everyday life in the urban which will lead to the urban revolution—an argument with which Castells (cited in Susser 2002: 49) disagrees with because of its lack of attention to structures of oppression.

Urbanization today constitutes not just the city but also a certain lifestyle that is held as being emblematic of the city. This particularly refers to exorbitant properties, most often in the form of gated communities and shopping malls. Such lifestyles, Harvey (2010: 24) argues, operate as commodities much as cities themselves do. In a neoliberal era, this has made fault-lines between the classes even sharper.

One of the most stark ways in which the urban process can be stated as having a differential class impact is through the very process of urbanization that entails what Harvey (2008: 33) terms as 'creative destruction'. Urban restructuring or transformations of the scale carried out by Haussman and Moses (Harvey 2008: 25–9), are dependent on the appropriation of resources of the working classes. The restructuring of Paris, for instance, took place after the slums were torn down. Displacement and the subsequent avenues it offers for the absorption of capital play a crucial role in urbanization under capitalism. Harvey (2008: 34) refers to this process as accumulation by dispossession.

Harvey (2003: 138–42) argues, contrary to Rosa Luxemburg's assertion, that the crisis in capitalism is not a product of under-consumption. For Harvey, surplus can still be extracted in the face of under-consumption, if cheaper inputs, such as land and labour, are available. Therefore, what is critical to the stability of the capitalist system is not keeping certain territories in a non-capitalist condition but rather the possibility to transform non-capitalist formations to capitalism. According to Harvey, it is this process which provides opportunities for the investment of capital when others are closed. It also ensures that inputs that were otherwise part of non-capitalist formations are now available for cheap to capitalists (Harvey 2003: 138–9). Non-capitalist formations can be reconsidered here since, as Harvey indicates, public and free resources being converted into 'pay for use' provisions is a form through which accumulation continues. Paid entry into public parks or privatizing mass transport networks are instances of this.

Critical to this would be the role of a labour reserve that is opened up when accumulation by dispossession takes place. A reserve army of labour is of significance to the capitalist who wishes to lower labour costs in the absence of technological change that can reduce the reliance on labour. There are several mechanisms through which the labour reserve can be created. This includes a general increase in population as well as a reserve introduced through external means such as drawing in the peasantry into wage labour or acquiring cheap labour through other external settings such as colonies. However, as Harvey (2003) points out, capitalism does not rely only on external mechanisms to enable its smooth functioning. This is contrary to Luxemburg's (1913b) position, which emphasized on the external nature of the 'fixes' that capitalism relies on to survive. Harvey stipulates the process is contingent and the significance of accumulation by dispossession lies in its ability to free up assets where capital can now be invested, at absolutely no cost. Taking over land, water resources, public services, and so on provide a means to now profitably invest surplus capital. These could be resources either held by the state or communities that are sought to be privatized. One of the most prominent changes brought on by accumulation by dispossession, according to Harvey (2003: 154), is that it renders modes of production other than a capitalist model redundant and therefore entails entry into a capitalist mode of development with strong backing from the state.

Harvey's discussions on the urban process under capitalism and its links to accumulation are pertinent when examining the case of urban commons. Commons are of particular interest to this work since its existence, often linked to resource-dependent livelihoods (as is the case with the coastal commons), disrupts the imagination of a city—a site otherwise integrally linked to surplus. Such disruptions do not merely occur on the peripheries of the city, as yet untouched by the onslaught of urban expansion, but also in koliwadas which exist in the heart of the city.

Land in the city is a critical resource and a vital commodity. Speculative pricing of land and its associated links to the high-priced real estate market has meant that dispossession contributes to a constant need for the commodity this market is built on. In such a scenario, the land occupied by economically and socially marginalized communities becomes one of the easiest targets, where relocation of large numbers of people is promised, if not guaranteed, to open up land for capital accumulation. Bhowmik (2010) discusses the issue when examining the case of the urban poor and their links to public space in Mumbai. In Mumbai, both the informal economy and its primary drivers—the urban poor—tend to occupy slums. Slum rehabilitation programmes led by the state, Bhowmik (2010) argues, have become one of the many ways to wrest control over the land occupied by slums, and the urban poor and make it available for consumption in the market. This is fuelled by a discourse that targets the urban poor by identifying them as 'squatters' and for 'stealing' essential services such as water and electricity.[6] Urban redevelopment projects that do not look to evict but seek to rebuild in situ also face the problem of being carried out in the public–private partnership (PPP) model. Private-sector involvement in urban redevelopment remains tied to aims of profiting from the real estate value of the designated lands. Such development then is rarely conceived with the intention of granting secure rights over housing and livelihood to the urban poor.

While the Kolis find an integral place in the history and culture of the city, the pressures of a speculative real-estate market and slum-rehabilitation measures continue to threaten them. The case of the Sion koliwada is evidence of a process that seeks to sever the links of Koli residents with the coastal land they held and which sustained their life and livelihood. At koliwadas such as the Sagar Nagar koliwada, Koli women engaged in fish drying as well as the local cooperative functionaries note how the fish-drying yard of the koliwada that lies across the beach is under severe threat from real-estate lobbies. Yards such as these, which lie in close proximity to the sea, can command high prices for the sea view they offer. Compounding the problem are legal measures such as the Coastal Regulation Zone (CRZ) notification which, although seemingly initiated to safeguard the coasts and in the interests of the fishing communities, do little to aid them. As Mathew (2008) argues, development projects such as mines and power projects which are permissible under the CRZ can pose a threat to the livelihood practices of fishers. Housing needs of the community

---

[6] 'The promise of free land, at the taxpayers' cost, in place of a jhuggi, is a proposal which attracts more land grabbers. Rewarding an encroacher on public land with free alternate site is like giving a reward to a pickpocket.' (*Almitra H. Patel* vs *Union of India*, 2000, Supreme Court. Available at https://indiankanoon.org/doc/339109/; last accessed in September 2019.)

too are threatened under the CRZ, which can limit the reconstruction of houses that lie on the seaward side. Several residents of the Sagar Nagar koliwada expressed anxiety around the issue, noting how the CRZ prevented them from rebuilding old houses or expanding older houses in order to accommodate their growing families.

Measures such as the CRZ, it can be argued, are primarily based on a discourse of ecological conservation. This does little, therefore, to either recognize or invest control in these spaces in the hands of local fishing communities who have otherwise made use of these spaces. A lack of understanding of how these spaces are held has also led to hasty measures being introduced, such as the Draft of the Traditional Coastal and Marine Fisherfolk (Protection of Rights) Act, 2009 (which the NFF has contested). A cause of concern for the Kolis at the Sagar Nagar koliwada is the fear regarding their inability to prove their private ownership of land on the coast, especially when threatened with eviction by the state and private lobbies of builders. While some claimed to hold documents dating to the colonial period regarding their ownership of the land, for others, this link was far more tenuous.

But it is not only through their ownership of valuable land that the Kolis find themselves immersed in the networks of accumulation that inform the city. Artisanal fishers and fishworkers in the city often eke out a living by fishing from lakes, creeks, and the sea, and supplying the catch to supermarkets, restaurants, and wholesalers.

The coastline of Bombay with its natural harbours and creeks had always primed the city for fishing to thrive. All this has substantially affected its ecology. Once densely forested, there remain only negligible forests within the district limits. Agriculture that was practiced, although to a limited extent compared to the interiors of the state, has also drastically declined—as per the 2011 Census, only 1.36 per cent of workers in the district are classified within agriculture (GoI 2014). Fishing, while it has continued, has been radically transformed. The efforts for this began early in the twentieth century with the development of new technology and with a colonial state that was keen to boost revenues. The policy continued in independent India, with jetties and harbours redesigned and reconstructed to enable industrial fishing and a new Bombay. The urban stamp on Mumbai is now indelible. And in the city's history we find the kernel that resides at the heart of urban policies of a liberalized India, one where urban growth is integrally linked to economic growth. The state, in its efforts to modernize the fisheries, also seeks to, by extension, modernize and urbanize the Kolis and Mumbai. Implied in this is the conceptual collapse, yet again of capitalism and urbanism with modernity and 'improvement'.

In the fisheries, the investment of private capital and the state's efforts towards transforming the fisheries as a site of capitalist production have taken place over the last five decades. The discovery of an export market with potential for revenue generation has underscored these moves by the state. Fishing, which was earlier primarily carried out on smaller non-mechanized crafts, employed a wide variety of nets that differed based on the fish they were used to catch. Such methods of fishing are referred to as artisanal fishing and continue to be practiced in some areas, although the number of those engaged in it is now dwindling, with a mere 2,783 non-motorized crafts in operation in Maharashtra.[7] With the discovery of a large export market for fish found in India, particularly prawns, the nature and scale of production within the fisheries changed completely, with an emphasis on suitability of the catch for the international market. This has significantly altered the manner in which fishing as an economic activity came to be organized. From being a caste-based occupation, where boat owners were also workers on their crafts, fishing is now increasingly organized as a modern industry, drawing workers and investors of different castes to it. A good indication of this change is the response of the state itself to the fisheries beginning in the 1960s. The planned outlay for fisheries for both centrally sponsored and state schemes, registered a significant jump between the third plan (INR 28.27 crores) and the fourth plan (INR 82.68 crores) (Ministry of Agriculture 2014). In Kerala, where this revolution began, John Kurien notes that the 'prawn euphoria' translated into a change in the state's plan expenditures: During the period 1961–9, out of the total of 110 million rupees spent on fisheries

> Rs 82.5 million (75 per cent) was spent on production oriented schemes; Rs 54 million of which went to for financing mechanized

---

[7] Out of a total of 17,362 crafts in fishery, 13,016 were mechanized and 1,563 were motorized (Central Marine Fisheries Research Institute n.d.).

boats equipped primarily to fish for prawns and Rs 20 million (18 per cent) was used to finance processing and marketing oriented schemes out of which Rs 18 million was directed towards creating facilities and organizations which were explicitly export-oriented or directly facilitating the export drive. (Kurien 2008: 71)

By the time of the sixth plan, the central government was investing up to 500 million rupees in a Trawler Development Fund; 7.67 per cent of the state outlays were to be directed towards mechanization, 18.12 per cent for deep sea fishing, and 5.84 per cent for processing, preserving and marketing of fish (FAO 1982) across coastal states. But even as the production of fish increased spectacularly (marine fish production rose from 534,000 tonnes in 1950–1 to 3,443,000 tonnes in 2013–14; the average annual growth rate of marine fish production went from 2.32 per cent in 1955–6 to 9.73 per cent in 1960–1), fish no longer remained the cheap source of protein it had once been, as its prices in domestic markets rose steadily. Ramesh (pseudonym), a member of a fishing co-operative in Maharashtra and organizer of the daily auction for the co-operative, recollected how, in the early 1970s, he and other auctioneers at the site would often be given large amounts of fish for free. These fish were mostly pomfret, a prime item of export now and one he can seldom afford in the domestic market. This corresponds to Kurien and Achari's study (1990) which highlighted the declining availability of fish for consumption in the local markets in Kerala. The NSSO data (Ministry of Statistics and Program Implementation 1990, 2012) on household consumption indicate that during 1989–90, the average monthly consumption of fish in Mumbai was approximately 3 kg and, by 2011–12, this fell to approximately 2 kg. This was a stark decline and surprising for an economy that was growing. The share of fish consumption remained the same (39 per cent) during the periods 1989–90 and 2011–12, indicating that costs of fish had risen in this period.[8]

With an export market which receives fish from both larger vessels with deep-sea fishing capabilities and smaller crafts (Parthasarathy 2011), the domestic market also stood changed.

---

[8] This is a calculation, made by Rahul Menon to whom I am grateful for pointing this out, based on the analysis of the NSSO data (based on Ministry of Statistics and Program Implementation 1990, 2012).

That state policies have ushered this change is clear, for instance, through the subsidies it provides on diesel but not kerosene. The state, by opening up deep-sea fishing and actively seeking private capital investment in it, has ushered into fishing, non-traditional players, such as entrepreneurs and corporates. Trawlers and large boats have thus been purchased by several entrepreneurs who see in it a lucrative business. This has led to the emergence of a new class of capitalists, and to an expanding scale of production. Fishing, which was earlier practiced for local consumption and subsistence and for exchange within a domestic market, now began to change dramatically. What we are witnessing is a steady accumulation in fishing, with technology now suited to larger scales of production.

The process, as briefly described earlier, can be understood as accumulation by dispossession for the simple reason that the accumulation taking place in the fisheries has contributed to making small-scale fishing increasingly unviable. Many can no longer afford to fish on their smaller crafts, and even those with mechanized boats find that they are on the verge of being pushed out of competition by capitalists who use technology, such as trawlers and purse-seine net boats, in order to sell at competitive rates.

For many, the problem was articulated as one disrupting the moral economy associated with the community. A constant refrain, for instance, was that a purse-seine net boat hauled enough fish to generate an income for at least ten families, but now this was being usurped by a single individual. The capitalist mode of production was in contradiction with an earlier moral economy that was based on smaller scales of production and norms of provisioning. In addition, the problem of the transition to capitalism also led to the generation of a pool of workers who, having been pushed out through competition, either hired themselves out as labourers or moved out of fishing altogether. But while local Kolis were leaving fishing as they were unable to sustain themselves, capitalist production in the fisheries remained in need of labourers. Increasingly, this labour came from migrants in the city. In many ways, the capital-intensive fisheries are able to continue and even thrive owing to their ability to hire from the large migration streams that make their way into Mumbai year after year.

Capitalism and Migration

Like any sector of informal labour, migrants are part of the work force hired on boats and trawlers in Mumbai and hail from other states as well as other parts of Maharashtra, particularly coastal districts such as Ratnagiri. Interviews with some migrant workers[9] revealed that they practiced small-scale agriculture in their native villages during parts of the year. The crisis in agriculture has contributed in no small way to this steady supply of labourers in Mumbai.

Migration and urbanization are integrally linked, not only because cities provide a wider range of economic and social opportunities but also because as Castells (cited in Susser 2002) notes, migration is a feature of capitalist development. This is because uneven development is not incidental but *central* to capitalism. Uneven development does not arise as a result of uneven distribution of resources, instead it follows from the logic of capital. Castells thus emphasizes that 'geographical and occupational mobility' (cited in Susser 2002: 78) is inevitable for the development of capitalism, since in the course of its development it must break up other sectors so as to not only create avenues for profitable investment but to also open up labour reserves. Migration can occur both due to a form of accumulation by dispossession that may be taking place in a site of low development and, as Castells (cited in Susser 2002) points out, because labour seeks to move to places with higher real and nominal wages which tend to be in places of high development.[10]

This was easily observed during the beginnings of capitalist development in Bombay. Uneven urban growth in colonial India led inevitably to migration to the few cities of the time. Chandavarkar (1994) and Bayly (2008) document the rise of Bombay and the migration capital and labour to it; working-class migrants were drawn by the employment opportunities, where they concluded that the shortage of work in one sector of the economy would be met with growth in another. Lawyers, scribes, merchants, and traders flocked to the city

[9] Personal interviews with migrant workers on 4 June 2013 at Sagar Nagar beach.

[10] Bonacich (1972) makes a similar assertion, elaborated upon in subsequent chapters.

with the decline of opportunities in Surat and Pune. Migrants came not just from neighbouring districts but from all over the country. A good indication of this is language; while Marathi was a prominent language in Bombay through the early eighteenth century (based on the 1911 and 1921 Census records), it never enjoyed complete dominance (Chandavarkar 1994: 33). Other languages spoken included Gujarati, Sindhi, Konkani, and so on. However, 1931 onwards, the number of people speaking Hindi gradually increased, and people in Mumbai learned how to speak the language, giving rise to a variation now typical of the city—providing a common tongue for those without one, as Chandavarkar claimed. Migration to Bombay in search of employment and food has been a continuing feature of the city. As a result of the Konkan and Deccan famine in 1803, when migrants came to the city, Bombay, with its trade networks, enabled them access to employment opportunities and food grains that were imported from other parts of the country. Streams of migration also took place during World War I, the influenza epidemic of 1918, Partition, as well as the agrarian crisis of the 1970s.

Castells (cited in Susser 2002) examines this phenomenon on a global scale, analysing the currents of migration to advanced capitalist countries. The role of immigration in a capitalist economy, for Castells, is to arrest the falling rate of profit. This falling rate of profit identified by Marx (2010c) is a broad tendency within capitalism, now countered through a number of means which include immigration or its new global avatar of outsourcing. According to Castells (cited in Susser 2002: 73–86), immigrant labourers help in minimizing the effects of cycles of boom and recession in capitalism, and aid in introducing deflation in a state where structural inflation is produced through an excess of capital seeking investment opportunities. Such inflation occurs because there is capital seeking to be invested, and profits must increase in order to justify this investment. However, the surplus cannot be generated through an exploitation of workers alone, since there is a limit to which this can be done. Surplus in such a scenario is extracted through a rise in price.

The availability of immigrant labourers enables capitalism to prevent such inflation through the exploitation of a vulnerable labour force, and thus counters the problem of the falling rate of profit. This is because immigrant labourers are usually paid lower wages than the domestic working class. With wages remaining low and housing conditions poor, it is often the young and unmarried who immigrate.[11] This immigrant labour then serves as a reserve army of labour for capital. Castells (cited in Susser 2002: 92) emphasises the significance of immigrant labour to the capitalist system, a significance that rests on the system's ability to hire and exploit workers, irrespective of the labour movement, which is typically concerned with domestic labour. This is because immigrant labourers find it difficult to organize because of their legal status and their political–ideological isolation. As Castells (cited in Susser 2002: 93) highlights,

> the racism and xenophobia diffused by the dominant ideology accentuate the cleavages derived from national cultural particularities and determine the ideological isolation of immigrants. They are thus separated from their class and placed in a balance of power so unfavourable that often they fluctuate between an acceptance of the conditions of capital and pure individual or collective revolt. This cuts them off still more from the labour movement, in a sort of vicious circle which tends to reproduce the fragmentation and dislocation of the working class in advanced capitalism.

As more populist parties come to power through Europe on anti-immigration agenda, Castells's words remain haunting. Although he argues from the point of view of global networks of migration, his arguments are useful in understanding the impact of domestic migration as well. Most significant is the downward push on wages that migrant labourers acting as a reserve army of labour can have. This is not only because they are an already vulnerable labour force willing to work at lower wages, but also because they migrate alone and thus do not have to bear the cost of raising families in the city—a point made by several Koli women against male migrant fish vendors. It must be noted, however, that questions over migrant entry are not an economic issue alone. Castells noted that migrant labourers in advanced capitalist countries faced xenophobia; in India, migrants faced the backlash of ethnic and nativist movements.

[11] Edna Bonacich's (1975) split labour market theory makes a similar argument.

Mumbai has a history of politics that has often granted primacy to claims of ethnicity and identity. And it is within the context of a long history of nativist politics in Mumbai that the politics of migrant entry in fishing must be understood. What makes this even more significant is the fact that the Kolis, both in popular imagination and in their own perception, demand rights for themselves under the claim of being the original inhabitants of Mumbai. Much of the early mobilization of Koli women was based on their apprehension towards migrants and took place under the leadership of the nativist party—the Shiv Sena.

Nativist Politics in Mumbai

It is not the case that migration in itself always results in conflicts between locals and migrants. For instance, the 2001 Census reveals that in-migrants from other states were higher in number for Delhi Urban Agglomeration (1.98 million migrants) compared to the Greater Mumbai Urban Agglomeration (1.57 million migrants), and the share of in-migrants to the total population was also the highest in Delhi (16.4 per cent), followed by Greater Mumbai (15.1 per cent) (Office of the Registrar General & Census Commissioner n.d.).[12] Migration as a whole has expanded according to the 2011 Census, with the total number of 'in-migrants' in Mumbai and suburban Mumbai reaching 5.39 million and those in the National Capital Territory (NCT), Delhi, numbering approximately 7 million.[13] Despite a large inflow of migrants, Delhi has not witnessed backlashes of the sort that have become common against migrants in Mumbai. But the political and cultural context of Mumbai is starkly different from that of Delhi. Significantly, as Jha and Kumar (2016: 69) indicate for Mumbai, the largest proportion of migrants come from Maharashtra (37.4 per cent), followed by Uttar Pradesh (24.3 per cent), Gujarat (9.6 per cent), and Karnataka (5.8 per cent). Yet it is the North Indian

---

[12] Data highlight, Tables D1, D2, and D3, Census of India, 2001. Available at https://censusindia.gov.in/Data_Products/Data_Highlights/Data_Highlights_link/data_highlights_D1D2D3.pdf.

[13] Available at https://www.censusindia.gov.in/2011-Common/Census Data2011.html; last accessed on 2 March 2014.

migrant (along with the Muslims) who has become the demonized political subject in the nativist politics of Mumbai.

The anti-migrant view is one that is seen as having grown with the rise of the Shiv Sena in Bombay, shaping a nativist assertion that also led to the change in the name of the city. The Shiv Sena was a party started by Bal Thackeray in 1966 with a specific agenda at that point of time—of protecting the rights of the 'sons of the soil'. As a nativist party, it proceeded with an anti-migrant strategy, arguing that most white-collar jobs in the city had been taken over and were controlled by South Indians. It led an agitation against South Indians, publishing in Thackeray's weekly, *Mamrik*, a list of companies controlled and owned by South Indians or with managers from the south of India, contributing to the perpetuation of the prejudice that South Indians had monopolized white collar jobs in the city (Lele 1995: 1523). As Katzenstein (1973: 391) notes, evidence for this prejudice was scanty, with data suggesting that during the 1960s, Maharashtrians were in fact proportionally represented in clerical jobs and it was Gujaratis and not South Indians, among inter-state migrants, who occupied a larger percentage of clerical jobs.

The Shiv Sena's anti-migrant stance can be traced to the culmination of the Samyukta Maharashtra movement (Katzenstein 1973; Lele 1995). This movement demanded the separation of Marathi-speaking areas, with Bombay as the capital city.[14] It, however, faced much opposition since it was believed that doing so would go against the interests of capital which was heavily invested in Bombay. This movement also enjoyed the support of Left groups who envisioned this problem not in terms of an ethnic issue of insider–outsider but as the problem of the entry of large capital from outside (Gujaratis) into the city. With the culmination of the movement in the linguistic division of the state and Bombay being declared as the capital city, the movement began to splinter. A common perception at the time, as Lele (1995) and Katzenstein (1973) point out, was that the success of the movement would dramatically improve the conditions of Maharashtrians, which was not the case. It is from this fertile ground

[14] In spite of over 40 per cent of the population of Bombay being Marathi speakers, none of them according to Lele (1995: 1520) occupied any position of significance.

that the Sena began its anti-South Indian agitation along with an anti-communist stance. With their identification of the problems being communists and the lack of white-collar jobs for locals, the party mainly drew support from the upper castes and middle classes. As Lele (1995: 1521) argues, what the Sena's politics, whether intentional or not, resulted in, was diverting attention away from the dominance of capital in Bombay, even referring to industrialists as *annadattas* (food givers) as compared to the 'criminal' South Indians whom they referred to pejoratively as *lungiwallas*.

The politics of the Sena, however, has close links to the urban (Hansen 2001). As Heuzé (1996) notes, even though the Sena is similar to other Hindutva organizations in terms of the importance cultural populism plays in its ideology, it is different from them. This difference, he argues, is born of its deep links with the city. Deteriorating economic conditions of working people in the city (the popular strata) led to a focus on 'insecurity of status and position' (Heuzé 1996: 216) and consequently the Shiv Sena paid keen attention to urban issues. In fact, Heuzé (1996: 216) points out that even the Shiv Sena's reach into rural areas has not been able to alter this trend. As Chandavarkar (2009: 26) also highlights,

> When, in 1985, the Sena secured a majority for the first time in the Bombay Municipal Corporation—which commanded the revenues of a medium-sized Indian state—it gained access to vast resources and extensive webs of patronage. The powerful position that the Shiv Sena established in the city's politics concealed its much slower advance in the Maharashtrian countryside. Bombay city was now no more the city of its region than it had ever been.

Since the city is where the Sena has grown in strength and from which it primarily derives its programme of action, migration has always remained a significant political subject. Mumbai's large streams of migrants and its constantly circulating population was seen by the Sena as a sign of non-commitment of migrants to the city, or as evidence of them being 'disloyal' to the city (Heuzé 1996: 229). The idea of a unified city with its own characteristics to set it apart dominates the vision of the Shiv Sena and it is from here that much of their politics stems. Heuzé claims that working with this ideology creates problems for the party, causing them to be ambivalent on a number of issues, playing up to the 'little bourgeoisie's fears and the big bourgeoisie's interests'. Located as he claims, 'between those who arrive every day in the city, make it and "live it", and the dominant classes who claim to possess it, cultural populism brings into light its own contradictions' (Heuzé 1996: 230). It is through making use of symbolic elements, according to Heuzé, that the party is able to win the support of people having contradictory interests. However, in doing so, the upper classes' rights to the city have never been questioned, not even on criteria such as origin and culture, which otherwise feature prominently in the Sena's ideological vision of whom the city belongs to. Thus, questions concerning a citizen's 'loyalty' to the city are never directed at Gujarati diamond traders or businessmen, but instead at poorer migrants. As Heuzé (1996: 233) notes, this is something that sets the Shiv Sena apart from other 'nativist' movements, such as the Jharkhandi movement of adivasi groups in eastern India. In Mumbai, it is the poor migrant who is constantly threatened with eviction.

Over the years, the Sena's conception of the 'outsider' enemy has constantly varied—South Indians, communists, people from the north, Muslims, and so on. Those who do not accept the Shiv Sena's ideology are treated to complete exclusion and expulsion. However, Heuzé (1996) is quick to add that this is more a theoretical stance. Political exigencies typically result in only the recent and weak migrants being targeted.

This has enabled the Shiv Sena to endear themselves to sections of the working class. According to Heuzé (1996: 219), it was perfectly acceptable to the workers to follow the call of trade union leader Samant during the 1980s and vote for the Shiv Sena. Chandavarkar contextualizes this, he points out that following the closure of the mill after the general strike of 1982, there were two fallouts. First, the workers' claim of having a stake in the city now came to be questioned. Second, the closure of mills led to the disintegration of the social organization of Girgaon (the locality where mill workers primarily lived). Instead they now had to rely heavily on caste and communal ties (Chandavarkar 2009: 26). In the light of this he claims,

> With its active neighbourhood presence, its readiness to do favours for its clients, to find jobs for the boys, to confront authority and to terrorize the powerful on behalf of individual members, its spectacular displays

of violence and its increasing access to state power, the Shiv Sena offered a kind of citizenship to workers, now seemingly disenfranchised and wholly subordinated, and created an arena in which they could at least fleetingly make a claim for dignity and equality, (Chandavarkar 2009: 26)

But securing their ties with the working class has not prevented the Sena from extending support to capitalists. Heuzé (1996) describes the Sena's relations with industrialists as ambivalent, since it not only supports industry and middle-class values but also continues to work with slum dwellers. However, it can be argued that much of the Sena's actions do not threaten or inhibit the functioning of capitalists, but in many ways aid them in maintaining their dominance. Targeting poor working-class migrants, for instance, contributes to the vulnerability of this class. This makes it even more difficult for workers to organize themselves, providing capitalism with a docile work force which is important for its functioning. It successfully endears itself to capitalists and the native working class.

The result can be understood in the context of what is happening with organizations of fishworkers in Mumbai, which by and large are hostile to migrants and unwilling to enrol them in their own organizations. It is in this context that women from the fishing community first organized under the mantle of the Shiv Sena to protest against the entry of migrants, who they claimed were taking over the vending of fish in 2004 (elaborated in Chapter 2).

The Sena has, according to Heuzé (1996), indulged in a politics that moved between paternalism and populism, but in which violence featured importantly. Since much of its politics was based on polarization, it was keen to enter into confrontations. This usually took the form of violent clashes, which as Heuzé (1996) notes, were often construed as 'heroic and virile' attacks against the state or groups that were considered the enemies. With violence central to their actions, strong links emerged between young men and the party, with the violence of the former leading to the development of and validation for '"*dada culture*": a culture of the goon, but also a virile and young power of the street' (Heuzé 1996: 225). He notes that it is through their violent actions that the 'son'[15] could assert himself. It is in this

---

[15] 'Son' here refers to the notion of 'sons of the soil', which also points to a culture of masculinity and patriarchy that the Sena subscribes to.

context that the Shiv Sena's early attempts to organize women and the resultant conflict must be understood. In 2004, Koli women sought to prevent male migrant fishworkers from working. The agitation which was to be peaceful, turned violent and led to several cases being filed against Koli women. Many Koli women, now part of fishworkers co-operatives and organizations, explained that violence was an important part of the protest against migrants in 2004. While they distanced themselves from the Sena after the agitation, ideologically and electorally, they remain ardent supporters. Rama,[16] a fishworker, noted how she has remained a member of the Sena (even after the 2004 agitation) and was well on her way to rising up the party ranks, even as she was increasingly involved in the MMKS, which was opposed to the Sena's nativist politics. To her, the Sena exemplified the question of fighting for the rights of those to whom the city belongs—in her eyes, the Kolis. Support for the demand for exclusive rights over fishing and allied activities is rooted in this ideology. Nativist politics, the crisis of migration to the city, and the process of accumulation of capital at work in the city have critically shaped the manner in which Koli's interpret the demand for exclusive access to fishing.

[16] Interview conducted 21 May 2013 at West Mumbai.

2

A History of the Commons

Regimes of Use and State Intervention

The continued existence and working of common property resources at a time when the logic of capitalism has taken over the world proves to be somewhat of an anomaly. Commons have come to be governed and administered in a variety of ways, some of which even find close resonance with the notion of private property and ownership.[1] Particularly important with regard to common property resources are questions not just of ownership or management but primarily of the regimes of use, the patterns in which use of the commons has been organized and has found social legitimacy. These regimes of use are built around the form of production that is employed to extract value from a resource. The fisheries in India which have undergone a capitalist transformation over the last five decades present us with an interesting vantage point in understanding the transformation of who can access the commons and how. Mapping these regimes of use also highlights contestations that emerge over access to the commons. In the case of fisheries, these contestations arise from technological and social changes introduced during the transition. And it is these

[1] Sea tenure treated in the same way as land tenure has been documented in Japan, Sweden, and Micronesia.

contestations between the labour force in fishing which have spurred demands of exclusive rights for traditional fishing communities to fish and, thus, to the seas.

This chapter will etch the connections between space, capitalism, and its impact on the commons. A discussion on state policy with respect to the fisheries, beginning with the interventions of the colonial state and its continuation by the Indian state, will shed light on the nature of changes and its consequences for fishing communities.

Reconfiguring the Politics of Space

It is interesting to note that academic work on the subject of the fisheries in India has witnessed a heavy focus on the coast and communities of southern India, with both Kerala and Tamil Nadu being well represented in such work. Questions of capitalist transformation in fishing, new technology employed, changing social relations on the coast, and implications of gender and caste in the fisheries have been addressed in such work. Of these, two books are prominent—Ajantha Subramanian's (2009) work on conceptualizing fisher politics from the prism of modernity and Kalpana Ram's (1991) work which looks at gender and social relations affected through capitalist transformation. Both works focus on the Mukkuvars, a traditional fishing community that lives on the Tamil Nadu coast in the Kanyakumari district as well as occupies parts of the coast in Kerala. A dominant theme in both Ram's and Subramanian's works is the marginality of the coast vis-à-vis the rural agrarian interior of the country. This marginality of space encapsulates other marginalities of caste and gender, all of which work towards inhibiting the mobility of members of the Mukkuvar community, especially women. More importantly, however, both Ram and Subramanian point to how the marginality of the coast can be traced to the perception of the coast, as primitive and in need of development. It was this notion of the coast and coastal communities as backward that guided many state interventions, and sought to introduce technological and social changes for the betterment of the community. Subramanian (2009) also points to how marking the coast as different and inferior influenced the political discourse of the Mukkuvars themselves.

The Kolis occupy, in contrast to the Mukkuvars, a part of the coast that is critically linked to the economic and socio-political growth of Bombay/Mumbai and that continues to be vital to Maharashtra (as Chapter 1 highlights). However, while the Kolis find themselves inextricably linked to the city physically and spatially, they continue to be politically marginal, with few resources to push issues that are of importance to them on a regional or national agenda. Many of them live and work under conditions similar to the urban poor of Mumbai, except for the fact that their claim to the city is never politically contested. This, however, has achieved little for them, with even small demands such as the extension of public transport to them being granted only after sustained agitations.

What is interesting about the Kolis and the study of the fisheries in Mumbai is that their presence, tied into the heart of the capital, has done little to lift the Kolis out of marginality. The marginality of space, of the difference drawn and relied upon by state policymakers between the agrarian interiors and the coast, is absent as a discourse among the Kolis in Mumbai. But while space conceived of in differential terms has had almost no impact on their livelihood and life, it now appears to marginalize them in new ways. Coastal land with its easy access to the sea (sea view being an important feature of most upscale housing in Mumbai) presents an irresistible opportunity for capital accumulation. Weak laws to protect the precarious ecology of the coast (such as the Coastal Regulation Zone Notifications of 2001 and 2011 [Ministry of Environment and Forests 2001, 2011]) and a neoliberal state that prioritizes the creation of an investor-friendly environment over the protection of the natural environment has meant that the coastal lands and seas, and by consequence, the Kolis are now under threat.

The critical difference, therefore, in how the politics of space intervenes in the lives of the Kolis when compared with the Mukkuvars, is also located in Mumbai's urban history and its importance to transnational trade—the coast is not inferior to its agrarian interior here— even as the Kolis themselves may be marginalized. At the Sagar Nagar koliwada, the drying yard for fish is under threat of usurpation. In a neighbouring koliwada which is surrounded by expensive residential complexes, redevelopment and beautification plans for the coast have been discussed for years. The proposal is to build a waterfront promenade in spite of the fact that currently the space does not adequately accommodate the fishers. Clearances for projects of this sort are sought by the government which increasingly seeks to ease access and control over such property for those willing to buy it. A similar sort of worry lies at the heart of Koli women's fiercely fought struggles over market spaces, and this is the reason why organizations such as the MMKS are seeking to involve Koli women in these decisions.

It is not the case, however, that moves to usurp coastal land have not been present in the past. From 1902, the Mandvi Kolis repeatedly petitioned the state to save their land that was under threat from the City Improvement Trust, which demanded they give up their land and houses for a development scheme (*Times of India* 1902: 3). Much of this land had already been threatened with encroachment by the East India Company, but ultimately spared. However, the construction of buildings and other development left them with little space for mending and repairing their boats, weaving nets, and stacking fishing gear. In a number of articles that appeared in the *Times of India* at the time, the issue of the Mandvi Kolis and their pleas to be spared of the move, and demands for good rehabilitation and compensation were discussed. It is staggering to realize that in over a century, the threats to the Kolis remain virtually the same. Even as the state itself is no longer driven by imperialist motives, that it seeks to push an agenda of capital accumulation at the cost of the poor is instructive and reminiscent of the history of Paris and New York.

But where there have been attempts to accumulate at the cost of the poor, there has also been resistance. In Mumbai, the Kolis are regarded as the original inhabitants of the islands and employ this strategically to highlight the irony of their current marginality. When Koli women are strident about selling fish from market spaces they are also drawing on a long history tying Koli women to the market space. Resultantly they are uncomfortable with both figures who disrupt this narrative—fisherwomen who sell from the streets and migrant vendors who sell door to door. Their access to the land they occupy has similar emotive value, even though many fishers have histories of migrating within the city when their villages were claimed for development.

Space, thus, is central to the politics of the fishers, although this gets articulated in differing ways. For supporters of parties such as the Shiv Sena and the Maharashtra Navnirman Sena, the city space is a critical site of power and politics. For the Koli women who primarily vend, space figures as access to public services, common drying lands, as well as to the markets that are increasingly under threat from the developmental gaze of the state and has to do with marking what are considered as legitimate spaces for their activity. For the male fishworkers and boat owners from the community, space features in terms of what they view as the commons they partake of—the sea—and their increasingly limited access to it owing to the technology they are tied to. This chapter will focus on the politics of space as understood through the commons. In light of this, it is important to lay out how spaces such as the sea, coastal lands, and even markets are accessed. The manner in which people come to use the commons and the changes it has undergone is central to understanding contestations, given that most concerns emerge from the question of access.

Regimes of Use, Access, and Ownership in the Commons

Much of the debate and contestations around the commons both in academic work and social and ecological movements relates to questions of managing and governing the commons. At the heart of these disputes lies the question of how the commons is used and by whom. The beginning of this debate in many ways can be attributed to the publication of Garett Hardin's essay the *Tragedy of the Commons* in 1968. It was a seminal essay that came to have a widespread impact not just on the question of common property resources but across a wide range of subjects.

The essence of Hardin's argument was that open access common property resources are not viable and sustainable. He argued that an examination of the commons at a time of relative stability of the population highlights the movement towards its ultimate ruin. For Hardin, all rational individuals act in their self-interest, and for individuals dependent on commons, this would translate into exploitation of the commons through over-use. The corollary to this argument is that there is no technical solution to this problem, requiring instead a change in our values and morality. Privatizing the commons, Hardin argued, would prevent the exploitation of the commons because its use could be regulated. One of the significant points that Hardin makes is that the notion of freedom cannot be tied into the concept of the commons, since it is bound to lead to the exploitation of the resource. He adds that it is imperative to recognize that individual self-interest does not translate into public good (an argument he attributes to Adam Smith) (Hardin 1968: 1244) and that in order to ensure that the resource does not meet with disastrous ends, it is crucial to put in place a system of what he terms as 'social arrangements', that would lead to responsible behaviour towards the commons. This social arrangement as he understands should be informed by coercion or an agreement that certain actions will involve costs for individuals, either economic or social. Hardin (1968: 1247) recognizes that the alternative he poses to the commons—that of private ownership—may not necessarily be a just one, but claims that 'injustice is preferable to total ruin'.

A significant counter to Hardin's thesis comes in the work of Elinor Ostrom (1990). Marking a departure from Hardin (1968), Ostrom, whose *Governing the Commons* is regarded as one of the most significant works in the field, argues for a policy on the commons that moves beyond privatization and state control (both solutions offered by Hardin). Ostrom, using 'an institutional mode of analysis' (Ostrom 1990: 2), highlights how communities can successfully govern the commons. These communities develop strategies that not only permit them to partake of the resources, but also to use them in an ecologically sustainable manner. She argues that communities all over the world have developed a diverse range of such techniques, but also analyses why some communities are able to develop such strategies while others are not, stating that this may depend on several factors, both internal and external to the group.

Linked to the management of the commons is also the question of who can access the commons. McCay and Acheson (1987: 8) argue that the problem with the 'tragedy of the commons' thesis is the inability to draw a distinction between the theoretical notion of the commons that assumes open access and the commons as a social institution where there are in-built restrictions to access determined by technology, residence, and social identity. They further contend that it is a misunderstanding around this question which has led the state and developmental agencies to impose codes of property rights over regimes of use that were never open access to begin with. Durrenberger and Pálsson's (1987) writing on the fisheries detail a history of the contexts and practices in which common property use and policy are determined, which indicate that the diversity in regimes of use do not emerge only from local ecological factors, such as the kind of fish caught or local cultures of fishing communities, but are also products of the larger social–economic contexts of which such commons are a part. Their central argument is that often restricted access to the commons does not translate into ownership, as is commonly understood.[2] What is meant by this is that notions of tenure or restricted access or ownership are social relations that characterize the systems of which they are a part. Thus, the communities' own set of rules emanating from their culture are not enough to understand how questions of access work. They must be located within the larger political economy in order to understand what tenure or ownership actually translates into, and how these rights are recognized or secured by these communities.

To do so is also to nuance our understanding of the commons. More importantly, it prevents easy generalizations that can emerge in such work, which pits the community against the state and, in doing so, adopts the position of 'virtuous peasant' versus the 'vicious state' (see Bernstein 1990, cited in Li 2008). Agrawal (2008: 48), making a similar case, points out that it is imperative in a study of the commons to pay attention to the politics around the resource, since it is also what he terms 'the structure of the situations in which resources are utilized which determines how resources are used and managed'.

---

[2] They argue that there are two reasons for this: the first being 'imprecise translations of indigenous concepts of restricted access' (Durrenberger and Pálsson 1987: 517); and the second that anthropologists, in their work with traditional fishing communities, often identify with them and seek to uphold their claims. Ascribing ownership to their claims is more of a philosophical position. In doing so, however, they point out that it is not necessary to counter the 'tragedy of the commons' claim that all restricted access to the fisheries be understood as a form of ownership: there must be a way to understand this social relation as it exists, without making use of the same vocabulary as supporters of Hardin (1968).

This is especially true of communities that are identified as being primary users or as having ownership claims over the commons. Such forms of community-based management demand attention to the hierarchies that exist within the community on the lines of class and gender and ethnicity, which can significantly determine questions of access. Jean-Platteau's (2008) and Li's (2008) works have adopted such an approach, particularly, to examine how migrant entry challenges the norms of restricted access. Both studies also highlight the role played by the state to whom appeals are made to convert customary practices of restricted access into rights.

As Durrenberger and Pálsson (1987: 518) point out, the notion of ownership makes little sense in a society without the presence of a state to legitimize that right. For access to operate as an exclusive tenure or as a form of ownership, it has to be backed by the state, evident in the demands by the traditional fishers of India who want the state to grant legal sanctity to the customary practice of restricted entry that was disrupted by the capitalist transformation.

The Trajectory of Changing Technology in the Fisheries

The fisheries are a distinctive common property resource. This has as much to do with the fact that common resources are most often understood in terms of land and that as a water-bound resource, it is difficult to conceive of territoriality as we can with land-based common resources. But the nature of thiw resource also contributes to its elusive understanding. As Subramanian (2009: 8) eloquently captures it, fish is a 'fugitive resource': It is not bound to an area, moves constantly, and not always in predictable patterns. It is, therefore, all the more interesting that territoriality becomes such a central aspect of regulating a resource that can be hard to grasp in terms of bounded territory. It is precisely because of this that the mode of production in fishing, that is, the technology used to fish, becomes significant. To return to the point that McCay and Acheson (1987) made, it is important to consider this technology too as embedded in socio-economic processes. Choice of technology and its deployment is dependent on the manner in which production is organized.

The change in technology and the move to capitalist fishing were introduced somewhat cautiously by the colonial state and unabashedly by the Indian state. Fishing involved, prior to these interventions, owners of crafts who worked alongside the labourers on boats, in addition to a merchant class (in some states) who financed fishing. Inequalities of class were accompanied by those of gender—women were excluded from fishing and restricted to allied activities such as drying and selling the fish. A capitalist transformation in fishing has meant that many of these divisions are now sharper (especially the owner–worker relation), while gradually pushing out small-scale fishers.

A significant difference between more recent forms of fishing and artisanal and smaller-scale fishing has been with respect to the gear used. Older forms of fishing used gear that was specific to the fish that was being caught. In Mumbai, which is rich in Bombay duck, prawns, silver pomfrets, eels, lobsters, and mackerel, different nets would be used for each kind of catch. A study commissioned by the Marine Department of the Bombay Presidency in 1910 (Lucas 2011: 4–6) lists the nets used in the area as *dol, bokshi, jal, waghul, kavi, vendi, pag*, and *gal*. Punekar (1959), in her study, recorded the preponderance of dol fishing in Bombay. Other nets used in the area and described by her include *bhokshi, dharan* and *tiboti*, all varieties of stationary nets which are employed in creek waters. In addition to these, she also lists the use of cast nets in deeper waters. Fishing with the dol net continues to this day, as was observed during fieldwork, through its use in stake fishing. Boats even today are known by the kinds of net and gear they use, such as gill netters, or purse-seine netters, as the case maybe. This difference in gear has been the major technological shift to have taken place in the fisheries. Older nets—primarily designed specifically for the fish they caught—meant that there was little wastage in the catch and the fish that were caught were the adult of the species, allowing for regeneration to take place. Most importantly, artisanal fishing followed a more passive principle in fishing, where one cast a net in an area considered rich in fish, rather than in active pursuit of fish, as is the practise now. This smaller scale was also more ecologically sustainable. Catches were large enough to meet the needs of the community and local economy, but not as large as they are today. Traditional communities that live off fishing, such as the Mukkuvars and the Kolis, do not and could not sustain themselves on fish alone; they necessarily traded within the local economy, and therefore produced more than just to meet their subsistence. However, it was in many ways the categorization of the activity as local, limited, primitive, and one tied to subsistence needs alone, that prompted intervention by the state for the development of the activity and the communities dependent on it. It was the misplaced assumption about the absence of a link between trade and artisanal fishing that paved the way for technological and socio-political intervention.

Technological and Social Intervention by the Colonial State

There is little difference in how both the colonial and the Indian states intervened to promote certain technology or to introduce certain forms of organization within the fishing community, even guided by similar intentions. This common motive was generating revenues for the state, which could be made possible through capitalist enterprise in the fisheries.

The colonial state monitored the fisheries carefully, with close interactions between the Madras and Bombay presidencies. Reports made by fisheries commissioners of the Madras Presidency, for instance, were relied on by the Bombay Presidency (Lucas 1911) to determine its own policies. The official documentation of the Marine Department in the Bombay Presidency that relied heavily on the writings of F.A. Nicholson, director of the Madras Fisheries Bureau, are indicative of the common approach of the Madras and Bombay state to the fisheries.

Subramanian (2009: 105) details the transition of fish from a commodity of food supply to a source of revenue within the Madras Presidency. She points out that after the devastating famine in Bengal in the late nineteenth century, fisheries came to be viewed as a solution to the problem of the food supply. This led to the emphasis on fish as a source of food supply and not revenue, a view espoused by Nicholson.

Consequently, the Madras Fisheries Bureau intervened through 'incremental social measures' (Subramanian 2009: 106) that were targeted at assuaging the chronic indebtedness that plagues fishworkers and continued maintaining a steady supply of fish to ensure food supply. Subramanian adds that it would be a mistake to assume that the colonial state's intentions were noble in this regard; rather it high-lighted the negligible role of revenues from the marine fish harvest to the immense riches of the empire. The emphasis on fish as food was only to minimize the damage caused by the famines which were a product of colonial policies.

The attempt to boost production for food supply informed colonial intervention in the Bombay Presidency. The *Times of India* (1933a: 8) reported that the fisheries in Bombay did not seem adequately developed, and noted the role played by the governor in seeking to revitalize the fisheries in Bombay to provide the city with an adequate supply of fish. It was reported that the fisheries ran more as a cottage industry rather than a typical large-scale industry. This limited expansion of the fisheries was reportedly a result of the inability of the Kolis to raise capital for the induction of trawlers and to expand fishing on commercial lines. Colonial disdain and racism underscored this belief.

> Unfortunately for Bombay—and this is true of the rest of India—only certain castes or races take to the fishing industry.... The result is that the industry is unable to provide from within the capital, the business capacity and the initiative necessary for exploiting to the fullest extent the harvest of the sea. As Mr. Sorley has pointed out after an exhaustive investigation, the boats, gear, curing-houses, and trade organisations necessary to give proper efficiency to the men and development to the industry can be provided only by large capital and business brains. (*Times of India* 1933a: 8)

This led Bombay Governor Sir Fredrick Sykes to intervene and invite experts to look into the problem, but the government's purse strings were also tied. This may have had something to do with the government's failed experiment in 1921 with the steam trawler 'William Carrick', which forced the Bombay Presidency to limit the expansion of the fisheries. Even so, further experiments in commercial trawling were considered by 'certain private interests', and in the meantime, it was believed that motor boats which worked well in Japan could also do wonders for the Kolis. A few months later in November 1933, the governor inaugurated the launch of motorboats in the village of Danda, Bombay. But what is especially important to note is that although Bombay Presidency's intervention was to ensure a steady food supply, it did not lose sight of the fact that the fisheries were extremely crucial for revenue earnings.

> It must be obvious to anyone that if the fisheries are developed to the fullest extent they should eventually add crores of rupees to the economic resources of the Presidency. Bombay's experiment will be watched with interest by other provinces, notably Madras and Bengal. (*Times of India* 1933a: 8)

In Madras, Subramanian highlights how Victorian bureaucrats viewed the fisheries as essentially a primitive enterprise that was in need of turn to modernity. To the colonial administrator, the fisheries were almost archaic in how they operated and they saw it as ultimately being swept aside by the tide of technological change. Their approach to it was therefore conservative, both in terms of how they perceived the fisheries and how they sought to tackle the issue of technological change in it, based as it was on racist assumptions regarding the ability of the community of fishers to adopt the technological changes. However, Nicholson also acknowledged the inevitability of change (Subramanian 2009: 106).

Since the fisheries in India were based and organized on caste, their eventual transformation for Nicholson was a certainty.

> An economy founded on caste, he wrote, could 'by itself never provide the essentials of development' because its seafaring population is 'born and not made'. The incommensurability of caste and capitalism, or of ascriptive, precapitalist social identities and the 'modern' identities of wage labourer and capitalist, would lead necessarily to the disappearance of the 'independent boatman with his catamaran and canoe, the petty individual curer with his pinch of capital and half a dozen baskets of fish, the small market dealer or buyer, and the fresh-fish runner', or to their subordination 'as the employees of capital'. (Madras Fisheries Bureau 1915: 36–7, cited in Subramanian 2009: 106–7)

But by 1909, Nicholson changed his point of view and claimed that a more gradual shift was better suited for the fisheries in Madras. Instead, he began to argue that a rapid shift to capitalism in fishing would reduce the previously independent fisherman to a mere wage labourer, and thus insisted on a gradual change as opposed to a sudden revolution. Subramanian points out that this change in opinion had much to do with his assessment regarding the technological and social backwardness of the fisheries. In addition, the presence of caste convinced him even more of the difference between India and West. This form of community he believed, would not allow for even small cooperatives to be established.

This lack of corporate sentiment, he believed, made the harvester of the sea 'less diligent and thrifty' (Subramanian 2009: 106–7) than the cultivator of the soil. Ironically, though, as Subramanian points out, fishers were constantly regarded as incompetent with regards to forming cooperatives, with evidence for it being sought in features of their social life that were seen as markers of corporate spirit among agricultural communities. Thus, she claims that panchayats, which were seen as typifying a corporate sentiment in agrarian communities, were seen as evidence for the opposite among fishers. This contradictory position was especially stark when the concept of private property was considered. Private property was seen as a testament of the difference between the West and the East, and as a sign of progress; in the case of the fishers, however, who possessed private property, this was evidence of their primitivism. Therefore, Subramanian (2009) claims, that both colonial and post-colonial administrators sought to end the social arrangement of private property, marking it as the culprit for the vulnerable position fishworkers found themselves in. Advocating for cooperatives, they claimed it was a better principle around which to organize production, and consequently uplift the fishers. However, the Travancore state's efforts towards the fisheries involved setting up cooperatives, not so much to provide technological aid but to help fishers with their debts. This was based on the assumption that cooperatives would grant fishers financial power where otherwise they were rendered vulnerable by middlemen and merchants (Subramanian 2009: 109). The history of the development of cooperatives in fisheries is particularly useful to understand the current political context of fisheries development in Maharashtra, in general, and Mumbai, in particular. In Mumbai, cooperatives are a critical part of the fisheries, and fishing villages often have several cooperatives functioning concurrently. Kolis often claimed that cooperatives are a mainstay of the fisheries because state aid continues to be mediated through cooperatives alone, as it is the only form of organization recognized by the Department of Fisheries. A conversation with a fisheries department official revealed as much, when he claimed that the law stated this, unaware though of why this was the case; Nicholson's legacy continues till today.

The persistence of cooperatives as a model of organizing is also responsible for the conversion of what began as a fisherwomen's trade union in Mumbai in 2013 into a cooperative a year later. This was the case, although at the early beginnings of this trade union, several fisherwomen argued how it was only a trade union that could grant them rights they had been previously denied. However, because the state only recognizes cooperatives as an intermediary institution to access financial aid and subsidies for technological inputs, fuel, and so on, Koli fisherwomen decided to establish a cooperative first.

Along with the institutional architecture to support it, technological change was introduced by the colonial state. The Madras Fisheries Bureau contributed significantly to fisheries development through the new technology they introduced. Replacing old crafts and gear, the Bureau now sought to introduce technology used in other parts of the world to boost productivity in fishing.

One of the important insights one gains from the rich archival sources on which Subramanian (2009) draws is that the direction adopted by the Madras Fisheries had much to do with its early directors, Nicholson and James Hornell. For Hornell, who succeeded Nicholson as director of the Fisheries Bureau and served for two years (1918–20), ecological conservation was a guiding ideology. Yet economic factors convinced him that the Indian fisheries were ready for trawling. But ecological sustainability was not the universal position of the fisheries bureau in Madras or in other presidencies. This ideology did not even gain currency when fisheries development came to be adopted as a project by the post-colonial state. Even now—in times of decline in fish catches owing to pollution and overfishing through new technology (Albuquerque 1995; Vohra 1980)—concerns over the damage to the environment come from outside of the fisheries department. The history of the post-colonial state's intervention in the fisheries indicates why this is the case.

The Post-colonial State and the Fisheries

In post-Independence India, natural resources were considered as national wealth. The ownership and control of these resources, according to Subramanian (2009: 126) was seen as being vested in the people of the country collectively. However, state-led development in India has only accentuated the differences between the haves and have nots, breeding new forms of inequality. The post-colonial state, it can be argued, has done more towards boosting capital accumulation in the fisheries. While at first this was guided by the idea of building a strong domestic market for consumption and led through an initiative to strengthen cooperative ownership of technology, this approach increasingly gave way to the notion of export-oriented growth in the fisheries and was boosted by the state subsidizing the purchase of new mechanized crafts and gear.

These interventions were legitimized as promoting national interest, as Rambhau Patil,[3] whose trawler was financed through state subsidies in 1969 recollected,

> according to the grow more food policy of the Government of India, they were providing subsidies for it and accordingly in the fishing sector they were providing subsidies and *they were giving everything to catch more fish and provide food for the people of India and to have a chance to export fish for revenue, in national interest* [sic]. (Emphasis mine)

The first steps towards introducing new technology were taken by India in 1953 when, in partnership with the United Nations Food and Agriculture Organization (FAO), it decided to introduce mechanization in the fisheries. Subramanian (2009: 133) argues that with the food crisis in the 1950s, the orientation of state policies shifted decidedly in favour of increasing productivity and generating surplus, as opposed to the policies in response to the early nineteenth-century food crisis, where the focus was not to be on revenue generation but on increasing productivity for subsistence.

As part of this, workshops were conducted where fishermen were taught to use mechanized crafts and gear, in addition to skills to be used on these crafts and theoretical knowledge. This contributed to

---

[3] Personal interview conducted on 9 June 2013 in Mumbai.

shifting the basis of livelihood from the experience of the fishworkers to the scientific knowledge now imparted by the state. This enhanced the inequality in development, creating pockets of well-developed areas distinct from the underdeveloped areas. However, it was the 'pink gold rush' that set-in-stone the divide between modern fish-workers and traditional artisanal fishers.

The 'pink gold rush' refers to the period during the 1960s when prawns were discovered as a prime item of export. The price of prawns that were used as manure in the southern states and in Maharashtra at one point now began to rise substantially, making the fisheries more commercially viable than they had ever been.

A livelihood practice that was limited to certain caste communities along coastal states transitioned into an exciting economic opportunity, ushering in new participants. Previous in-built barriers of skills, technology, and social barriers, such as caste background, which had previously limited the entry of capital and labour from outside the community was fundamentally altered (Kurien 1993).

What this meant for the fishery policy was that, as opposed to building the cooperative movement to increase productivity for domestic consumption, the vast revenue generated by the export earnings of prawns led the state to expand and commercialize fishing. Trawlers, which were suitable to this new form of fishing, were introduced on a large scale, given that they allowed for indiscriminate fishing through the nets and gears used.

Subramanian argues that orienting production towards the export market led to the predictable outcome of a large influx of capital in the fisheries—'private capital drove the mechanization drive far more than did state capital' (Subramanian 2009: 169). State efforts at providing subsidized trawlers only aided a small minority in the community and since most fishing communities were not able to command such vast amounts of capital, these flows could be traced to those from outside the community. Furthermore, Ram notes that in Tamil Nadu, the government gradually began phasing out the sub-sidies extended for trawler purchase. In addition, certain pockets, owing to the political patronage they may have garnered through kin-ship and other networks, were larger beneficiaries of these subsidies than others (Ram 1991: 133). The presence of a small group that was able to switch to trawlers meant that the divide between trawler

Table 2.1 Total Planned Expenditure, Department of Fisheries, Government of Maharashtra (in Rupees Thousands)

Planned Schemes	Total Planned Expenditure (in Rupees)			
	2006–7	2007–8	2008–9	2009–10
State	98,732	95,861	83,776	30,441
NCDC	255,606	245,942	456,319	387,186

Source: National Cooperative Development Corporation (NCDC). Data sourced from the Department of Fisheries, Government of Maharashtra Budgets. Available at https://fisheries.maharashtra.gov.in/Site/Common/ViewPdfList.aspx?Doctype=E13A259D-E7AC-4281-8212-C5C17088EF3C; last accessed on 1 January 2015. The data account for the expenditure under the planned schemes of the budget.

Table 2.2 Share of Expenditure on Installation of Modernized Equipment on Mechanized Trawlers

Schemes	Share of Expenditure (in Percentage)			
	2006–7	2007–8	2008–9	2009–10
State Schemes	10.64	13.61	11.84	39.37
NCDC Schemes	71.73	93.40	73.66	84.01

Source: Data sourced from the Department of Fisheries, Government of Maharashtra Budgets. Available at https://fisheries.maharashtra.gov.in/Site/Common/ViewPdfList.aspx?Doctype=E13A259D-E7AC-4281-8212-C5C17088EF3C; last accessed on 1 January 2015.

owners and artisanal fishworkers remained in place. State support for such mechanization and capital-intensive technology waned in Tamil Nadu but continued to remain prominent in Maharashtra. Tables 2.1 and 2.2 highlight that state support for the introduction of such technology remains strong.

As seen in Table 2.1, between 2006–7 and 2007–8,[4] the total expenditure was actually falling for both state and NCDC schemes, and yet expenditure on mechanization registered an increase (Table 2.2). The NCDC's total expenditure was rising in 2008–9, but

[4] For 2009–10, the expenditure figures are shown up to December 2009, which does not give the entire picture.

the total expenditure for state schemes was still decreasing in 2008–9. Even though the total expenditure for the state in 2008–9 was lesser than that in 2006–7 (by nearly 15 per cent), the share of mechanization expenditure was higher in 2008–9 as compared to 2006–7; this reflects the strength of Maharashtra's commitment to mechanization. Additionally, the state expenditure on mechanization fell between 2006–7 and 2008–9, but not by as much as the total expenditure did.

Under these conditions, trawler owners grew into a new powerful class and there continues to be a palpable tension between trawler owners and small-scale fishers. Several fishers in Sagar Park spoke about the attempts made by a cooperative dominated by trawler owners in the area to popularize purse-seine nets and resist efforts of organizations such as the NFF and the MMKS, which have filed legal petitions for purse-seine nets to be banned. At the Sagar Park koliwada, fishermen also complained that in spite of the Department of Fisheries's attempts to regulate the number of purse-seine nets, a number of such crafts continued to operate without licenses or were able to evade legal action owing to the political influence they commanded.

The state's clear commitment to the goal of modernizing the fisheries has led directly to the marginalization of artisanal and small-scale fishers. Artisanal and small-scale fishers are often forced into abandoning fishing or reduced to working as labourers on trawlers under such conditions, but direct confrontations between trawler owners and small-scale fishers have also raged around the coast of the country.

In the 1970s, small-scale fishers faced declining catches owing to the large numbers of trawlers. It was under these conditions that the NFF emerged—from a previous collective National Forum for Kattumaram and Country Boat Fishermen's Rights and Marine Wealth comprised of 13 regional fishermen's unions—and took up their cause. Along the southern coast, as well as the coast of Maharashtra (encompasses five coastal districts[5]), conflicts raged (see also Joshi 1991). In response to this issue, the union legislature issued a Marine Bill in 1980 that regulated and demarcated marine

---

[5] In addition to Mumbai, these include the districts of Thane, Raigad, Ratnagiri, and Sindhudurg.

fishing, by establishing broad guidelines to which state governments could introduce further notifications. In 1981, the Maharashtra Marine Fishing Regulation Act came into effect; it aimed to regulate fishing 'to protect the interests of different sections of persons engaged in fishing, particularly those engaged in fishing using traditional fishing craft[s] such as country craft or canoe'[6] as well as in the interest of maintaining law and order. In order to do so, the Act mandated the establishment of an advisory committee which would regulate fishing by restricting or prohibiting specified kinds of fishing activities in particular areas. As per the decision of the advisory committee, for the districts of Mumbai, Raigad, and Thane, the zone from the shoreline to 5 fathoms was prohibited for trawlers and reserved for traditional crafts, whereas for the districts of Ratnagiri and Sindhudurg, the zone reserved for artisanal fishers was up till a distance of 10 fathoms. The regulation, which was seen by the state as a neat solution, in effect complicated matters further. For one, it rested on the assumption that trawlers and mechanized boats would confine themselves to their zones, as would artisanal fishers. However, the species that trawlers and mechanized crafts were especially interested in were present in inshore waters as well, drawing them to these zones. Further, the assumption that artisanal or small-scale fishers and gears could not handle deeper seas was also a mistake. Resultantly, frictions continued. Mechanization and the new regulations also disrupted earlier customary practices where territoriality in the seas and on land were linked. For coastal villages, their territory extended to the part of the sea that was adjacent to it. Fishers would therefore traditionally not enter the waters of neighbouring villages or districts to fish. But in the tussle of older customary practices and new law, confusion and hostility reigned. Several fishermen noted, for instance, the hostility that exists even now between fishers from Ratnagiri and Sindhudurg districts, where trawlers are accused of entering the waters of the other district to catch fish. A similar conflict plays out between Sri Lanka and India every year, when mechanized crafts from India are caught by Sri Lanka for violating its waters and regulations on the

[6] See Maharashtra Marine Fishing Regulation Act, 1981. Available at http://bombayhighcourt.nic.in/libweb/acts/1981.54.pdf; last accessed on 1 October 2020.

use of such gear, leading to international conflicts. The conflict in Maharashtra, however, plays out within Kolis themselves given that the state encouraged large-scale production.

In 1991, the problem was compounded when the state opened up a 200-mile Exclusive Economic Zone in the deep seas to foreign capital, with an eye on boosting economic growth. This was accompanied by establishing exclusive terms of tenure in the seas. Regulations in the form of zones of operations were demarcated—foreign vessels in collaboration with Indian firms were restricted to a zone beyond 12 nautical miles from the coast, while the territorial waters that lay closer to the coast were meant for domestic fishers.

The emergence of such regulation, a feature of the commons being opened wider for use and the intense conflict that took place in coastal states was an interesting development in understanding how customary practices, which until then had operated as de facto law, came to be altered. Subramanian (2009: 188) points out that the reason for the state not playing an authoritative role prior to this was not out of respect to customary practices, but because until the conflict these practices had not affected their agenda of capital accumulation in the fisheries.

This capital accumulation followed predictable patterns. In Tamil Nadu, Ram (1991) indicated that technological change led to the fishers of Kanyakumari becoming workers as opposed to owners, which was not the original intention of such policies. Ownership of trawlers, she argued, was concentrated in the larger port towns in Kerala and Tamil Nadu, where fishworkers migrated to find work (Ram 1991: 12). Despite the passage of over two decades, a very similar pattern could be seen in Mumbai. Here the large proportion of operational mechanized crafts, trawlers, and purse seiners attract labour from smaller coastal villages in other districts, such as Ratnagiri, in addition to those coming from outside the state. Ram points out that while artisanal fishing involved hard labour, the intensity and pressure of work can be much higher in mechanized fishing, owing to the fact that technological interventions bring a control over production that is absent in artisanal fishing. Yet migrant workers in Mumbai noted that the physical labour of small-scale fishing was more arduous, even if the intensity of work was high on trawlers. Most significantly, technology transformed fishing in the most fundamental way—a shift away from the vagaries of the sea to the certainty of catch, drawing to it more people than before but on unequal terms. The demand for exclusive access is in many ways a reaction to this.

Technology and Ecology

Perhaps one of the most significant impacts of the changes that have taken place in the fisheries is the resultant practice of overfishing. Kurien and Achari's (1990) work in Kerala documents this. They elaborate that overfishing needs to be demarcated on two grounds.

> It is customary to distinguish between two types of overfishing: economic and biological. Economic overfishing occurs when marginal costs of an additional unit of fishing effort are higher than the marginal revenues. The economy experiences loss (even though total fish catch may increase) because of a misallocation of capital and labour which might have produced higher economic yields in alternative activities. Biological over-fishing occurs when the yield of an additional unit of fishing is negative. At such a level of effort the fish population stock is prevented from generating its maximum sustainable yield. (Kurien and Achari 1990: 2011)

Ecological overfishing, as Kurien and Achari (1990) document for Kerala, was devastating. Between the years 1971–5 to 1981–5, the harvest of prawns alone in Kerala registered a 51 per cent decline (Kurien and Achari 1990: 2013). A similar decline was found in other demersal species of fish as well. The impact of such overfishing is felt on a number of fronts. A decline in fish harvests means that the wage and income of those dependent on this suffers a decline as well. In addition, as mentioned earlier, a significant impact is that fish, which was a cheap source of protein in coastal areas, now becomes increasingly difficult to access. This is a result not merely of overfishing but also of the primary cause of overfishing in the first place, which is that of a large export market available for fish. As Kurien (1984, cited in Kurien and Achari 1990: 2014) notes, both the availability and quality of fish in the local retail market in Kerala suffered a decline, and the price of fish has increased substantially as compared to other products. He also argues that the middle and upper classes transition to other cheap and easily available sources of protein in the face of a declining fish harvest. This means that the brunt of overfishing is suffered by the working-class population. According to Kurien and Achari (1990: 2014), 'The per capita availability of locally consumed fish has declined from 19 kilograms in 1971–1972 to 9 kilograms in 1981–1982'.

A key point to remember in deliberations about the ecological impact of technological changes is to make note of the fact that technology must be appropriate to the environment. It must also take note of the complex inter-relations that are part of any interaction of humans with the natural environment. It is interesting to note that communities of fishworkers as part of their livelihood practices did not render the environment vulnerable, owing to their scales of production. Other sustainable practices were also incorporated, in several fishing communities one would discover a decline in fishing during the monsoons, a period during which several species of fish reproduce and regenerate. In Kerala, where communities of fishworkers had organized themselves politically quite early, there were several struggles and agitations demanding a ban on trawling activities during the monsoon. A complete ban was not brought into effect until June 1989, when the state government finally implemented it. Kurien and Achari (1990) note that although a large number of people were unemployed during the course of the ban, several others who belonged to local fishing communities made use of the opportunity to work on their motorized boats during the monsoon. When the ban was lifted, the prawn harvest of the year had increased substantially. Kurien and Achari (1990) hasten to caution that the increased yield must not be attributed to the ban alone, but would also have had something to do with the rain and weather patterns. However, they do agree that the impact of the ban on the increased yield would have been significant. Since then, the Kerala government has continued with the monsoon ban on trawlers. A similar ban was introduced in Maharashtra 1992 onwards. Again, it was small-scale fishers who demanded the ban but as they recollected, the ban took a long time to be introduced and as they emphasize, it was only through sustained pressure on politicians that it was finally implemented.

This notion of ecological damage is one that is slowly emerging as a significant issue, as a ground for mobilization among the Kolis (see Chapter 5). The damage caused to the community through the use of technology is echoed in Rama's (pseudonym)[7] anger, who says: 'Everyone has rights over the sea, how will it work if only one person retains the right?'[8] Several Koli fishers also claimed that 'one boat robs a dozen households of a living'. For Subramanian (2009: 162) this was:

> the expression of moral economy based on an opposition to the immoral material advance of a few at the expense of the majority. It was based on a notion of the common good that ruled out unfair competition, but not a critique per se of technology or development.

However, in Mumbai, both at Sagar Park and Sagar Nagar koliwada, there was a coherent argument being made against the use of a new technology. In both koliwadas, respondents drew on the norms of the community to substantiate a position that essentially saw the seas as a common resource now monopolized by a few. But the discourse around the question of the commons incorporated critiques centring on both ecological destruction as well as suitable technology. The work of the MMKS has been significant in this regard. While mobilizing support on the grounds of ecological concerns and a common morality of the community has led to some success, one consequence has been the concern regarding who can participate in this moral economy.[9]

---

[7] Personal interview conducted on 21 May 2013 in Western Mumbai.

[8] See also, Subramanian (2009: 160) for a detailed discussion on the fierce and violent contestations that broke out between trawlers and artisanal fishworkers in Kanyakumari over questions of destruction of artisanal boats and nets by trawlers, and the violation, by trawlers, of the regulated zones of fishing for trawlers and artisanal crafts established by the state.

[9] Even as the moral economy is rooted in values that determine the norms for provisioning (fair and unfair limits), these norms in their original conceptualization by Thompson (1971) were not associated with a single community but defined the political economy of a time and place. In linking morality with a single community alone, there has been the accompanying tendency to see only members of the community as demonstrating allegiance to these norms.

3

The Kolis of Mumbai

Life, Livelihood, and Identity

It was not by the paths of the sea, but from landward that the earliest inhabitants of Bombay journeyed. At some date prior to 300 A.D. and prior perhaps to the Christian era, our desolate isles became the home of certain lithe dark men, calling themselves 'Kulis' or 'Kolis'.... One would fain speak with more certainty of the date of their arrival on these shores; but so remote, so shrouded in antiquity is the Koli Hegira from the mainland, that no definite statement is permissible. (Census of India 1901: 3)

This introduction to the Kolis is an indicator of their well-acknowledged history and their links to the western coast, particularly the islands that comprised Mumbai. The relationship of the Kolis to Mumbai is one that is of special significance to the community, especially at a time when they see their traditional link to fishing threatened. The Kolis, described in the Census and gazetteers as a distinct community, came to be characterized as distinct tribes (GoI 1901, 1909). There are the agricultural Mahadev Kolis who occupied the interior (Ghurye 1963: 2–3), while the islands of Mumbai were inhabited by the Son Kolis or Meta Kolis who practise fishing. The detailed descriptions in colonial accounts are testament to how location and livelihood fundamentally inform the Koli identity, but also leave an imprint on the city.[1]

In a context where to be Koli was also to be fundamentally linked to fishing, it is not hard to imagine that the capitalist transformation in fishing brought in its wake a series of changes that have produced new imaginations of what it means to be a Koli. Critically, both gender and class have shaped the manner in which labour has been reconfigured within the fisheries and determined new arrangements of relations of production and social reproduction. Consequently, in the city of Mumbai, it is often Koli women who have been strident in their demands to have fishing restricted to traditional fishing communities.

Two significant changes have taken place in the fisheries in Mumbai as a result of the state's initiation of the capitalist transformation of the fisheries. First is the change in labour practices and social relations in the fisheries, and second is the emergence of a populist agenda that is rooted in hostility towards migrants and the responses to it. An exploration of these two developments is critical in order to engage with the NFF's demand for exclusive access to traditional communities of fishing; the manner in which the demand is framed can produce different responses and repercussions in Mumbai. In other words, whether one can read Koli fisherwomen's resistance to the entry of migrant men as resistance to an agenda of accumulation is a question that demands investigation. But first the question arises: Why is it that it is Koli women who have typically been at the forefront of this agitation? It is imperative to understand the world of work in the fisheries to answer this question. Changes that have taken place, not merely in the livelihood but also in the city itself, have played a role in this. Koli identity has been shaped through the close interaction between livelihood and locale, and this chapter will unravel this relation.

[1]   The Census introduction notes, 'They undoubtedly existed in two southern islands; which thereby acquire the title of "Kola-bhát" or "Kolaba" the Koli estate' (Census of India 1901: 4). Additionally, it argues that the name Mazagon, the fourth of the seven original islands of Bombay, is derived from the title *Machva-Ganv*, that is, 'the fishing village' (Census of India 1901: 5). Both islands mentioned continue to be important parts of Mumbai and continue to have fishing villages located in them.

Koli Life and Livelihood

For a community which has had a long, historic, and complex relation with the city of Mumbai, it is surprising to note the dearth of work on the Kolis. Vijaya Punekar's ethnographic account, *The Son Kolis of Bombay* (1959), and descriptive accounts of the Kolis in the Imperial Gazetteers and the Colonial Census provide the bulk of information on the community (Census of India 1901; GoI 1901, 1909).

Punekar notes that the earliest reference to the Kolis can be found in a text called *Mahikavatichi Bhakar* published in 1819 (cited in Punekar 1959: 3) and in the historical sketch by Govind Narayan who describes Bombay in 1530 (cited in Punekar 1959: 4). The Census of 1901 documents the Kolis as both agriculturalists and fishers 'from time immemorial', but notes that those who settled on the island of Mazgaon found fishing to be more profitable than agriculture, and thus became 'wedded to the pursuit' (Census of India 1901: 5). The terrain and layout of Mumbai certainly made the development of fishing a strong possibility, with the creeks of Mumbai providing safe anchorage for the boats, especially during the monsoons, and being a site for fishing (Punekar 1959: 13).

Much of this has changed at a time when creek and territorial waters are plagued by problems of pollution.[2] Boat owners from the Sagar Nagar koliwada noted that fishing near the shore, which was once practiced between the Hindu festivals of Dussehra and Diwali, is now nearly impossible owing to water pollution. Plastic bags in creeks and waters near the shore also prevent fish from entering these waters. This has prompted the fishers to move into deeper waters in order to fish, bringing them into competition with mechanized trawlers and boats, even as the declining catch in deep seas cause trawlers to move inland.

Much like fishing itself, koliwadas too have transformed over the years. Changes in patterns of work have altered the koliwadas. Constructions on small jetties in koliwadas such as the Sagar Nagar koliwada are indicative of the scale of change that is coming

---

[2] For example, the Mahim creek is infamous for the pungent smell of sewage it carries, but fisherwomen of the area mentioned how it was a popular spot for creek fishing earlier.

to these shores. Koliwadas remain predominantly populated by the Kolis. The Sagar Park koliwada[3] is a relocated one, which shifted to its current location sometime in the 1970s. According to the chairperson of one of the large cooperatives of the koliwada, many settlers came from the east of Mumbai because of an agitation over land reclamation, while others moved in from Colaba. The exact time of the move and the reason could not be ascertained; however, most respondents did confirm this history. Consequently, most residents of the koliwada have lived in Mumbai for over a decade—approximately 92.6 per cent of households in Sagar Park record a presence for over 10 years, and a mere 7.4 per cent households in the area can be considered as migrant families who have lived in Mumbai for less than 10 years. A significant number of migrants hailed from Palghar[4] and its surrounding villages, all part of Thane district, moving in search of better opportunities in the city. Critically, low education levels have meant that most of those seeking employment outside of fisheries do so in low skill wage employment with networks of kin aiding the move.

While most of the residents of the koliwadas at Sagar Park and Sagar Nagar are Hindu, there are Son Kolis who follow Christianity and Islam as well. The 2010 Marine Fisheries Census for the state notes that 85 per cent of the families in involved in fishing are Hindu by faith, while there are 8 per cent Muslims and 7 per cent Christians among the local Kolis (Central Marine Fisheries Research Institute n.d.). This representation is in some contrast with the southern coast where a large section of the fishing community tends to be Christian.

This played a significant role in early organizing that took place among the fishing communities of Kerala and Tamil Nadu. The local parishes of the fishing communities helped forge the initial fisher organizations and were looked upon by the state as one of the chief representatives of the fisher community during times of conflict.[5] With a majority of fishers in Mumbai being Hindu, the Church has

[3] The koliwada lies at the southern tip of Mumbai.

[4] Palghar is a major centre of fisheries in Maharashtra; it was once known for its large catches of pomfret. Currently, Palghar falls under the Mumbai Metropolitan Region.

[5] See Subramanian (2009) for a discussion on this.

not been as significant a figure. Organizing fishworkers through solidarities based on religion also takes place in Mumbai, but remains distinct from the South.

Kailash[6] from the Sagar Park koliwada—a young activist and Ambedkarite—claimed that members of the community were divided across lines of religion and that for many young adults, participation in local Ganesh mandal activities was important because it led to associating with political parties. Mandal activities therefore would transition eventually into party campaign work. The Ganesh Chaturthi festival, celebrated widely in Maharashtra, has had a long association with Hindu revivalism. Consequently, several parties, prominently Hindu right-wing parties such as the Shiv Sena, have played an important role in organizing mandals across localities.[7] Support for the Shiv Sena is widely acknowledged by several of those who were interviewed for this study, with a number of women, especially, being members of the party as well.[8] This support led to the Shiv Sena establishing one of the first fisher cooperatives for women in the fisheries. Typically, much of the support that the Sena enjoyed among Koli women also came owing to their nativist politics; with an anti-migrant position, Sena politics and Koli fisherwomen's assertions of their rights came together decisively in the early 2000s in Mumbai.

Social institutions, such as the local parish, which have remained both strong and relevant in the context of the Mukkuvar fishing community in Tamil Nadu and Kerala do not have an equivalent among the Kolis, even in areas where the Koli population is predominantly Christian in faith. While older accounts such as Punekar (1959) record the presence of an institution termed the *jamat* (with a recorded presence since 1882), this was primarily an administrative unit and not a religious body. It did, however, enjoy social legitimacy. Comprised of

[6] Personal interview conducted on 31 April 2013 at Sagar Park.

[7] For a detailed analysis on the links between the celebration of the festival and the construction of the Hindu Right (that is, the political project combining Hinduism and right-wing ideology) in Mumbai, see Hansen (2001: 20–35).

[8] The Shiv Sena also played an important role in forming the first women's cooperative for female fishworkers in Mumbai, as elaborated in Chapter 4).

several families and with a male head of the unit, termed the *Patil*, the jamat worked through the *Panch*, which was made up of elderly and respected members of the community, all of whom were men. At the time of her study, Punekar was already documenting the decline of the institution of jamat. As a community entrenched in the life of the city, other public institutions have assumed the role that the jamat played in the life of the Kolis.

One of these institutions which now occupy a prominent place in the life of the Kolis is the local cooperative. While the local cooperative is not the administrative overseer of the community in the way the jamat was, its role as the intermediary between the state and the community has meant that it plays a critical role for most Kolis, who continue as fishers. Cooperatives, however, are notorious for being dominated by boat owners, and, consequently, their composition is overwhelmingly of men constituting the elite of the community. In some koliwadas, the case for cooperatives as one of the central institutions of the community can be made more strongly. For instance, at the Sagar Park koliwada, one of the prominent cooperatives, in addition to its regular function, also extends credit facilities to members for purchasing household items during the monsoon months when fishing is banned. They also grant scholarships to young students from the community and play a role in mobilizing the community in alliance with the MMKS on issues of technology and its impact. But as relevant a role the cooperative might play, its administrative role has been conceived of and remains restricted to concerns from the labour of fishing alone.

Embedded as the koliwadas and the Kolis are in a highly urbanized site, they have also been subject to the administrative exercises and political imaginaries of those who govern the city as a whole. Municipal governance has, thus, played a significant role in shaping the community's presence in the city. One of the biggest threats that koliwadas have been facing is, the threat of eviction from the spaces they occupy. The absence of the necessary regulation required for the CRZ notifications as well as a misclassification of koliwadas have contributed to the threats they face from processes of gentrification. The Sion koliwada episode was instructive of the pressures of urban policies felt on communities such as the Kolis whose life and livelihood do not map neatly over the grand visions of Mumbai's future. The construction of the Bandra–Worli Sea Link, the proposed Coastal road, and the Shivaji statue are all projects that will be severely detrimental to those fishing in inshore and territorial waters and within the 5 fathom zone as stipulated by the Maharashtra Marine Fishing Regulation Act, 1981. Processes of gentrification, growth of the informal economy, and environmental concerns have spelt doom for the urban poor, but for the Kolis whose livelihood is inextricably linked with the city and the sea, the effects have been amplified.

The Labour of Fishing

This insistence of young Koli parents that their children must not follow them into the profession of fishing contradicts the otherwise routinely expressed pride in their traditional labour, that many Kolis claim. Much of this contradiction can be explained by the changes that have taken place in fishing over the last few decades, which are seen as contributing to the immiseration of the community.

In response to this, and in order to understand why the Koli community's popular perception of the demand for exclusive access in fishing has found articulation through hostility to migrants, there is a need to understand the social and economic background of the community. The works of scholars such Castells (cited in Susser 2002) and Bonacich (1973, 1975, 1976) have been important in pointing out how xenophobia that is rife in urban spaces has come on the back of much social and economic misery. The context is familiar for the case of Mumbai and the Kolis. However, what is important to note is that it has been Koli women who have opposed migrant entry in the fisheries (and Mumbai), while Koli men seem to have varied positions on this. It is impossible to understand why women have been at the forefront of the agitation against migrants without understanding how labour in fishing is organized and how links to education have shaped the Koli experience of negotiating the capitalist transformation in the fisheries.

The link between education and mobility is especially crucial in regard of the conflicts that have emerged between Koli women and migrant men. Production in fishing has always followed a strict division of labour between the sexes, one in which access to the most critical resource of livelihood—the seas and the implements of fishing—is restricted to men alone. Women's work in fishing is in the nature of post-harvest work, where they purchase, process, and sell the catch. This division of labour, in many ways, frames the positions which fishers take on the question of exclusive access rights for the community.

The technological makeover in the fisheries did little to dismantle the gendered division of labour, and the technology introduced was restricted primarily to men's work in the fisheries. These technological changes in the nets (nylon based, purse-seine), boats (fiberglass based, trawlers), and aids (GPS, Sonar) used have caused a major upheaval in the mode of production in fishing. As discussed in Chapter 2, the advent of trawlers in fishing—supported and subsidized heavily by the Indian state—transformed fishing into a capital-intensive venture. The introduction of such technology was accompanied by a change in the relations of production, most significantly in the development of a distinct class of owners and workers. Many Kolis view the recent decline in fish catch and the gradual decline of small-scale fishing as resulting from the use of such technology; the NFF too argues that it has led to ecological destruction and this has set the ground for the exclusive access demand.

Men's Work in the Fisheries

It has been one of the most understated but significant problems of the community that in both common perception as well as the state's imagination, fishing has been understood in its most limited sense— as the act of fishing itself.

Fishing was based on the customary knowledge of navigation, seas (tracking which species of fish can be found at which place), and technology. This knowledge was passed down to the male members of the community who would use it in their work as either workers or owner-workers. Incomes were earned and calculated as a share of the catch, with owner-workers receiving two shares instead of one. The two shares were to compensate them for the boats and equipment that they owned. In this scheme, the typical fisher household resembled the peasant household in many ways, where ownership combined with participation in work and where family labour was heavily relied on.

Even as class divisions, therefore, existed within the Koli community, owners participating in work led to the belief of an equitable community. It is, however, this category of the owner-worker and therefore the relation between the property-owning class and labour that has undergone a shift with the capitalist transformation.

The Rupture of the Owner-Worker Category

The question of whether owners of boats operate as owners alone or as owner-workers is the subject of much debate now among the Kolis. Owners almost always refer to themselves as owner-workers, arguing that this has historically been the manner in which they have operated. The practise of dividing the earnings based on equal shares further reinforced the idea of the owner-worker category.[9] The fact that this practise continues even today is often used to differentiate owners in fisheries from the category of owners in other industries. Remuneration being fixed in shares is viewed by many owners as evidence of providing for their workers well, since—they argue—remunerations could be extremely high if the catch is large. The converse, however, also holds true; if little is caught, workers are left with low incomes. This has turned into an increasing possibility at a time when rampant use of purse-seines and trawlers have led to decline in the catch.

Typically, a wage system is indicative of a capitalist system. In the case of Mumbai, incomes that are not termed as wages could lead one to the conclusion that capitalism has not completely arrived in the fisheries, even though workers do sell their labour and receive a remuneration for it. This payment is termed as a 'share' (and not as wages) by boat owners and workers often engage in negotiations around this payment, which is typically decided at the beginning of the fishing season. Increasingly, those who can command capital and influence in order to secure subsidies for purchasing mechanized crafts and trawlers operate as owners alone and not as workers. The basis of the capitalist turn is the erosion of the category of the owner-worker and its fracture into two distinct classes. The capitalist transformation in the fisheries can be inferred from an increasing reliance on capital-intensive technology, an increasing need to rely on investments of large amounts of capital, and on the presence of a large pool

[9] The implication of this on the political discourse around the exclusive access demand of the NFF is discussed in Chapter 5.

of labour that does not have access to the means of production. The absence of a clearly defined wage system should not be taken as the only indicator of whether or not a capitalist transformation is occurring in the fisheries.

In the case of Mumbai, many young and old Koli males who do not possess capital or networks of influence and patronage to purchase boats, even through state aid, eventually take to working as labourers on boats. Such work is often coupled with other jobs (outside of the fisheries), such as working as watchmen, life guards, or speed-boat drivers for water sports companies. Notions of customary work play a strong role in retaining the Kolis within the fisheries. But increasingly, owing to the expansion of the fisheries, a large section of younger men taking to fishing comprise migrant labour. Young boys and men travel from the interior and coastal districts of Maharashtra as well as from other states looking for such work. Skills required to find work on mechanized boats are different and no longer based on customary knowledge of navigation, where to fish, and so on; they have been replaced through the use of technology such as GPS and Sonar systems, enabling the entry of migrants with no previous knowledge of fishing. Such migrants, however, move between jobs in the informal economy, searching for such work during the lean agricultural season. Migrant labourers working on boats in Sagar Nagar, who largely hailed from Uttar Pradesh, claimed that they also travelled to other states in search of work, often picking up jobs in construction or pipe-manufacturing industries. They work in Mumbai on boats during the fishing season (not on fixed contracts) and return to their homes to pursue agricultural work during the rest of the year. Many of these migrants could be characterized as what Breman (2010) refers to as 'footloose labour'.[10] This entry of migrant

---

[10] Discussing migration from rural to urban areas, Breman argues that very small numbers of such migrants find work in urban manufacturing, in the form of either factories or sweatshops. Most of them end up finding work in the informal economy, marked by low wages and skill levels. Such migrants, however, do not always settle in urban areas due to limited employment opportunities as well as the intolerance of the urban rich for the poorer residents of cities. This leads to a 'circulation of labour', resulting in the footloose nature of such migrants (Breman 2010: 2–3).

labour in fishing was also contributing to the distinction between owners and workers.

The Business of Fishing

The emergence of this distinct class of workers can be observed in spite of the fact that the state initiated the capitalist transformation through cooperatives to enfranchise those who could not individually finance their ownership of boats. The mechanization process which began in 1949 did not lead to greater access to new technology: Since loans and subsidies for mechanization were given against the security of boats and other kinds of assets, loans were often unaffordable to many fishers (Punekar 1959: 217). Punekar's observations are pertinent, especially because this inequality persists even today. The Department of Fisheries, however, officially promotes the cooperative principle in fishing,[11] through an extension of loans for mechanized crafts to those who form a cooperative of seven individuals. Advances are also given through the National Cooperative Development Corporation for this purpose. However, a trawler owner stated[12] that while finances for these boats came from multiple sources—including both state and central government funds—at least 10 per cent of the finances have to be secured by the individual loan applicants themselves. Since purse seiners and trawlers are expensive technology, this amount can be substantial, with most boat owners estimating the cost of construction of a trawler as between 40 and 50 lakhs.[13] While the Department of Fisheries mandates such loans being sanctioned only to cooperatives, it is more often the case that there is one primary owner of the business who eventually buys the shares of other members to retain exclusive ownership of a trawler. While most boat owners claimed they worked through the cooperative, they rarely included their partners in discussions on how the trawler business was run. Some, however, later admitted that over time, trawlers could

[11] As discussed in Chapter 2, the cooperative model replaces individual ownership with collective ownership.

[12] Personal interview conducted on 8 June 2013 at Sagar Park.

[13] This set of personal interviews were conducted on 28 May 2013 at Sagar Nagar.

be bought off by one member of the cooperative. This especially holds true for those boat owners who purchase more than one trawler. The dominant trend in such cases was one where the first trawler or purse seiner boat was purchased through government loans, while subsequent acquisitions were financed privately. In some cases, later purchases were in the names of the owner's children who pursued work outside the fisheries.

This is not to suggest that there are no cooperatives of trawler and purse-seine net owners. In fact, a discussion with the local cooperative board of the Sagar Nagar koliwada revealed that several members of their local cooperative could only purchase boats after forming these smaller cooperatives. These loans were also valued, they added, because they incorporated a diesel subsidy which could be availed for the craft. The chairperson claimed that these loans were subject to a strict verification procedure and, therefore, there was minimal scope of cheating the system.[14] The opinion of members of the Sagar Nagar cooperative, however, remained divided on whether such loans should be granted to cooperatives or individuals. While some members argued that the system was beneficial because it allowed for 'seven households to earn an income from one trawler', others disagreed. Notable among those disagreeing was a middle-aged man who had entered the cooperative office during the discussion. Introduced as the biggest boat owner of the area, he proudly noted that he owned a fleet of 10 trawlers and disagreed with the loans being handed out to cooperatives and not individuals. But as he clarified later, his first purchase was made through government aid and he privately financed his later acquisitions.

The divided opinion on the question of loans being handed out to cooperatives alone can be attributed in some part to Subramanian's (2009) argument on the imposition of cooperatives on a community that was accustomed to private ownership. However, cooperatives now enjoy a long history in the state of Maharashtra and dominate not merely the fisheries but also sectors such as agriculture. This makes it a prevailing feature of the political landscape in Maharashtra, and

---

[14] In the course of this research, non-Koli individual trawler owners who had made use of the system to secure financial aid for themselves via the cooperative model were found.

one in which older classes and dominant castes remain prominent. The discontent brewing against such enforced cooperation could also be explained by looking at the quarters from which they emerged. More often than not, it was those who owned more than one trawler who rejected cooperatives and had much to do with how the business of fishing is run today. Clearly discernible among trawler and purse-seine netter owners is the notion that their work is no longer just a traditional occupation—'originally theirs'—but is also a *business* similar to other enterprises prominent in the city, and retaining private ownership is important for this. And while many have gained from the new business, it came at the cost of other castes entering the business of fishing. A commonly held view in the community is that non-Kolis were able to enter the fisheries business through state aid to purchase trawlers. This, they argued, was achieved by non-Kolis establishing a fake cooperative, fronted by Kolis who were paid for their 'service'. A Maratha trawler and purse-seine net owner, Santosh (pseudonym),[15] admitted that this was how he began his business. He claimed that initially he was casually associated with the members of a koliwada cooperative that rejected him when he proposed that he would like to be made a member of the cooperative, to start his own trawler business. He was told that since he was not a Koli, he was not eligible for membership. An angry Santosh decided that he would not let this stop him. Eventually, someone from the cooperative itself introduced him to a government official, whom he bribed with alcohol and money. Following this, Santosh was able to secure membership to a 'cooperative' and was able to get a loan for his trawler. The Koli man who helped him in this work, he claims, has now progressed to become a boat owner himself.

Santosh perceives his actions as being magnanimous. He claims that he has provided 'these people [the Kolis]' with the confidence and ability to take risks, which has enabled them to do better. He claims that his cooperative was not bound by notions of community, and in building a cooperative where membership was not tied to community identity, he portrays himself as modern and industrious. His pejorative views on Kolis and on small-scale fishing reflect this: Small-scale fishers are those 'who don't want to progress in life'. Even with the government

[15] Personal interview conducted on 5 July 2013 in South Mumbai.

willing to provide them the finances to expand the scales of operation they do not do so, Santosh feels that it is merely fear that holds the Kolis back. He regards only one southern koliwada in the city as having 'progressed', with the Kolis finally expanding on their operations, declaring that it is only profits from trawlers which has led people out of poverty. 'Progress', 'technology', and 'modernity' were therefore values that Santosh embraced and claimed to embody through his entrepreneurial spirit. He defined himself as fundamentally different from the Kolis and was secure in his belief that the *business* of fishing would ultimately triumph.

But the notion that fishing is a business was not one espoused by non-Kolis in fishing alone. It was especially evident in how boat owners referred to their work as 'business', often using the English word for the same. The use of the English term 'business', with all its attendant meanings of a large-scale trade and an infusion of capital, can be contrasted with *dhanda*, which can colloquially stand in for business but is most commonly associated with occupation. The transformation from occupation to business was perhaps also the reason why the upper class among the Kolis did not see themselves as leaving fishing. The chairperson of the Sagar Nagar cooperative argued instead that the trawler business was thriving, and the Kolis who 'are from Mumbai, its original inhabitants' are thus returning to fishing. He claimed that they do so to establish a business in their 'traditional occupation'. He pointed to the increased number of loan applications to the Department of Fisheries as evidence of the fact that the trawler business was doing well. Boat owners from the Sagar Park koliwada also made the same point. A trawler owner at the Sagar Park koliwada, for instance, had bought his first trawler only in 2008. In his early thirties, he declared how, prior to his trawler investments, he used to manage the family business of a popular restaurant and bar in South Mumbai. In 2008, realizing that the business of fishing was thriving, he decided to invest in it and began by purchasing two trawlers. Although a Koli, he had no experience in the fisheries, but decided to return to the 'traditional work' of the community in a manner that was commensurate with his vision of running a profitable business. This was not a return to the labour of fishing, but a business investment, the notion of 'traditional work' was being reconfigured by a class of Kolis who could participate as owners and not as workers.

This reconfiguration is perhaps one of the most significant outcomes of the capitalist dynamics that have entered fishing and it has the potential to open up new possibilities. The cooperative chairperson at Sagar Nagar, in response to young men abandoning fishing, claimed that Kolis alone will continue but it could now be Koli women who would do this. They will shift to 'trawlers and purse-seine netters which are run like businesses from the docks with management decisions'. It will be 'work done from a chair' ('*chair pe baithke dhanda karenge*'), but run as efficient export businesses, with the processing and packaging undertaken at the same location, much like how it is done in Japan, he notes.

This formalization and reconfiguration of fishing for him would draw an even closer link between the Kolis and fishing because it held the possibilities to break out of the traditional sex-based division of labour, where women were not involved in fishing itself. It was precisely the business-like management of fishing and the absence of physical labour that, according to this new class of Koli men, would allow women to play a role in fishing-related activities too, in addition to post-harvest work. In the formal business of fishing, owners were now restricted to back-end operations of the business. This includes ensuring a supply of ready capital which is required for purchasing fuel, hiring labour on boats, and processing the fish. In addition, they must engage with auctioneers who determine rates for the kinds of fish depending on the volume of the catch. Of these, securing finances is critical to work in mechanized fishing. The cost of running a trawler lies in the range of 2–3 lakhs for a single trip to the sea, which lasts between 10 and 12 days. Operational costs of purse-seine netters are comparatively higher, with the general consensus being that it could be as high as 12 lakhs for a single trip. The pride associated with labouring on boats was now gradually being replaced by the ability to command capital and employ it successfully for the business. Work on a boat is generally acknowledged as constituting hard and rigorous labour which continues for several hours at a stretch. Therefore, with the ability to hire labour easily, it is not surprising that boat owners have given up working on boats. Yet, there is a great reluctance in letting go of the notion of themselves as owner-workers. This reluctance cannot be attributed to a sentimental attachment to the term alone. On the contrary, it can be argued that at a time when differentiation between owners and workers has increased, the term must be clung to even more steadily, so as to prevent the existing divisions from being turned into political fault lines.

This was reflected in a meeting of the MMKS held in a koliwada in the outskirts of the Mumbai Metropolitan Region. A point of discussion on the agenda was whether the organization was to be registered as a trade union, similar to its parent organization—the NFF—or whether it should take another form. Many members contended that instead of a union, the organization could take other forms, such as charity.[16] They believed that there was no requirement for a trade union, because owners and workers in fishing shared an amicable relationship and worked together. In many koliwadas of Mumbai, a similar claim by boat owners would be repeated—of working on the boats—but this was contrary to empirical evidence. Pressed on the matter, they would describe themselves as 'occasionally working' on the boat when labour was short in supply. However, workers claimed this was not the case, insisting that it was they who had to take on additional work when there was a shortage of labour. The only work that some owners were observed as doing was that of net repair.

Relations between owners and workers were also not free of antagonism. A problem this research encountered—an inability to talk to migrant labourers at length—was born in part from the tense relationship between owners and workers. Most workers had hectic schedules and this posed a problem in finding time to speak to them; many of them also lived on the boats. Furthermore, the presence of owners on the shore along with the workers prevented conversations from taking place. At times, owners would scuttle efforts to speak to workers and would be agitated if workers discussed organizing in collectives. The workers, in response, claimed that relations with owners were not hostile, although confrontations with the owners over remuneration did take place.

More importantly, the reluctance of owners towards workers organizing can be attributed to the sharper distinction emerging between owners and workers. This was linked with labour in fishing

---

[16] The stated reasons for this included tax benefits for those who donated money to the organization, and the ease in maintaining membership accounts if it was not registered as a trade union.

being increasingly composed of migrants. These migrants included the ones from other districts of Maharashtra—most prominently Ratnagiri—and also those coming from the states of Gujarat, Uttar Pradesh, Andhra Pradesh, Karnataka, and so on, who find such work through networks of kin and friends. Thus, the changing mode of production introduced through the flows of capital has led to a clear division of classes between owners and workers, which differences of language, ethnicity, and caste fortify.

Purse Seine Net Fishing and the Moral Economy of the Fisheries

In the fisheries, the entry of migrant workers into low-end jobs and the presence of capitalists from other castes were not the only external threats perceived by the community. What marked the capitalist transformation was technology that reordered the manner in which the commons were used, and how access to fish as resource and product was impacted. While mechanization had initiated this process, it was the entry of purse-seine nets that altered the scale of fishing radically, producing in its wake disruption in the moral economy and affecting the labour of both Koli men and women.

Purse-seine net fishing entered India in the 1970s.[17] The nets are vast, spreading to a radius of up to a kilometre, and possibilities of several nets being linked and cast enable a large catch. These nets cost between 10 and 20 lakhs, making it the hallmark of the capitalist shift in fishing. In addition, its use is accompanied by the employment of technologies such as cameras to locate vast schools of fish that can be caught, all of which adds to the expense of the technique.

While it has generated vast amounts of wealth[18] for some, this mode of production is one that is perceived as being against the

[17] A seine net is one which hangs in the water, forming a vertical wall. The purse-seine net is so named because of the shape the net takes when the bottom of the net is pulled together to shut it, in a manner similar to pulling a drawstring to seal a purse.

[18] While in the field, discussions around large catches and their worth were common. Several members of the Sagar Park koliwada were discussing the recent haul of a purse-seine net boat that sold for INR 1 crore. 'Evidence' for the claim was in the form of a short video showing a large haul of catch on a

morality of the community.[19] A closely knit relationship with their labour in the seas has meant that the Kolis have come to view the sea as a resource that can provide sustenance to all through techniques of fishing employing customary knowledge and practice, knowledge of tides, and use of nets for the passive capture of specific kinds of fish. The participation of the community in the livelihood was woven into customary practices, such as the territorial divisions of the sea, where fishers from one village do not fish in the waters of the other. A mutual understanding on the matter built over the years had resulted in some measure of equitable fishing practices, even as class divisions within the community existed.

This is likely one of the reasons why arguments against ecological destruction were preceded by how purse-seines nets ran against the fabric of moral economy, with fishworkers arguing that its use profited a single individual at the behest of others. Boat owners at Sagar Nagar koliwada argued, 'What we all used to share and eat, the purse-seine takes off alone.'[20] The sentiment was echoed by small-scale mechanized fishers, workers on boats, and retailers of fish, for whom purse-seine and trawl nets represent a form of technology that is at variance with how they envision fishing—a livelihood that provided for the community. This is not to suggest a romanticized vision of how fishing was pursued prior to the introduction of such technology. It also does not suggest that a community operating on the broad principle of common good was not internally divided. However, despite the internal divisions in the community, the technology employed by the Kolis prior to shifting to more capital-intensive forms, one which

---

purse-seine net boat, which was forwarded among young boys of the wada. Other cases with fish catches earning up to INR 8 crores were the stuff of urban legend in the koliwada.

[19] As a caste-based practice, the impact of changing terms of production and exchange were concentrated among the Kolis and also affected those from outside who were embedded in the moral economy of the fisheries, such as consumers of fish, workers in markets, docks, and so on. Even with this concentrated impact, it would be hard to discuss the moral economy as linked to the Kolis alone.

[20] Personal interviews conducted on 17 June 2013 at Sagar Nagar.

enabled equitable access to fish, or what Subramanian terms as 'distributive justice'.

Purse-seine nets disrupted these older practices by enabling single boats to usurp vast amounts of fish, and indiscriminate fishing has threatened the fragile ecological balance of the seas. Purse-seine boats deploy technology to discover large schools of fish, and the nets trap young fish that are smaller in size and weight. This juvenile fish has no value in the markets and often end up as waste. As a senior activist of the MMKS explained, losses incurred through a catch composed of smaller fish which fetch lower prices are compensated by the quantity of fish caught. This overfishing and the severe pollution on the coast, inhibits fishing in creek and inshore waters, compelling small-scale fishers to venture into deeper waters in search of fish. However, the technology they use limits their ability to traverse long distances and limits their quantity of catch. At the same time, purse-seine net boats which are legally supposed to fish in the deep sea move inwards, having exhausted the deep seas, bringing both groups into the same zone and in competition with one another. This is in violation of the regulations of the Maharashtra Marine Fishing Regulation Act, 1981, which sought to address this issue by designating zones for fishing for different kinds of crafts. Further, while only a restricted number of purse-seine nets are legally permitted to operate (with passes issued by the Department of Fisheries for the same), this regulation too is frequently violated. It is widely acknowledged in the community that a large number of such boats operate off the coast of Mumbai without permits. In addition, fishers also point to the presence of purse-seine net boats from neighbouring states which also fish in the waters near Mumbai.

Small-scale fishers who are crippled by the advent of technology argue that shifting to trawlers and purse-seine nets might be the only way for them to survive in fishing (discussed in Chapter 5). But the problem also affects workers on boats, who also bear the consequence of decline in fish catch. A middle-aged fisherman who had worked on a trawler claimed that his decision to move out of fishing was rooted in the declining catch because of which he could not earn enough. Incomes were reduced to INR 3,000 or 4,000, he claimed, and even trawler owners at the Sagar Nagar koliwada, agreed that while 'business' flourishes with the use of purse-seine nets in the short run, the fish catch registers a decline over a period of time.

The apologetic tone with which several trawler and purse-seine net owners explained their use of the technology was indicative of the coalescing of opinion around the notion that purse-seines were detrimental in the long run. The owner of a purse-seine net boat agreed that wastage of fish through the use of these nets was a problem. However, the real problem according to him was that of a single individual making gains from this kind of fishing, at the cost of others. Using better technology enabled him to catch fish, he argued, which may have otherwise been taken by several other smaller boats. But, in spite of his sympathies towards the problems caused as well as towards his local cooperative's position[21] against it, he continued to employ the technology: 'If the people around me do it why not me', he reasoned.

It is interesting to note that much of the widespread derision for such new technology is directed at purse-seine nets alone and not towards trawl nets.[22] Many claimed that while trawlers were also a problem, the sheer quantum of catch that a purse-seine net allows for made it much more culpable in their eyes for their predicament. Blame was also laid on the government who they believed contributed to this situation by providing financial and infrastructural aid to enable the use of this technology. Boat owners at the Sagar Nagar koliwada, claimed that the government sanctioned large loans for the construction of such boats and nets, pressuring fishers who undertake them to flout regulations regarding zones, including the ban during monsoon, in order to pay back the debt. Arguments on ecological harm, customary notions of common good, as well as state policy, were all marshalled, therefore, to highlight the problems with purse-seine net fishing.

However, despite the adverse impact on ecology or the depressing wages in the fisheries, for Koli men avenues remained opened. Those with social and financial capital could look to convert themselves in to

---

[21] The cooperative was affiliated to the MMKS and supported its demand for a ban on purse-seine net fishing.

[22] The type of net makes a significant difference to the amount of catch: Of the two, purse-seine nets are seen as generating larger catches.

new capitalists, aided by state policy. If this was not an option, many armed themselves with an education and sought work in the city.

Typically, the change in technology in fishing has been seen to impact fishing itself, without adequate attention this affected the domain of women's work in the fisheries. This neglect of women's work informed state policy as well as the fisher movement itself, which addressed the impact of the transformation on women's work belatedly. This neglect of the women's question contributed in no small part to shaping the early alliance between the Koli women and the Shiv Sena in Mumbai.

4

The Other Half of the 'Pink Revolution'

Koli Women's Work and Its Discontents

It is important to note that even though the transformation did little to dismantle the sex-based division of labour or change women's work in the fisheries, fisherwomen were still fundamentally affected by it. The sex-based division of labour restricted women's work to post-harvest/fishing work, such as that of fish processing and retailing. It is the entry of migrants into this work, a consequence of the transformation, that triggered the hostile response from Koli women. But by no means was this a 'natural' response. I argue that the absence of state aid and lack of institutional support from cooperatives, coupled with blocked avenues of mobility, led to Koli women responding in xenophobic terms.

State interventions in fishing did not address the question of gender at all. This was both by means of commission and omission. Even though there were stray references[1] in Mumbai of women fishing and

---

[1] An employee of the International Collective in Support of Fishworkers (ICSF) working with Koli women recounted an anecdote mentioned by one of the older women regarding how Koli women would sometimes fish while travelling on boats between the islands that comprised Bombay.

having limited access to resources, such as ownership of boats and other implements, the state made no attempts to enable women's participation in fishing directly. Linked to this division of labour is what Ram (1991) identifies as incorporeal property[2] in fishing communities, which also mediates a relation to space. This has implications, particularly, for women in the community. Mukkuvar women, as Ram (1991) points out, do not have access to beaches and sea fronts, which are occupied by men. While this has not been noted in Mumbai as a norm, it is certainly true that the division of labour makes male presence along the coast and beach dominant. It was rare to see a woman present in these areas because their work would mostly require them to be at the drying yards (which in places such as the Sagar Nagar lay at some distance from the shore), markets, or in their homes. Even during hours of leisure, the shores and beaches were used primarily by men.[3] But while fisherwomen were absent from the shores, they enjoyed wide mobility in other spaces owing to the division of labour. This mobility, which is an important part of fisherwomen's work as both Ram (1991) and Subramanian (2009) argue, was not available to women who participated in agrarian labour. In contrast, fisherwomen travel widely in the course of their work, frequenting markets.

> Women's ability to travel with impunity and even authority within the coastal belt and to the markets and shrines of the agricultural hinterland stems from a collective understanding that they are carrying out the tasks as duties proper to them as *women*: that is in the name of domestic responsibilities associated with a cultural model of femininity. (Ram 1991: 206)

[2] 'These privileges may include the proprietorship of certain skills, knowledge of rituals, songs, and legends. Among the Mukkuvars, the incorporeal property comprises the transmission of specialised skills, astronomy, and so on. These skills are essential in working and utilising the natural resources of the ocean' (Ram 1991: 47).

[3] An interesting anecdote recounted at the Sagar Park koliwada highlighted how the shore was a space primarily occupied by men for leisure and work. Several residents recollected that had there not been an important televised international cricket match on the evening of 26 November 2008, the day of the terror attack in Mumbai, the men from the village, who otherwise spend time on the shore after their dinner, would have definitely spotted the attackers landing their boat on the shore of the koliwada.

Ram's observations are relevant because they recognize and reiter-
ate that domestic work spills outside of the home into other spaces,
such as agricultural land, and in this case, distant markets, fishing
yards, trains, and so on. This is in contrast to the general conception
of domestic work as restricted to the space in and around the home.
Several women would also take up the work of processing or curing
fish, which would be located away from home. For those who did
not cure or process large amounts of fish, this work would often be
performed at the threshold of the house such that the lanes and alleys
would often be occupied by women engaged in this work during the
day. In light of this, Ram (1991: 208) echoed concerns raised by the
women's movement on domestic work, arguing that such work was
not completely 'privatised and unrecognised', as it had been understood in the West.

The case of Koli women is similar, with mobility and access to space
not threatened. But this does not suggest that Koli women are treated
as equals to their male counterparts (the difference in education levels highlighted later in the chapter are indicative of women being
disadvantaged). However, it does require us to nuance our arguments
regarding unpaid domestic work and paid work with its ascriptions
of femininity, and thus complicates older arguments regarding wom-
en's domestic labour, which is often assumed, as Ram (1991) pointed
out, to be constrained within the home, unrecognized and devalued.
Punekar (1959) alludes to this complexity by highlighting that their
paid work grants Koli women economic independence, which, she
argues, explains their stronger presence in fishing as a livelihood
compared to the men who were seen as leaving this profession.

> At the young age of twelve or thirteen a girls [sic] starts earning. For a
> few years she sells from her mother's stock of fish. The mother gives
> her earnings from the fish she sells. Within three or four years she has
> her own separate seat in the market. (Punekar 1959: 154)

Interviews with Koli women who vend, highlighted continuities in
this pattern of work. Parvati (pseudonym),[4] a fishworker, recollected
how she began working while still studying in the 8th standard and,
in addition to fish vending, also took tailoring classes. Earning and

---

[4] Conversation with Parvati on 3 July 2013.

working from a young age, she soon left school to pursue fish vending full time. Most fisherwomen began fish vending at a young age and often began from the same markets in which their mothers and sometimes grandmothers worked. Besides the historic connection they retained with these spaces, women come to attach great symbolic and economic value to the site of the market since it was linked with their customary practice.

It is important to note that this gender-based division of labour is one that continues to be reinforced by the state. Training imparted to members of the community at the Fisheries Institute at Versova in Mumbai,[5] for instance, differs for men and women. Men are given classes on engine maintenance, repair, and so on, while women are given courses on preparation of what are termed as 'value added products', such as fish crackers, pickles, chips, and so on.

This kind of value addition or post-harvest work done by Koli women, according to Punekar, had granted them primary control of household income as a consequence of men being out at sea and women engaging in retail. But with men shifting to salaried jobs in the city from the 1950s onward, this changed (Punekar 1959: 154). Punekar argues that much of this had to do with the effects of urbanization because, for the men in the city, the need for money indicated a desire to participate in the leisure economy that the city had to offer (Punekar 1959: 154). Currently, with opportunities for wage employment available both within and outside the fisheries, household income is not completely under the control of women. Since most women worked, they retained some control over their earnings. Men who worked as labourers on boats also supplemented their income through employment in low skill jobs which granted them a salary. Such kind of supplementary labour is usually not taken on by women, but that could be attributed to the long hours of work in fishing itself.

New Technologies and Altered Markets

Women's work linked to fish retail is integrally tied to market spaces. In the absence of ownership or control over any resource directly

[5] Those who take government loans for the purchase of boats must attend these courses.

related to fishing, markets have become central to their identity. Rooted in their occupation and the politics around it, in the face of urban policies of gentrification, they have come to define their political actions. Markets hold historic relevance for Koli women. This is not merely due to their personal associations with it, such as daughters vending from the spaces where their great grandmothers and mothers used to work. It also emerges from the relationship they forge with the market itself.

Built over the years, many markets saw their humble beginnings with Koli fisherwomen. In the collective memory of Koli women, markets came to be established when they began vending from these spaces; with other vendors such as those selling spices and vegetables joining them, gradually the space came to be recognized as a market. The technique is often still used to establish new market spaces. In addition to the markets from which the retail of fish would take place, Koli women also travelled to the larger whole-sale markets from where the produce for sale was purchased. In South Mumbai, the Crawford Market is the site of large wholesale fish markets from where the daily supply of fish makes its way to local markets scattered through the city. The auction of fish held early in the mornings was one where women were predominantly active. However, the capitalist transformation in fishing has also altered the process of purchase from an auction. Traditionally, fisherwomen would often purchase fish at the morning auctions on credit, repaying when they had sold their stocks. But with the entry of new technology and its orientation towards an export market, there has been a rise in the price of fish. Additionally, fisherwomen are no longer the only agents participating in the business of fish retail. Export companies have emerged as significant players in this field, often hiring middlemen who offer money in advance to boat owners for their catch. This translates into high-quality fish being immediately procured for international and domestic regional markets, as opposed to finding their way into smaller local markets for immediate consumption.

As discussed earlier, new technology has severe effects on the amount of fish caught. Women's work has particularly been hit by this. With a dwindling catch, female fish vendors who operate on smaller profit margins are left competing with medium-scale and large-scale exporters.[6] It was precisely to deal with these problems plaguing fisherwomen that one of the first collective organizations for women emerged.

Purnima Meher, a senior activist of the NFF and MMKS, noted that to respond to the credit crunch fisherwomen were faced with, a voluntary organization called the Shramik Sadhana was established.

> At this point of time, there were several savings groups being established by the government and we also made one of our own. This organization, which worked for female fishworkers, primarily fish vendors, as well as for people from tribal communities who were engaged in fishing, ran for around two years. For this savings group, money was collected from the women. Around this time, we were given the suggestion that it would be good if a credit cooperative of our own was to be established. The women who worked with us on the savings group also worked on a voluntary basis. But now they came together in the credit cooperative that was formed. This took place in 1999 when we established this women's credit cooperative. A number of women both from the fishing community and the tribal community came to be a part of this. Once this happened, the issues pertaining to women started emerging, such as market issues and even national-level issues.[7]

Purnima's observations are especially pertinent to realize the slow pace in drawing attention to the problems fisherwomen faced in their labour. But as these activists noted, fisherwomen's problems were obscured from vision by an exclusive focus on men's work alone by both the state and fisher organizations. For instance, another problem that fisherwomen encountered has been with regard to transportation. Once the fish is bought at the wholesale market, fisherwomen have to transport it to their local market from where they vend. As fish is a highly perishable commodity, both speed and insulation are critical to its transportation, yet both have been out of reach for most women. In states such as Tamil Nadu and Kerala, where fisher organizations had an early start, these questions eventually came to be addressed. As Subramanian notes,

[6] Ram (1991: 220–1) highlights a similar process at work.
[7] Telephonic conversation with Purnima on 19 June 2013.

for fisherwomen, mobility was mediated through material concerns of transport as well as caste.

> Compounding the inland caste aversion to the 'polluting' labor of handling fish is the censure against fisherwomen for their transgression of gender norms. The stereotype of women fish vendors as filthy, uncouth, argumentative, and lewd are ubiquitous. Not only are such pejorative assessments of their bodies and behavior insulting, but they also have serious effects on coastal women's livelihood. Until their demand for special coast-to-market buses with racks for fish vessels was granted by MGR's government, women vendors were routinely denied passage on public transportation. Many older vendors recounted tales of daily struggle to get their fish to the market before it spoiled. (Subramanian 2009: 182)

The problem was similar to the one which Koli women continue to endure. In the absence of public transport, Koli women who travel with fish must make use of local trains and also hire taxis/tempos and so on to transport the fish. An activist with the MMKS, Ujjwala, notes that the fisherwomen in Mumbai are permitted to travel in the luggage compartment of local trains.[8] However, their travel in the 'ladies' compartment' often lead to fights with other working women, who complain if the water from the fish baskets/containers falls on them. She argues, therefore, that there is a need to arrange for better transport for fisherwomen. But it is not merely fisherwomen from the city who are affected by this; fishers from neighbouring regions also rely on the train network. Koli women from neighbouring districts of Thane, as well as fisherwomen from Gujarat travel to purchase fish from the Crawford Market. These women travel through the night to Mumbai, returning in the day to their villages to sell the fish purchased from the city. As another activist, Suresh, notes, travel for Koli women has always been a challenge.

These problems, which were severe for the residents, were especially difficult for those travelling to Mumbai. Purnima recollected that women travelling from the town of Palghar to Mumbai would often be prohibited from travelling in the trains. Leaders of the MKKS,

---

[8] The right to travel with their fish loads in luggage compartments was itself a hard-won right.

Rambhau Patil (the chairperson of the MMKS at the time) and N.D. Koli had to meet with railway authorities to resolve this problem.

In addition to fish retail, fisherwomen also undertook the drying of fish, some pursuing this exclusively. Fish drying is a critical part of the post-harvest work in the fisheries, especially necessary to ensure a supply of fish during the monsoon months when fishing is not actively pursued (mechanized fishing being banned by the law during the monsoon season). Dried and cured fish is also cheaper to purchase for those who can ill afford fresh fish. Additionally, sometimes, smaller fish are dried and used as manure (which was also the primary use of prawns prior to the discovery of an export market for them). This work involved days spent in sorting, cleaning, and stringing fish up to dry in yards demarcated for this purpose. At Sagar Nagar, poles were erected, on which Bombay duck were hung and dried, while shrimps were usually laid out on the ground for this purpose. Punekar's (1959) descriptions of the process highlight the continuities in the work, indicating the absence of technological change in this sphere of work in the fisheries.

Migrant Labour in Post-Harvest Work

In addition to the primary occupations of fish vending and drying practised by fisherwomen, there has been an area of work that has emerged in response to the capitalist transformation. The export market and the changing scales of production have resulted in a need for fish processing to be undertaken on a large scale. Following from the traditional division of labour where cleaning and processing of fish was constituted as women's work, processing work continues to be performed by women but has attracted a large number of migrant women to it.

Kumari (pseudonym),[9] who works at a fish processing unit at the Sassoon Docks, hails from a tribal community in Karnataka. She migrated to Mumbai a few years after getting married and her search for work in the city led her to the docks, where she is now one of the hundreds of women involved in cleaning and sorting fish, typically prawns, before they are packaged for export. Even after spending

[9] Personal interview conducted on 20 August 2013 in South Mumbai.

over 30 years in the industry, fishworkers such as Kumari continue to labour in oppressive conditions, under the supervision of contractors employed by export companies. On a typical work day, contractors purchase the prawns and transport them to warehouses, where women like Kumari begin their days at 8 a.m. and continue till around 6 p.m. They have no fixed wages, and their incomes are dependent on the amount they process in a day, with the rate being determined on the basis of the amount of catch that is purchased by the company on that particular day. The usual rate is Rs 10–12 per kg. This amount can increase by Rs 1–2 on days when the quantity of the catch is large, with the maximum amount being close to Rs 25.

The women who work in the industry suffer immensely, owing not only to the low wages but also the physical demands of the work. Their hands are often injured due to the shells, which causes swelling. Further, in the absence of proper seating, they sit hunched for long hours, and get breaks only to have lunch and use the toilet. This leads to backaches and other health problems. Kumari adds that the work is also difficult because they must fend for themselves during the months of the ban, when work is minimal to negligible. As a result, many women who work in fish processing seek out other employment, such as domestic and construction work, as common alternatives taken up during the period of the ban. Working conditions are precarious and the absence of unions has contributed to the vulnerability of the workers. Kumari and workers like her are unable to negotiate for increased wages since they are threatened with dismissal, and with a surfeit of those looking for work, the threat seems potent.

Much like migrant men in fishing, workers such as Kumari have remained tied to the informal economy in fishing. It is significant to note that it is with the capitalist transformation in the fisheries that one also notes the rise of precarious work with low wages and exploitative conditions that have been taken up by migrants in the city. But the transformation also affected Koli women's work in the fisheries. The change in market relations, the rising prices of fish, and the decline in fish catch have been central in weakening Koli fisherwomen's links with their traditional livelihood. In the face of these changes, Koli fishermen are seeking to become new capitalists and, if pushed out of the fisheries, they have taken up employment outside of it. The same patterns have not been visible for women. Typically, occupational mobility is tied to education and this emerges as an important difference between Koli men and women; it remains significant as an explanation for why it has been Koli women who have been at the forefront of protesting migrant entry into fishing and have been strident about strengthening the rights of the Koli community over fishing and its allied activities.

Education and Mobility among the Kolis

The large flows of migrant labour in fishing raise the question of what is happening with local labour. Punekar (1959) identified education levels and economic dependency on others as one of the reasons why men abandoned fishing for other work. Migrant workers, though, were not entering fishing in substantial numbers at the time. The current context, however, with a decisive shift towards capitalism and the ecological stress caused, has shaped how Kolis are able to access work in the fisheries. For Koli women, the entry of large businesses in fish retail squeezed them out of the credit they operated on[10] and the diminishing quality and quantity of fish in domestic markets are further threatening their position. In a city with one of the highest costs of living, the threats to their livelihood have rendered the Kolis vulnerable. In these circumstances, accessing work outside the fisheries has been critical to their survival. Even as many young Kolis access some form of employment in the informal economy of the city, it is through education that many have been able to access such work.

Listed as a 'backward' caste, the community has historically had a fraught relation with education; expanding on education has always been part of the agenda for the Kolis. As early as 1914 (*Times of India* 1914: 8), a conference of the Son Kolis was held at 'Kolaba', where resolutions were passed on promoting education among the Kolis. Newspaper records also point to public meetings organized by the Municipal Schools Committee. One such meeting held at the Worli

---

[10] As elaborated in Chapter 5, big businesses in fish retail often purchased fish by making advance payments to boat owners. However, traditionally, Koli women bought fish on credit and made the payments later. With the entry of big businesses, Koli women lost the ability to access this credit.

koliwada in 1932 (*Times of India* 1932: 13) was to urge the spread of education among the Kolis, asking them to avail the government facilities for education. The community repeatedly petitioned the state to intervene to improve the education levels of the Kolis. Yet Koli education levels have remained low, as indicated in detail by Punekar (1959) and this book.

As early as 1935, the spread of education among the Koli youth had led to 'a distaste among them for their traditional profession and they now prefer service to fishing' (*Times of India* 1935: 7). Punekar's work on the Kolis documents the same, pointing to how education for young boys was not encouraged because it was seen as drawing them away from manual work that was essential to fishing (Punekar 1959: 121).

This did not mean that young boys began acquiring the skills of fishing as soon as they quit school. That process did not begin until they reached 15–20 years of age. Punekar (1959) claims that the boys who began work on boats did not receive an income, since their income was retained by their fathers. According to Punekar (1959: 121), their economic dependence on their fathers was the primary reason why educated boys sought to move out of fishing. Moreover, with an increase in education levels, fishing was seen as a 'low occupation' and many refused to take to it up, instead seeking employment outside. Their lack of skills led them to take up jobs such as that of fitters and welders. Therefore, she argues, with higher levels of education in a locality, the fishing industry registers a decline in that area (Punekar 1959: 125). Contrary to the men, Punekar noted, women of the community continued to participate in allied activities of fishing even if they attained higher levels of education. She attributed this to girls working in fish retail being given a share of the day's income by their mothers. In contrast to men, the economic independence fishing offered to women led them to continue in it. Today, the reasons for women's continued participation in fishing are different and rooted more in their access to education, which affects their occupational mobility. This is established by the correlation between education levels and employment choices, which, contrary to what Punekar's (1959) study highlighted, reflect that educational advancements for *both* men and women pave a way for them to exit the fisheries and seek work elsewhere.

Koli Women and Education

Punekar (1959) records in her work that Koli children are sent to school at the age of six or seven, but the girls are quick to leave school, usually within two to three years of joining. Of the 260 women surveyed by Punekar (1959: 119), only 68 had received primary education, but with recent improvement in education, the numbers were improving.

The survey conducted for this work also testified to recent improvements in education for females. But even as a general trend, female education remained low in both absolute as well as relative terms compared to men. In 2013, of the 268 females who were surveyed for this study, excluding toddlers (of whom there were 7), only 13 females (that is, 4.9 per cent) had completed their primary education (defined here as between the 1st and 8th standard), while 28 females (that is, 10.4 per cent) were in the process of pursuing primary education (see Table 4.1) and 17.9 per cent of the women had not received any education.

Table 4.1   Completed Level of Education for Females

Level of Education	Total	Percentage
Completed primary and upper primary education (1st to 8th Std)	13	4.9
Did not complete primary and upper primary education (1st to 8th Std)	65	24.3
Pursuing primary to upper primary education (1st to 8th Std)	28	10.4
Completed secondary education (8th to 10th Std)	24	9.0
Did not complete secondary education (8th to 10th Std)	15	5.6
Pursuing secondary education (8th to 10th Std)	13	4.9
Completed higher secondary education (11th to 12th Std)	12	4.5
Did not complete higher secondary education (11th to 12th Std)	5	1.9
Pursuing higher secondary education (11th to 12th Std)	12	4.5
Completed graduation	8	3.0
Pursuing graduation	14	5.2
Did not complete graduation	4	1.5
No education	48	17.9

Source: Author's fieldwork.

Punekar (1959) found that few girls continued their schooling beyond primary education and that, generally, they dropped out after the fourth standard, with only 3.85 per cent of those surveyed in her study having received a secondary education. She also notes that illiteracy was at a minimum between the ages of 11 and 15 for girls (Punekar 1959: 121). In comparison, in this study, 24.3 per cent of the women had dropped out of school while pursuing their primary education, compared to 5.6 per cent who dropped out during secondary education (8th to 10th standard), and 1.9 per cent who dropped out during higher secondary (11th to 12th standard). Thus, Punekar's argument regarding females dropping out from school earlier continues to remain valid even after a gap of 54 years.

However, an age-wise break up of the levels of education for females in the current study reveal that in the age category between 4 and 20 years (see Figure 4.1), there are no females who have dropped out of school. Of these, the highest numbers, that is, 35 per cent, are those pursuing their primary education. It is also important to note

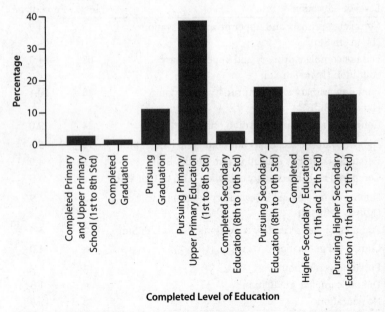

Figure 4.1   Level of Education among Females between 4 and 20 Years of Age
Source: Author's fieldwork.

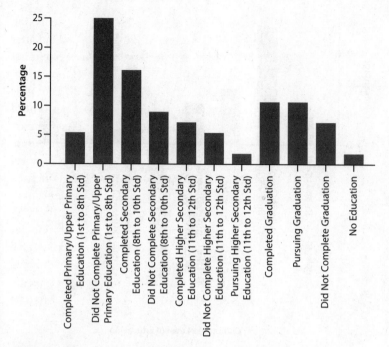

Figure 4.2   Level of Education among Females between 21 and 30 Years of Age
Source: Author's fieldwork.

that 10 per cent from this age bracket are pursuing their graduation.[11] These indicators signify that education among women is reasonably well-established now. Comparisons with older age groups of women also point to how this improvement in education levels is a recent phenomenon.

In the age bracket of 20–30 years (Figure 4.2), for instance, only 5.4 per cent women completed their primary education, while 25 per cent of them dropped out. The percentage of women pursuing their graduation was just a fraction below the previous age bracket and stands at 10.7 per cent (see Figure 4.2). Of the 56 women who were

[11] Certain individuals listed themselves as pursuing a diploma course. This has been clubbed with graduation for purposes of convenience since the aim was to estimate the number of women pursuing education after school.

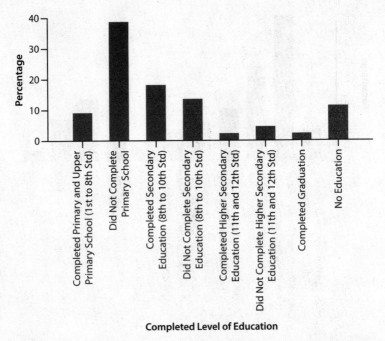

Figure 4.3 Level of Education among Females between 31 and 40 Years of Age
Source: Author's fieldwork.

in this age bracket, only one did not receive formal education. As one moves up the age brackets, the number of women who dropped out of primary education and who are illiterate increases. This is accompanied by low numbers of women who pursued higher education. Thus, in the age group between 31 and 40 years of age, 38.6 per cent did not complete their primary education, 11.4 per cent had no education, and only one woman (2.3 per cent of the sample) had completed her graduation (see Figure 4.3).

Between the ages of 41 and 50, the number of women who did not complete their primary education rises to 52.5 per cent and those with no education stands at 25 per cent. None of these women pursued higher secondary education, and consequently none of them pursued or completed their graduation. Only 7.5 per cent women from the age cohort of 41 to 50 years completed their secondary

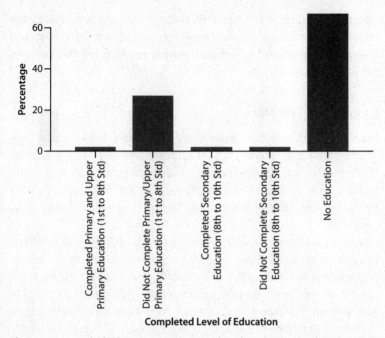

Figure 4.4   Level of Education among Females Above 50 Years of Age
Source: Author's fieldwork.

education (8th to 10th standard), as opposed to 18.2 per cent women between the ages of 31 and 40.

Finally in the bracket of women above the age of 50, the difference in education levels from women of other age brackets is stark and revealing. Of these women, only 2.1 per cent had completed their primary and secondary education. Interestingly, a large proportion of the women in this age group (that is, 66.7 per cent) had received no formal education (see Figure 4.4).

This data, therefore, highlights that there has been an emphasis on female education only in the recent times, with a surge especially in the last 20 years or so. Much of this can be attributed to the parents' desire to educate their children in order to enable them to move out of fishing (a point that will be elaborated upon later). Also, the penetration of the schooling system, with the mushrooming of private schools, has led to increased access to education. But most importantly, such an increase would not have taken place without a corresponding willingness to spend and invest on education for females, which has defined the last two decades for Koli women.

Education of Koli Males

Punekar (1959) noted the tendency of Koli boys to not continue their education for long, leaving school within a couple of years of joining. Skills for fishing, she argued, demanded a regular routine through which young boys could be familiarized with the techniques and this interfered with regular school, resulting in their low levels of formal education.

In this study, of the 243 males surveyed, excluding 11 toddlers, figures for education reveal significant improvements in the education levels of Koli males. Just like education among young girls, these improvements have also taken place recently, although compared to Koli women, education levels among men have always been better. In the category between 4 and 20 years of age, 10.9 per cent of the males were pursuing their primary education, and only 1 among 64 males in this age group had not completed his primary education, dropping out mid-way, and this too was because the child in question was cognitively differently abled and was not being sent to any school.[12] However, 46.9 per cent of males in this category were pursuing their primary education, this indicates the significance education has assumed in recent times.

The age cohort of 21–30 is of particular interest in this regard, since 21.2 per cent of the 52 males in this group are graduates, while the other 7.7 per cent in the process of pursuing their graduation. A single individual (1.9 per cent) is pursuing a post-graduate degree, while 3.8 per cent have completed their post-graduation. The representation of young adult males in higher education is an important milestone for a community that has historically had low education levels. Evidence for this can be found by looking at the number of

---

[12] The results for the ages between 4 and 20 also highlight an instance of a child not being enrolled. This was the case of a five-year-old child, who had not entered school at the time this survey was conducted.

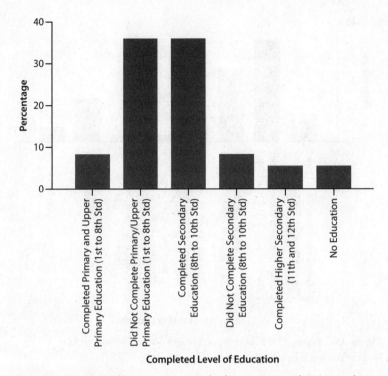

Figure 4.5   Level of Education among Males between 41 and 50 Years of Age
Source: Author's fieldwork.

those who drop out during primary or secondary education as well as the number of illiterates among older males. For those dropping out during primary education, the figures stand at: 30 per cent for those between the ages of 31 and 40; 36.1 per cent for those between the ages of 41 and 50 (Figure 4.5); and 34.1 per cent for those above the age of 51 (Figure 4.6). While all[13] males between the ages of 4 and 40 have received an education, among men between 41 and 50 years of age (see Figure 4.5), 5.6 per cent did not receive an education, and in the age bracket of above 51 years, this percentage rises to 14.6 per cent.

---

[13] With the exception of two young males, one of whom had not been educated at a special needs or regular school since he was differently abled whilst the other was yet to be enrolled.

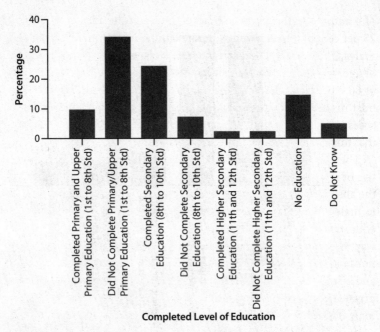

Figure 4.6   Level of Education among Males Above 51 Years of Age
Source: Author's fieldwork.

Gender Differentials in Education

Regarding the gender difference in education, Punekar (1959: 122) observes that boys 'as a rule have been taking more education and from much earlier times (since the end of the last century)[14] than the girls'. Punekar's observations continue to hold true. However, a feature common to the education of both boys and girls is the recent decline in the number of illiterates. With regards to secondary education, Punekar observed a wide difference between the sexes, with a larger number of men entering and completing secondary education.

The difference in illiteracy, however, remains prominent between the sexes. In this study, the percentage of women who were illiterate between the ages of 21 and 30 was 1.8 per cent, and this rises to a significant 11.4 per cent for those between the ages of 31 and 40. Comparatively, there are no males who are illiterate between the ages

---

[14] That would translate to the end of the nineteenth century.

of 4 and 40. In the next age bracket, between the ages of 41 and 50, 25 per cent of females were illiterate compared to a mere 5.6 per cent males. This number swells in the last category of those above 51 years of age, where female illiteracy stands at a tragically large percentage of 66.7 per cent compared to 14.6 per cent for males. The stark contrast in these figures reveals how men have generally enjoyed better access to education than women, and it is only in the last few decades that this gap has reduced but not been bridged.

The absence of illiteracy among the younger generation irrespective of sex (between the ages of 4 and 21), however, cannot be read as the absence of a preference for male education. Entitlements granted to male children have now taken a new form, that of the *medium* of education. English-medium education is viewed by many as the gateway to employment outside of the fisheries and into better paying, non-manual work. As a result, a great importance is accorded to it and several households surveyed mentioned how they also employed private tutors for English for their children. Around 26 per cent of the male children received an education in English compared to 19 per cent of the females. This difference, however, does not extend into a preference for public or private schools. With the mushrooming of private schools, including several which used Marathi as a medium, parents sent their children, both male and female, to them.

Another interesting development was the high prevalence of households hiring private tutors to assist the children in their education. Out of the 100 households surveyed (excluding those who do not have school-going children), 61 employ private tutors for their children in addition to sending them to either public or private schools, indicating that education has gradually taken on greater significance in the community. Thus, while the aspiration for education may have been a long-prevalent desire of the community, substantial improvement has been registered within the community only in the last few decades. For those seeking to improve their circumstances, the calculation that better education can lead to mobility has been responsible for the investment in their children's education. Several parents, thus, declared that they spent large amounts of money on their children's education to enable them to move out of fishing.

Mobility in the context of Mumbai, for most Kolis, is therefore based on their ability to move out of fishing. Education is regarded as the most important resource to enable this. But what was made evident through the survey was also that achieving mobility through the means of fishing was not a feasible option. Most parents were of the opinion that fishing could no longer sustain a household, compared to older times. Around 49.2 per cent of the respondents claimed that they did not see fishing as providing adequate sustenance in the future. A significant number of respondents, that is 26.2 per cent, wanted their children to move out of the manual labour involved in fishing and seek regular, formal employment, and 6 per cent saw fishing as being too expensive to pursue.

The relation between education and labour is therefore a critical one, and in the case of the Kolis, especially, has played a fundamental role in determining who remains in fishing and who does not, as will be discussed further.

The data in Tables 4.2 and 4.3 clearly highlight how, in the age group between 18 and 30 years, considered as the prime working populace, there is a tendency to move out of fishing by attaining higher levels of education. This is especially evident in the case of males who move out of fishing in higher numbers compared to women, as their education levels rise. Thus, for instance, among those who have completed their secondary education, 10 men (out of a total of 41 in the age category of 18–30) have moved out of fishing. At the same education level, only 4 women (out of a total of 43 women in the age category of 18–30) have moved out of fishing. Furthermore, all graduates, of whom there are 10 men and 2 women, are employed outside of the fisheries. Education typically translates into employment outside the fisheries, irrespective of sex. However, since education levels register a significant difference based on sex, there is a tendency for more men to move out of fishing compared to women, leaving a higher concentration of Koli women working in fisheries compared to men of the same age.

This difference in educational achievements and the ability to translate this into a route out of the fisheries is critical in understanding why it has been the Koli women who have been strident about strengthening the link between the community and the occupation of fishing. While fishing has been central to the identity of both male and female Kolis, education, technological change, and state aid to access capital have come to men and their labour, but not to women. For Koli fisherwomen, their domain of work has remained

Table 4.2 Cross-Tabulation of Education and Work Details for Men between Ages 18 and 30

Level of education	Boat owners	Work as hired labour on boats	Fish vending and/or drying/processing fish	Allied activities such as net repair/supplying fish to hotels	Employed outside the fisheries
Completed primary and upper primary school (1st to 8th Std)	0	0	0	0	1
Did not complete primary school	2	2	0	0	1
Did not complete secondary school (8th to 10th Std)	1	0	0	1	0
Completed secondary school (8th to 10th)	1	0	1	1	10
Completed higher secondary (11th and 12th Std)	1	0	0	0	5
Completed graduation	0	0	0	0	10
Pursuing graduation	0	0	0	0	1
Completed post-graduation	0	0	0	0	2
Pursuing post-graduation	0	0	0	0	1

Source: Author's fieldwork.

Table 4.3 Cross-Tabulation of Education and Work Details for Women between Ages 18 and 30

	Details of work	
Completed level of education	Fish vending and/or drying/ processing fish	Employed outside of the fisheries
Completed primary and upper primary school (1st to 8th Std)	1	1
Did not complete primary school	15	1
Completed secondary school (8th to 10th Std)	3	4
Did not complete secondary school (8th to 10th)	3	1
Completed higher secondary (11th and 12th Std)	0	3
Did not complete higher secondary (11th and 12th Std)	0	3
Completed graduation	0	2
Pursuing graduation	0	2
Did not complete graduation	0	3
No education	1	0

Source: Author's fieldwork.

technologically backward and low levels of education have hindered their movement out of fishing and into more formal forms of employment which are desired. Owing to this blocked mobility, Koli fisherwomen have rallied even more strongly to safeguard fishing and its allied activities as the domain of traditional communities alone. In doing so, Koli fisherwomen have focused their ire on the figure of the migrant, whose entry they perceive as a threat to their livelihood and community identity. Their actions are typical of many working-class movements which have responded to the loss of job and identity in xenophobic terms. Given that the identity of the Kolis as the original inhabitants of Mumbai affords them prominence within the nativist politics, the simmering discontent of Koli fisherwomen had put them on a warpath with migrants in the early 2000s.

5

The Struggle around Identity

Organizations and Politics of the Kolis

The entry of migrants into fish vending has ruptured the traditional division of labour that defined retail as Koli women's work. Koli women see themselves as competing with migrant men in a finite market, which has led to much antagonism between them in both fish retail as well as claims to the city.

Migrant labourers, many of whom escaped low wages and productivity in the agrarian sector, moved across cities in search of work. In Mumbai, which has witnessed popular currents of nativist movements, migrants (although the specific kind of migrant has varied over time) have often been the target of the locals, who hold them responsible for the dismal economic conditions they find themselves in. Parties such as the Shiv Sena and its splinter, the Maharashtra Navnirman Sena (MNS), have come to power by not only riding the wave of popular discontent among locals but also by sharpening this discontent into active hostility. These parties have also played a significant role in organizing the Kolis (*Times of India* 2003, 2004c), especially Koli women, into a position of hostility against migrant labourers from North India.

The question of migration is currently central to the fisheries, so much so that it impacts not only how organizations such as the

MMKS work in Mumbai but also how the NFF's demand—for exclusive access for traditional fishing communities—is interpreted on the ground. Strikingly, that hostility towards migrants as well as fears regarding their position in fishing are most visible and vocal among Koli women.

The fact that there have been gender differentiated outcomes of the capitalist transformation in fishing must be considered here, as it reflects the difference in the position of Koli men and women on migrants. In the absence of cooperatives where typically only Koli men find representation, Koli women found support from parties such as the Shiv Sena, and only later from organizations such as the MMKS, to define their political position.

The history of organizations among the Kolis, combined with the differential impact of the capitalist transformation contributes to a situation where Kolis define their rights in opposition to the rights of the migrants. This meant that emerging organizations for fisherwomen had to foreground the community identity. Migrants as a result are increasingly left out of participation in existing and new fisher organizations. Even as hierarchies among fishers—between Koli men and women as well as locals versus migrants—harden, there is an attempt by the NFF and MMKS to bring all fishers together.

The Original Inhabitants and the 'Outsiders'

One of the most common refrains to be heard from the Kolis is that they are the original inhabitants of Mumbai. In a city such as Mumbai, which has historically witnessed large streams of migration, staking claim to belonging can seem imperative. It is particularly interesting to note that for the Kolis, laying claim to their status as original inhabitants is part of the repertoire of political strategies used to retain rights/control over spaces, and this has become frequent in the last two decades. Their recourse to this claim is not merely an effort to thwart the attempts of newer claimants. It can also be seen as a strategy employed, especially in cases of disputes over land,[1] where, in the

[1] Articles that have appeared over the years in *Times of India* have relied on and cited the claim of Kolis as the original inhabitants (*Times of India* 1994c, 2004c, 2005a. See also *Times of India* 1994d, 1995c, 2000b, 2001, 2003b, 2005b).

absence of evidentiary documents such as land *pattas* or ownership documents to prove their long use and/or ownership of the spaces, Kolis must rely on collective memory and history in order to secure their rights.

There are two main reasons for the vital link established between rights and claims of being the earliest inhabitants. These reasons emerge from the context of recent political moves, which have enabled the Kolis[2] to fashion an argument for rights (over land, fishing, and so on) that can play on very different emotive and political registers. These two reasons are the popularity that nativist politics enjoys in Mumbai and the passage of the Scheduled Tribes and Other Traditional Forest Dwellers (Recognition of Forest Rights) Act, 2006, which acknowledged rights of the forest-dwelling communities giving them access to resources from protected areas, such as forests. These reasons are distinct from one another but form the uneven terrain on which such claim-making exercises unfold.

By relying on indigeneity, the Kolis have drawn from a repository of meaning already in existence at the level of the politics of the city, on what it means to be the earliest inhabitants. As Xaxa discusses, the term 'tribe' has many different meanings and claims, so much so that its current usage by marginalized communities who refer to themselves as tribes often stands in contrast to the meaning ascribed to it by the state, administrators, and so on (Xaxa 1999: 3589). Xaxa's argument is important because it enables us to understand Koli political action that seeks to argue for rights based on claims of indigeneity. This has positioned them close to parties such as the Shiv Sena, which too have made similar claims (for Maharashtrians and not Kolis specifically). However, it raises the critical question of whether there is a difference in the usage of this claim by the Sena and communities such as the Kolis. Xaxa's argument that the imprecise definitions around categories such as tribes as well as fuzzy boundaries being drawn around claims of

[2] It is critical to point out that currently, there is move towards mobilizing the community for petitioning the state government to be recognized as a tribe aside from their listing as a backward class. For Kolis, the acknowledgement of their status as the earliest inhabitants should find its logical conclusion in their demand for status as a tribe to be recognized.

indigeneity have contributed to a limited understanding of the term is relevant in this context.

For instance, claims of indigeneity deployed by groups—or ascribed to them—are often hard to validate, given that migration has always existed. Xaxa advocates adopting a cautious position for claims of original settlement (when used to categorize communities as tribes), stressing the redundancy of such criteria. But what is important to note is that even though it may not resemble empirical reality, it does hold relevance through its use as a political category by communities who identify as original inhabitants. He highlights that communities see their relationship with territory as distinct and, thus, claim exclusive or preferential rights (Xaxa 1999: 3593). The crudest form this expression may take is when dominant groups such as sons-of-the-soil movements demonstrate a fear of outsiders and the loss of control over social, economic, and political sources of power (Xaxa 1999: 3594). However, the same expression has also been the political cry of several marginalized groups, especially tribal communities, that have increasingly been dispossessed of their control over resources. This is the reason that this nomenclature, initially used as a descriptive category, has now taken on a more political role. Therefore, Xaxa's argument regarding the clumsy categorization of communities as indigenous points to this problem where dominant groups can often define themselves and their rights in a manner very similar to communities who have actually been impoverished.

In Mumbai, the early alliance between the Shiv Sena and a section of the Kolis was a particular instance of this, as it brought together a dominant and marginalized group as one. Although the Sena spoke in the name of the Maharashtrians in general, they came to be largely supported by middle-order castes. The Kolis in contrast are a marginalised caste that has witnessed disenfranchisement over resources. The coming together of these two on the grounds of indigeneity, thus, produced a potent and charged political atmosphere.

The Shiv Sena was already a mainstream force by the early 2000s, when this alliance was beginning to take concrete shape. It was especially influential in terms of its control over institutions, such as municipal bodies, and had a long history in a political practice that relied on violence. When the Sena began to play an active part in organizing Koli women, the anti-migrant ideology came to be the foundation on which they sought to build a wave of support. This coalition between Koli women and the Sena reached its peak during the 2004 Bhaiyaa Hatao Andolan (Oust the Bhaiyaa[3]), where Koli women took to the streets to protest against the work of migrant men in fish vending. It is this movement that sparked the beginning of active political participation for many Koli women, who until then had been relegated to the margins by cooperatives that were dominated by boat-owning Koli men.

The Split Labour Market, the Anti-migrant Agitation, and Its Roots in Fisher Politics

According to Padmini (pseudonym),[4] a Koli fish-vendor in suburban Mumbai, 'There is no point being a Koli in Mumbai.' She attributes the problems she faces in her work, in part to migrant men who undertake the work of fish retailing, and in part to the demolition of the market she worked at (claimed by a local church as an encroachment of their property). The hostility towards migrants in fish retail is widespread, but what is significant is that in the recent years this hostility has been shaped specifically against the North Indian migrants. This is in spite of the fact that there is no evidence to sustain the claims of Koli women that most migrants in fishing come from the North. As mentioned earlier, migrants in fishing come from different parts of the country, and even in fish retail, it is not only migrant men but also migrant women and other local non-Kolis who participate (although many of these women vend from market spaces, unlike the male migrants).

The figure of the North Indian migrant as being the primary focus of anti-migrant agitations can be traced to the influence of the Sena in constructing this narrative for the city. Although there has been

---

[3] The term 'bhaiyaa', which translates as 'brother' in Hindi, is used to refer to not just kin members in North India but is also commonly used in Hindi-speaking regions for young men, particularly working-class men such as autorickshaw drivers, daily wage workers, and so on. But in Mumbai, the term is also used as a derogatory reference and a slur for North Indian migrants.

[4] Interview conducted on 19 April 2013 in North Mumbai.

scholarship[5] to discuss why the shift away from South Indian migrants took place, there is little to suggest why they now target those travelling for work from the North. One of the reasons for this could be that as migration, in general, to the city increased, leading to a strain on the existing resources and infrastructure in the city, poor migrants—many of whom hail from the North—became an easier target. Over the last two decades, the number of migrants to Maharashtra from other states has been rising, though the share has reduced in the last decade. In 2001, migrants from outside Maharashtra constituted 57.43 per cent of the total migrant population. Their share dropped to 45.92 per cent in 2011 (Shaikh 2019).

In 2001, 3.2 million people migrated from other states into Maharashtra; of this, migrants from Uttar Pradesh constituted the largest stream, at 0.9 million or 28 per cent of all inter-state migrants. Of the 3.2 million inter-state migrants, 2.6 million (79.6 per cent) moved to urban areas (Office of the Registrar General & Census Commissioner, India n.d.[6]). Around 35.51 per cent of the population of Mumbai was made up of migrants at this time. This percentage increased to 43.02 per cent in 2011, with Uttar Pradesh sending the largest share of migrants (41 per cent) to Mumbai.[7]

The Sena and the MNS have, since the late 1990s, launched an aggressive politics against North Indian migrants, not excluding physical assaults on them. It was as a part of building this groundswell of support that in 2004 the Sena actively worked with Koli women. A fish vendor and Sena party worker, Rama (pseudonym),[8] describes:

> I was involved in the Bhaiyaa Hatao Andolan in a coalition, but it didn't work … *bai log* (Koli women) said we are not able to manage, not able to sell in the markets. So, we thought if we stop the vending done from

---

[5] See Chapter 1 for a discussion on this.

[6] 'Data highlights Tables D1, D1 (Appendix), D2 and D3'. Available at http://censusindia.gov.in/Data_Products/Data_Highlights/Data_Highlights_link/data_highlights_D1D2D3.pdf.

[7] The share of inter-state migrants into Maharashtra, however, dropped between the two Census periods, indicating the rise of intra-state migration (Shaikh 2019).

[8] Rama's quotes in this chapter have been taken from the personal interview conducted on 21 May 2013 and in 2014 near western Mumbai near Sagar Nagar.

here and there by the bhaiyaas, we will get customers in the markets again. All this began with meetings in Worli, there were 10 meetings. We addressed all the markets, not just our own. But there was a problem and we ended up in trouble.... People started getting calls from *bada* saabs [big people] in Delhi saying don't remove the bhaiyaas, they are working. *But it is not their work, it is ours.* (Emphasis added)

The agitation was a remarkable event for many fisherwomen and was seared in their memory as one of the first steps towards safeguarding their livelihood. Meetings held to bolster support often involved the Sena, such as in early 2004, when the Sena corporator Ramkrishna Keni addressed a meeting held by the Koli Mahila Sangharsha Samiti and said: 'The north Indians seem all set to grab every job and trade opportunity in Mumbai. The Kolis, however will not tolerate this encroachment. The "bhaiyaas" are fishing in troubled waters' (*Times of India* 2004c).

The atmosphere was clearly charged. Triza Killekar, a fish vendor, is reported to have declared that Koli women would physically prevent the North Indian vendors from entering the fish market. The hostility against migrant vendors was attributed to their practise of buying fish from the wholesale market and selling it through a kin network of retailers, as well as their mode of selling fish by weight and not by lumps/'*kaudi*', as was the traditional practise. The problem was, thus, described essentially as an economic one (*Times of India* 2004c).

The issue continues to provoke, Koli fisherwomen in the Shakti Mandi (pseudonym) in southern Mumbai claim they have been impoverished by the migrants. Negotiations did not work, and Lata (pseudonym), a fisherwoman,[9] claimed, 'Kolis even beat them up', but this too did not convince migrants to leave. They also believed that boat owners preferred to sell fish to migrants who would not haggle, compared to Koli women who did. Rama, who left the city during the agitation and narrowly escaped being charged by the police, claimed that even as the movement began to whither owing to the political storm they found themselves in, they were encouraged to continue with it. The 'party' (Shiv Sena), she claims, told them to carry on the

---

[9] All of Lata's quotes in this chapter have been taken from personal interviews conducted on 23 April and 30 May 2013.

agitation and that they would support it; ultimately, however, as a result of the cases filed against Koli women, the agitation crumbled.

However, the alliance the Sena was building with the Koli community on the broad agenda of nativist rights continues and includes parties such as the MNS making overtures by sponsoring a Koli festival every year in Mumbai, where 'Koli culture' is celebrated. In spite of the fact that overt alliances of the kind witnessed in the early 2000s are not taking place anymore, many of those who participated in the agitation remain sympathizers of the Sena or MNS. Despite her experience of the agitation, Rama remains a loyal Sena party worker:

> Balasaheb was very good for Maharashtra, if there was injustice to Maharashtra, he made a noise and people were scared by that noise. He worked for all castes and particularly for women's welfare. The party would do a lot for women.

The more fundamental impact of the alliance and the agitation that emerged from it has been the adoption of the nativist ideology. It has resulted in many Kolis, especially women, viewing their inability to command resources (monetary, over spaces such as markets, as well as 'traditional rights') as stemming directly from the presence of migrants in the work that was once their exclusive preserve. This is not to suggest that Koli women are unable to understand the impact that the capitalist transformation has had on their work. Rama herself remains a strong critic, 'Purse seine boat people [owners] fill their own stomachs but that is not how it should be, everyone together should be able to fill their stomachs.' But, it is precisely in the event of the massive changes that have taken place in the fisheries and in an effort to grasp on to the little control they currently hold, that Koli women agitate against the migrants. They see themselves as competing with them in an increasingly narrow market, and it is this perception which nativist parties have built on in order to elicit support for their exclusivist agenda.

An indication of the strength of this nativist ideology can be gauged from the almost identical terms and phrases used to describe the work and life patterns of migrants. First, irrespective of the fact that migrants come from different parts of the country, ire is reserved for the male migrants from North India—the 'bhaiyaa' as they would be derogatorily referred to. This is in spite of the fact that in most markets, Koli fisherwomen share space with non-Kolis. For instance, at the Shakti Mandi in South Mumbai, vendors who hail from West Bengal are present in addition to many Maharashtrians, both Kolis and those of other castes who vend from here (the chairperson of the market association claimed that only a small number of vendors—around 20 were Koli women). Second, Koli women argue that the number of migrants in fish vending swells constantly because '1 "bhaiyaa" brings along 10 more people with him'. This line repeated verbatim by women across the city and from different markets reflects the force of the idea that Koli women stand to be expelled from their work by an exponentially increasing number of migrants, thus constructing a provocative economic argument for survival. Parvati (pseudonym),[10] a fish vendor, participant of the 2004 agitations, and trade union activist, claims that migrants do not contribute anything to the state of Maharashtra.

> They earn money here and send it back to their state. They do not pay taxes. They stay in 15' × 15' rooms, 15 in one room, pay INR 100 per head as rent, sometimes sleep at the market, and buy fish early in the morning and reach the customers door by 7 a.m.

She compares the lives of the women with this, pointing out how 'they must prepare food for the whole household, pack tiffins for their children, and then set out on work'. Drawing on how women must perform paid work along with bearing the burden of unpaid domestic labour, Parvati points to how migrant men who devote themselves exclusively to their paid work do better than them. In addition, she and other Koli fisherwomen point out the additional costs they bear compared to the migrants working in fish retail. Fisherwomen vending from market spaces have to spend on transporting fish to the market and must pay a license fee to the municipality in order to use the markets. Additionally, they must pay for ice to be brought daily to keep the fish fresh, due to the unavailability of refrigerated spaces in the market. This is coupled with the expense of paying someone to clean their allocated space and for the provision of water in the market, since the municipality does not ensure either, despite charging

[10] Personal interview conducted on 3 July 2013.

money for the same. Parvati, Lata, and Rani (pseudonym)[11] claimed that negotiations with boat owners on restricting migrant fishers' access to fish for purposes of vending failed precisely because they apparently agree to pay the price that the boat owners demand, unlike the fisherwomen who bargain owing to these additional expenses. Koli fisherwomen argue that their prices cannot remain competitive, since they must bear the cost of living in the city. They argue that since migrants spend little on themselves—sometimes even living on the streets—they are able to sell fish at lower rates, earn more, and send most of the earning home as remittance. The fisherwomen use the precarious conditions under which migrants exist as the very reason why they are able to sell at lower rates compared to them.

It is noteworthy that Koli fisherwomen's positions are strikingly similar to those highlighted by Edna Bonacich (1972, 1975, 1976) in the case of a split labour market in the United States, where competing groups in a labour market are divided along lines of ethnicity or race. Bonacich's theory seeks to examine what occurs in a situation where high-priced and low-priced labour in a market also happen to be divided along ethnic or racial lines. She contends that both Marxist and non-Marxist scholars attribute ethnic antagonisms to cultural and racial or ethnic differences alone. Challenging such a point of view, she points to how economic processes can be fundamental in spurring such conflict (Bonacich 1972: 547). This is not to suggest that any ethnically varied circumstance in a labour market automatically leads to antagonism. It arises primarily as an outcome of a price differential, where one group of labourers can sell their labour power at lower rates than the other. An influx of new entrants in the labour market who command the same price as existing labourers, even if they are ethnically varied, will not lead to a split labour market. However, even when there are no existing ethnic differences, a split labour market can occur. She states:

During the depression years, 'Old Stock'—that is, white, Protestant, anglo-Saxon Americans, from Oklahoma, Arkansas, and Texas—were roundly denounced in California as 'interlopers'. The same charges

---

[11] Personal interviews conducted on 3 July 2013, 23 April 2013, and 30 May 2013 at Shakti Mandi, western Mumbai.

were made against them that were made against the Japanese: they were 'dirty'; they had 'enormous families'; they engaged in unfair competition; they threatened to 'invade' the state and to 'undermine' its institutions. (Bonacich 1972: 557)

The hostility between groups of high-priced and low-priced labourers is specifically a function of the differences in the price they command and is driven by the need for capitalism to avail cheap and docile labour. It is precisely these attributes often associated with lower-wage labourers that make them a more attractive option to capitalists. As Bonacich (1972) argues, the main conflict is the one that is visible between the two groups of labourers and not between the labourers and the capitalists. In the scenario of the antagonism between migrant fishers and Koli fisherwomen, it could be contended that these are not groups engaged in selling their labour power to a capitalist. But the split labour market approach also applies, Bonacich (1972) argues, to the smaller entrepreneurs or the self-employed, where price differentials may operate similarly. For instance, the price differential at which the migrants sell fish is perceived to be lower than the rate at which Koli fisherwomen can.

The reasons stated by Koli fisherwomen for why it was possible for migrants to sell fish at lower rates than them echo Bonacich's (1975) arguments for why a price differential exists between competing groups. These reasons can be categorized as factors of resources and motives. Of the three kinds of resources which play a role in determining the price of labour, the first is the 'level of living' of migrant labourers (Bonacich 1975: 550). For a migrant to be induced to move, wage levels must be higher at their destination. Poor migrants are willing to sell their labour at a wage lower than that of the locals, but even the wage they earn at the new location is typically higher than what they could have earned at the place they come from. A second criterion of resources is the information migrants may have access to, where a lack of information can also keep them at depressed wage levels. The third is political resources or mobilization. The ability of labourers to either organize themselves or to be able to command political resources to protect their vulnerable status from the powers of capital is critical if they are to enjoy bargaining powers (Bonacich 1972: 549–50). The inability to command political resources is particularly pertinent in rendering migrants susceptible to pressures of being ousted. Bonacich (1975: 558) indicates that this a common feature for split labour markets in which a section of the labourers share their ethnicity with those who control such resources.

Despite this, migrants continue to seek work in destinations with lower prospects of income. Migrants are often willing to tolerate bad working conditions and low pay because they do not see themselves as participating in such a labour market for long periods. This is rooted in the fact that often migrants are men migrating alone and their income does not need to pay towards costs towards education and housing for their families.[12] This was one of the crucial factors identified by Koli fisherwomen as the reason for the migrants' ability to sell at lower rates. Further, the precarity of work and the easy replacement of workers—especially in a labour-intensive economy—also compel migrants to put up with unequal and often difficult working conditions. Another reason why migrant workers might be willing to work at lower wages could be because they are supplementing their income with the work they do as migrants (seasonal migrants)[13] or working towards an immediate payment. Due to the temporary nature of such migration, there tends to be rapid turnover in labour.

The end to the ethnic antagonism that defines the split labour market is usually sought through means of either preventing the entry of migrants or by seeking to make work exclusive to higher priced labourers alone. In launching the anti-North Indian migrant movement, Koli women had attempted the former strategy. Owing to this, migrants have been subject to violent agitations and the target of hate speech, not only by Koli women, but at other instances by the Shiv Sena and MNS.[14] The move for preventing migrant entry, therefore, relies on extra-legal tactics of such violence and harassment.

---

[12] However, Bonacich (1975: 551) adds that even when they migrate with families, they are often willing to endure low wages.

[13] This was certainly the case with the migrants working on boats, who worked in Mumbai as fishworkers for only part of the year to contribute to their meager family earnings, which come from small subsistence farming in their native villages in Uttar Pradesh.

[14] Attacks on migrants from North India have been occurring since the first decade of the 2000s and continue till date. See news articles (*IANS* 2008; PTI 2008a, 2008b; Thevar 2015) on the MNS attacking migrants from North India.

However, even though they can lay strong claim to the political dis-course of nativism, as a community the Kolis too could not escape the consequences of their tactics. The cases filed against them led to an abandonment of this strategy. And it is towards the latter tactic that they now turn their attention.

Hostility towards migrants continues, but Koli women now claim that even though migrant entry has depressed their income levels, their main grouse has to do with their method of fish vending. Most migrants, they believe, sell fish door-to-door, and in doing so, save costs associated with markets and are able to secure more custom-ers because they deliver at great convenience—at their doorstep and at lower rates. Koli women perceive that the number of customers frequenting the market has declined and they are running into losses because of their inability to compete with this method of vending. Significantly though, migrant vendors are not the only fish retailers who sell fish directly to the homes of people—several Koli women participate in this method too. However, market-based fisherwomen claim that since Koli non-market vendors do so at fixed areas, it poses little threat to their own trade. In contrast, the migrants who are viewed as being 'footloose' do so without entering into any prior arrangement with the women from the neighbouring markets, and are therefore viewed as troublesome. Koli fisherwomen claim that what particularly threatens their work is the manner in which the migrants in fish vending make redundant the space of the market which holds immense social and political value in the lives of Koli women.

Market Policies and Their Significance to Koli Women's Political Life

The womenfolk have one place—the market. Traditionally this has been our practice. Even before Independence, women would sit, sell fish and make a market [sic]. Then after the Independence came the Municipality which took over [these] markets and constructed new markets. Our people—the Kolis—are the ones who established these places which would otherwise have been lost. That is why, in my opin-ion, Koli women deserve the right to the market. And this tradition should continue. Even women from the community should not be allowed to sell their place in a market, their children or daughters-in-law will eventually take over. So, it shouldn't be sold.

Rama's comments are an indication of the threats that Koli women face, not only through new methods of vending, rendering the market redundant but also through new urban policies.

Over the last two decades, the market development policy introduced by the Brihanmumbai Municipal Corporation (BMC) has led to Koli women realizing that their control over the markets, which they assumed to have by virtue of a history of use, would now require recognition from the state, as licensees of the property. The policy drafted in 2004 allotted markets to developers without calling for bids, where 70 per cent of the licensees of a market could consent to its redevelopment. Under the initial draft, the Floor Space Index (FSI) was to be shared between the BMC and the developers, however, later the BMC determined that it would retain the FSI but would offer the Transferable Development Rights to the private developers. The policy was one of urban regeneration, however, it posed a threat for the Koli fisherwomen, many of whom were not registered licensees even though they had used been using the space for decades.

Many fisherwomen, vending from the markets, as well as activists noted that after Independence, the BMC sought to administer the markets by assuming control over the private ones and regulating the ones that passed to them from the colonial state. As markets came to be regularized under the BMC, vendors were charged a daily rate for using the space. Recounting the history of the BMC's foray into market governance, Suresh,[15] an activist says:

> In 1956, the BMC took control of all these markets and started issuing daily passes to the vendors sitting at these markets. In Marathi, this is called *baitha shulga*—that is sitting charges. These were only for single days ... they started going around collecting the money from every woman. This started from 5 paise. Then gradually it increased to Rs 5, then to Rs 10, and so on. After this, they started looking into the water supply, cleanliness, and so on. They hired staff to look into these things. They hired 2–4 people, then assigned an inspector. And that is how they began. In this season,[16] by collecting Rs 5–10, they earn a total of up to 5 crores from these markets. So then we realized that

[15] Personal interview conducted on 19 April 2013 in western Mumbai.

[16] Referring to the fishing season prior to the period of the ban, which is in effect from June to August in Maharashtra.

we generate so much revenue for the BMC but what do they do for us? Wherever there was a shed, it was built by us. They should have at least made improvements to it. Whether it was question of lights or fans, they did very little. They never looked into ventilation. They just let things continue as is.

The BMC was, thus, viewed by most of the women as a largely ineffective and corrupt organization. Suresh claimed that the BMC officials appointed to the markets would often demand extra money and fish from the fisherwomen, which the women had to comply with in order to continue vending from these markets. The broken relationship with the BMC meant that women reposed little faith in the institution and imagined the continuance of such ad-hoc functioning. Thus, in 1992–3, when the BMC declared a new policy of shifting away from the regime of daily passes to one where licenses would be issued to all those who vend from the markets, the fisherwomen refused to comply even as other vendors did. The Koli fisherwomen also refused to acquire the licenses owing to their high rate, and in the belief that their right to the market would not be threatened if they did not take licenses. However, in 2004, when the BMC announced its new policy of market redevelopment, they saw why acquiring the licenses would have been beneficial for them.

The ambitious market redevelopment project envisaged by the BMC seeks to redevelop older markets, many of which were established prior to Independence and most of which occupy land having a high potential value. In the land-starved Mumbai, futuristic visions of urban development[17] could now be projected onto spaces such as older, crowded markets to refashion them for the times into upscale, modern commercial spaces. Seeking to involve retailers—who had long ties to the markets—in this new vision of development, the BMC required that any project of market redevelopment be pursued in association with those from the markets. The redevelopment project was to involve three parties—the BMC itself, a private developer who would undertake the project and to whom control over the sellable

---

[17] In 2003, McKinsey submitted a report to the Maharashtra government on developing Mumbai into a 'world class city' like Shanghai. 'Mumbai to Shanghai' has since became a slogan for those demanding urban development of the city (Sharma 2003).

area would pass on once the construction was over, and a retailers' organization from the markets.

Suresh claimed that a key BMC regulation for the project was that a sum of close to 10 crores be set aside by each market as a deposit with the BMC for the redevelopment project. For the women who had no prior history with organizing, these announcements set off waves of confusion. First, they discovered that holding licenses to the markets was critical in order to be part of the redevelopment project. Second, there was bewilderment as to how to establish their stake in the proceedings. It was at this point of time that a union called the Maharashtra Machimaar Masivikreta Sangh (Maharashtra Fish-Vendors Organization, henceforth the MMMS) was formed for the fish sellers, which began to intervene over the question of licenses and the redevelopment project.

Prior to the MMMS, there was another women's organization that had emerged among the Kolis. This was the Mumbai Zilla Cooperative established under the shadow control of the Shiv Sena. The dire need felt by Koli women to lay claim to the compensations handed out by the state government to the fisheries at times of natural calamities or ecological disasters led to the formation of this cooperative. According to the Department of Fisheries, the only recognized organizations in the fisheries were cooperatives, and therefore, schemes, subsidies, and more importantly compensation packages were handed to registered cooperatives in the state for distribution. However, since most cooperatives in the city were dominated by men and usually owners of boats, women's membership and participation in the cooperatives was more of an exception than a norm. The Mumbai Zilla Cooperative was envisaged as a solution to the lack of representation that women found in koliwada cooperatives. However, members of its executive board came to be viewed as corrupt, and gradually the organization came to be defunct with one of its primary members leaving the organization and associating with the MMMS and MMKS.

More importantly, both the MMMS and the Mumbai Zilla Cooperative found a foothold among the women by addressing themselves to what was widely perceived as being the biggest problem of the time—the issue of migrant vendors. Rama and Parvati, now activists with the MMKS, attribute the beginnings of political action with the 2004 anti-migrant agitation and claim they were associated with the MMMS and the Mumbai Zilla Cooperative, respectively, from then on. Despite the 2004 agitation ending with the Koli women on the back foot, as well as discrediting of their leader, an ex-Shiv Sena corporator, the issue of the licenses and the redevelopment project brought the party back to the fore. Koli women found the Shiv Sena to be a powerful ally. Rama recounts:

> In 2004, we heard that women were going to be asked to leave the markets. There are 61 women's fish markets and they wanted to convert this market into a mall and did not want to involve the women. So, we formed a union called the Machimaar Masivikreta Sangh and through it began organizing.... Not everyone joined the union but through the union we were able to do some good work. We held a meeting with the BMC. Through the union we were able to negotiate with the BMC; it was a Shiv Sena government at that point and we met with their representatives in the BMC office.... During this meeting the Shiv Sena claimed they had issued licenses for the markets earlier and that the fish vendors had not responded to this. The fruit and vegetable sellers at markets had already applied for their licenses but the fish vendors were unaware of this. Us women, we wake up early, do all the work, and return home late. We were busy with this and no one paid attention. Women aren't educated, that is how the others took out the license and women didn't.... The BMC claimed that Sulochana Thanekar[18] was approached regarding this issue, she was one of the main women who had started a women's organization. She claimed the women would not take a license but would merely pay the daily pass for vending. We asked the BMC whether they had any of this correspondence in writing and they replied that it was a verbal discussion. The union informed the BMC that this was not acceptable, we created a furore until the BMC agreed to grant licenses again to these women. But in some markets, women were left out and could not get licenses. Some women who sat for 20–30 years did not receive licenses.

It was during the course of organizing the women for licenses and handling the redevelopment issue that the MMMS came to be embroiled in a case of embezzlement. The redevelopment process which almost came to a standstill after this embezzlement issue was also embroiled in much confusion regarding the process to be

---

[18] Thanekar was recognized as an early leader among the women.

followed. The markets which were to be redeveloped were to include a fish market; the MMMS was to negotiate with the BMC with regard to the layout of this new fish market, seeking to include changes in it that they believed would improve the women's work life[19] as well as position them to be strong contenders in a gentrified commercial space, through an assurance of a 30-year lease. Questions regarding a corpus fund to hand out compensation amounts to women during the period of construction of these new markets when they would be unable to operate led to much heated discussion and dispute among the women in the market; it was in the ensuing period that accusations were levelled against the MMMS as well as its affiliates in each market.

The period was, therefore, rife with confusion, anger, and distress among the women on what the future course of action was to be. The issue of licenses was viewed as critical not only because it was linked to the question of redevelopment but also because the women came to view the licenses as a way for their customary practices to be recognized and legitimized by the state.

Rani (pseudonym), a vendor and chairperson of the Shakti Mandi fish market earmarked for redevelopment, argued how it is imperative that licenses be treated as property to enable women to legally transfer the license to another female member of their family upon their death or when they so choose. This demand was a way to not only ensure their links to markets through which they are connected by patterns of use from generations before, but also an assurance against the threat of being ousted if the new malls replacing the markets exerted pressures of gentrification. However, in the absence of a unified organization to fight for these rights, the women saw their position as vulnerable.

Ujjwala claims that it was in the context of the women stranded without licenses (she and others quote 900 fisherwomen in Mumbai who had still not received a license after re-applying for it in 2006)

---

[19] Health complaints were common among women vendors who faced poor sanitary conditions in most markets, with no access to clean toilets and water. In addition, unclean workspaces and uncomfortable sitting positions assumed to carry on the work caused problems for the women. The MMMS, thus, sought to intervene over the question of designing the new markets to ensure that the women would be able to access better workspaces.

that some women approached her for help in resolving the issue.[20] Following this, she demanded that her organization, the MMKS, play a more active role in organizing the women, an issue she felt had been relegated to the margins. It was in this lacuna created by the absence of the MMMS that the MMKS emerged as the forerunner in organizing Koli women.

Political Formations and the Women's Question in the Fisheries

The MMKS was established in 1965 under the leadership of Bhai Bandarkar. Recognized as one of the earliest leaders of the community, he is credited with bringing the community together on a variety of issues, ranging from the rehabilitation of those displaced by urban development projects to highlighting the plight of small-scale fishers at a time when state policy was aggressively pushing towards mechanization and large-scale capital-intensive technology. Organizing under the banner of the Maharashtra Machhimar Kruti Samiti (Maharashtra Fishermen Action Committee), the MMKS which was an affiliate of the NFF[21] was, thus, guided by aims of promoting and protecting small-scale and artisanal fishing. In Maharashtra, the focus was on questions of 'traditional and customary rights over sea for fishing and coastal lands (coastal commons) for residing and for fisheries activities'.[22]

As a result, this has been the focus of the MMKS and NFF but had come with singular attention paid to fishermen, relegating the issues of female fishworkers. Consequently, the MMKS was caught unaware at a time when the dispute around market development was raging and threatening the livelihood of fisherwomen. Ujjwala declared that when she was approached by female vendors for help regarding the issue, it lay outside the purview of work that the MMKS usually did. She recounted:

No, they [the MMKS] never picked up any of the issues relating to these women. On the coastline there are smaller fishworkers, they worked

[20] Ujjwala's quotes in the chapter are from the author's conversations with her from April 2013 to January 2014.

[21] See Chapter 2 for a discussion on the NFF.

[22] From the Maharashtra page of the National Fishworker's Forum website, available at http://www.nffindia.org/nffmaharashtra.php.

on them. Those issues were so many that they kept fighting the government on them. The MMKS was different. The MMMS was made for the women. But then they made a mistake. In 2010, when the big ships, *Chitra and Khalijia*, struck each other, it became a big issue.

The MSC Chitra–MV Khalijia collision that Ujjwala refers to came to be the turning point for the role that the MMKS was to play with regards to Koli women's mobilization. The collision, which led to an oil spill off the coast of Mumbai and an advisory by the Maharashtra government cautioning people against consuming fish, leading to the financial ruin of several fisherwomen who had invested significantly in purchasing fish from other states, as this was the period of the ban on fishing in Mumbai. The state government at this point, ironically, announced a compensation package for local fishermen, indicative of their lack of knowledge of the fisheries. The compensations were channelled through local cooperatives with the aim to cover only the losses of fishermen which given the ban should not have been operational anyway. Even if the Department of Fisheries had announced the relief with the aim of compensating the loss borne by a fisher household, using the cooperatives as a medium to do so was blind to the fact that women had extremely low representation in the cooperative.

Ujjwala claims that cooperatives at the time were extremely reluctant to add fisherwomen as members. She approached the MMKS on the issue and Rambhau Patil (then president of the MMKS) actively advocated along with her the need to mobilize women, leading to the MMKS taking the lead on the issue. They began to enlist Koli women as members of the MMKS and explored the policies of other coastal states that could be introduced in Maharashtra to benefit fisherwomen. As Ujjwala recollects, interaction with members of the International Collective in Support of Fishworkers (ICSF)—that works for the rights of small-scale fishers—alerted her to the schemes and facilities available for fisherwomen in other states, especially Kerala. Prominent among these were the facilities extended to transport fish, which has been a long-standing issue for the Koli women.

Realizing that the absence of a concerted effort to highlight the issues of Koli women and their absence from the cooperatives had led to a severe neglect of their problems, the MMKS decided to dedicate a separate organization within, for women. Ujjwala and Purnima,[23] activists with a long history in the MMKS, took on the responsibility to organize women. In the summer of 2013, meetings were held in the city to formalize an organization for the women who would be affiliated to the MMKS and by extension to the NFF. Both the NFF and MMKS, which are trade unions and politically ally with a pro-labour position in fishing sought to now organize a community of women whose earlier political forays had been shaped by the nativist Shiv Sena, which historically has been opposed to communism and left-of-centre positions. Contradictions, therefore, seemed imminent.

The Formation of Renewed Women's Organization

There was a dire need for a cohesive organization for women fish-workers, according to several activists. As Shuddawati,[24] associated with the ICSF, noted:

> The mainstream fisheries movements know little about the women because they not get anything from the women. However, when they aid in acquiring boats or getting resources for boat owners they receive something, hence they pay no attention to women fishworkers. There was also no representation of women and those who were present were weak leaders. In 2004, when the BMC market redevelopment policy came out, that was when women's organizations came up highlighting fisherwomen's issues. The first of these was the Mahila Masivikreta Sangh, which was almost like a trade union.... The good work of the old union was that they put forth a set of demands regarding what they wanted from this market ... but what they did was aggressively articulate women's issues in the larger fisheries movement. And, thus, they were able to attract the attention of the mainstream fisheries movement towards women's issues.

Shuddawati claims that as part of their work, the MMMS built committees comprised fisherwomen in each market. The committees were strong and withstood pressure from real estate lobbies. This

[23] Purnima's and Ujjwala's quotes in the chapter are from the author's conversations with them from April 2013 to January 2014.

[24] Personal interview conducted on 8 July 2013 at East Mumbai.

was crucial because in some markets builders had slyly managed to bypass the consent of the women for market redevelopment, by taking consent from the other vendors. In cases such as this (for example, the Matunga Market), fisherwomen were able to stop the builder and file cases against them.

The political readiness, thus, already existed by 2013, when a series of meetings were held to discuss the renewal of a women's organization. One of these was the meeting held in June 2013 near the Sagar Nagar koliwada, attended by approximately 60 women. The meeting organized by the MMKS and Shuddawati, was called with the aim of introducing the women who came from different parts of Mumbai, to the idea of developing a trade union for female fishworkers. The meeting introduced fisherwomen to several ideas—the MMKS and its policies, a trade union, and specifically a women's trade union. Although the MMMS had worked as a women's trade union prior to this, it had failed to develop as a cohesive collective, functioning largely through the smaller units it established in each market for the purposes of negotiating with the BMC. The new organization, it was hoped, could unify the women to address their problems, not limited to the redevelopment and license issues alone but with wider aims. In doing so it was seeking to ally with the larger agenda of the MMKS, which was to promote the interest of small-scale fishers.

Two clearly articulated ideas in the meeting were that the organization was to be exclusively for women and that it was to take the form of a trade union. The first of this was discussed as a question of representation. Ujjwala highlighted that though women were fishers, their issues found little representation in fisher organizations. Most importantly, it was noted that most schemes, subsidies, and facilities extended by the state to the fisheries, purportedly for all fishers, was in fact directed towards fishing practiced by men. It was noted how cooperatives were also ineffective in granting representation to women, and the MMKS's own inattention to the issue was also remarked upon. The formation of the new union in alliance with the MMKS was, thus, seen to be the way to correct an old wrong.

The more crucial part of this meeting was the discussion on why the form of the collective should be a trade union. Some of the MMKS activists, who had interacted with members of the NFF from

Kerala, revealed how they were told of the prevalence of schemes for women being available for female fishers in states such as Kerala. These schemes, they told the hall of women, came to them through agitations led by unions. A critical connection being forged in the discussions in the hall that afternoon was between struggles and unions: 'Trade unions can solve problems better and faster' was heard often.

The decision to form a union, an organization with a relatively recent history in the political landscape of the fisheries in Maharashtra, stood out. This was especially so since the functioning of the trade union was viewed to be in complete contrast to that of the cooperatives. Cooperatives, which are imperative in order to secure aid, were viewed as a medium between the state and the individual fishers. In contrast, the trade union was viewed as a collective that would be aimed at 'agitating', as the fisherwomen said, for a better deal from the state, and to draw the attention—of both the state and other cooperatives—to the predicament of female fishers. Parvati claimed that cooperatives did not do anything for the women and did not raise issues important to them. The women, she argued, are so distanced from the idea of cooperatives that they do not even know what the term means. For women who are illiterate, the word 'cooperative' is itself alienating:

> Societies are usually termed as 'so and so *sahakari* society'. It is only the word 'sahakari' that they might understand. Why would women participate in cooperatives where nothing relevant to them would come up? That is why the MMMS came, but even there the chairperson did not do enough.... We will fight for the women who have been wronged.

Parvati believes there is clear distinction between cooperatives and unions. Cooperatives, she suggests, 'ask us to hold their hand but only give us what falls through the fingers. But we realize that actually we have a right over the whole hand.' The trade union, for her is the organization that allows for this recognition of rights, which is why she believes it is vital to form a union for fisherwomen.

A list of key demands of women—including the introduction of basic technology—is a good indication of how one-sided technological improvements pushed by the state have been in the fisheries. While the government has aggressively championed mechanization in fishing, it did so with an exclusive focus on fishing. In an economy where work in most sectors tends to be divided along the lines of gender, it is tragically common for technological improvements to be initiated into areas of work performed by men.

Documenting a similar process in agrarian work, Prem Chowdhry (1993) noted that the technological changes that were part of the Green Revolution introduced mechanization in the tasks performed by men. Agrarian labour performed by women continued to be in the form of manual labour (Chowdhry 1993: A135). As a result, women's burden of work remained extremely high, while their work was undervalued. The same remains true of the fisheries, where there is little change in how women's work is performed. This is not to suggest that no technological improvement has occurred—usage of solar dryers for fish drying is one such change. However, compared to the efforts made by the state in introducing technology for fishing, there has been no equivalent effort made towards mechanizing women' work in the fisheries.

The application of technology towards one side of the gender-based division of labour highlights the patriarchal mindset of the state as well as of the cooperatives which did not demand such change.

As a result, the objectives of this proposed organization were to highlight the urgency of bringing about changes to fisherwomen's work, both in terms of actual retail work as well as value-added work. It was believed that this would also align with the aim of promoting small-scale fisheries. These objectives discussed in subsequent meetings[25] included:

1. Aid women vendors and allied fishworkers.
2. Develop new ways to market and sell fish, as well as to get facilities for those who engage in retail.
3. Aid women who work in fish processing (linked to export industries).
4. Introduce solar dryers and other instruments for fish drying and initiate classes for women to educate them about the new technology.

[25] These objectives were discussed at the women's trade union meeting held on 21 July 2013 in Western Mumbai. The meeting was organized by Purnima and Ujjwala.

5. Introduce the use of cold-storage boxes, fans, and other facilities for the convenience of those vending from markets.
6. Introduce insulated vans for transporting fish from auction sites to markets across the city.
7. Establish representation of women in cooperatives and government boards to promote and implement schemes for women fishworkers.
8. Develop a policy for compensation in case of natural disasters and other calamities.
9. Introduce social-welfare policies of insurance and pension for female fishworkers.
10. Strengthen the rights of women in the market redevelopment policy.
11. Educate and promote fisheries in their communities.
12. Undertake village-to-village education of dry fish and other products and techniques.
13. Make mandatory protective gear for women working in fish processing.
14. Undertake protection of the CRZ notification.
15. Prevent environmental degradation.
16. Working towards the development of a national policy for fish vendors.
17. Undertake the protection of their traditional rights.

In order to secure these interests, some of which would be dependent on state aid, the fisherwomen's collective decided to create both a cooperative to interact and be a recipient of state funds, as well as a union. It was especially interesting to note that at a time when the MMKS itself was struggling to be registered as a union, they were able to push the case for a women's trade union. A sense of urgency was assumed in forming the union, with the driving motive being that they could no longer wait for the state to catch-up and devise schemes for their benefit.

As mentioned earlier, attempts at registering the MMKS as a union were thwarted by protests claiming that this would introduce a class divide among the fishers. In contrast, class differences seemed dulled within the women who engaged in fish vending. Although some women who engaged in retail came from households having ownership of trawlers, by and large the women who vended from markets and other spaces were those who depended on the income generated through selling fish to run their household. Class differences between them were thus minimal and it was perhaps this that led to the fault-line developing elsewhere. Resistance, therefore, to the notion of a trade union was not present, or at least not articulated by the women at the meeting. Instead, most of those present at the meeting seemed invigorated with the idea of political action.

Purnima, an MMKS activist, who was present at the meeting, said in a later discussion that introducing trade unions to the women took time. According to her, between NGOs and corporates entering fishing, the modes of organizing have changed, and in this regard, trade unions seem to be the only way to go forward. She added that this was not an idea that held immediate appeal for fisherwomen and that many of them did not understand the logic of organizing under unions. Much of this had to do with the lack of a history of trade unions in the fisheries here. The notion of agitation is something that is not well understood, she explained, in spite of the fact that Koli women are familiar with 'fighting'. But 'how to fight', she believed, can take on different meanings, and the political, social, and cultural aspects of what it entails was not clear to most. The impact of the Shiv Sena and its prominent leader Bal Thackeray denigrating trade unionists by referring to them as 'red flag people' was also severe. She argued, however, that the MMKS cannot follow in the line of the Sena, especially in their agitations against those from the North.

Purnima's efforts towards marking a difference between the kind of agitation the MMKS was advocating and the kind the Koli fisherwomen had previous exposure to under the Sena's leadership highlighted that for the MMKS, building a certain kind of political consciousness among fisherwomen was viewed as critical. They saw their work as drawing the women closer to a political position that was distinctly more progressive than the one they had been exposed to earlier. It was perhaps because of this, and in spite of the fact that the question of migrants continued to remain a volatile subject with most Koli vendors, that Purnima addressed the question of migrants in the meeting, pointing out that many of them come from fishing communities in the North and are, therefore, fishers much like the Kolis themselves. Most prominently, when she was addressing the meeting of fisherwomen, she stopped to correct herself to address those present as 'female fishers' rather than 'Koli women'.

An Organization for Fisherwomen or Fishworkers?

The perception of threat from migrants continues despite the fact that the MMKS activists discuss how lower footfall in markets occur due to reasons other than male migrants who sell door to door. According to Shuddawati, the anti-migrant discourse was pushed by the Sena, who also pit it as a male incursion of women's work. For the community, this held resonance as it was seen as vital that women retain control over fish vending. The matter was complex, according to Shuddawati, because Koli women's work had suffered in the recent years. But based on her study, she attributed this to fish becoming expensive, door-to-door vending/home deliveries being carried out by shops (different from male migrants who sold in the slums), app-based delivery services, and mall-based markets. This, however, is not a popular analysis and she claims that Koli women continue to be aggressive towards the migrants.

Purnima also believes that the anti-migrant stance was crafted by political parties seeking to capitalize on it, pointing to how a wide range of migrants work in the fisheries in various states, from Orissa to Andhra Pradesh.[26] However, she too argues that the issue remained volatile among Koli women. In this differentiated and complicated scenario, activists with the MMKS who are keen to organize Koli women and bring them on par with fisherwomen from other states and also Koli men, now have to consider whether gender and ethnicity should play a role in such mobilization. Activists of the MMKS said that it was impossible to organize the women as fishworkers alone, given the continuing resonance of the anti-migrant rhetoric they prioritized to come together as Koli fisherwomen.[27]

In a situation where two prior attempts at instituting organizations exclusive to women have failed, and there has been an absolute dearth of representation for women in community institutions, it is

[26] Telephonic conversation on 19 June 2013.

[27] Author's conversations with various MMKS activists during fieldwork in 2013.

of little surprise that the MMKS viewed establishing fresh organizations exclusively for women as a priority. But this was underscored with efforts at building a new political consciousness. For instance, Purnima and Ujjwala asked new women members to stop using the word bhaiyaa to refer to migrants from North India.

Given the dire straits the female fishworkers of Mumbai found themselves in, the need to organize in order to catch the state's eye on the issue was an urgent matter. But the question also arises about the conditions of work of migrants—both women and men—and whether political choices made between Koli or non-Koli are necessary.

In a split labour market, Bonacich argues, resolution comes either through exclusion, replacement of higher priced labour or through a suppression of the wages of all or when higher priced labour operate as a 'caste' and reserve certain kinds of jobs for themselves, making it hard for capitalists to replace them with lower priced labour. But for this, state intervention becomes important (Peled and Shafir 1987). Here the state will ease the 'burden' on the capitalist, who may not want to hire higher priced labour, by subsidizing higher cost labour through social expenses and by preventing lower cost labour from entering the market and imposing discriminatory immigration practices.

The scenario is similar to where the Kolis and the MMKS find themselves today. Not only are existing cooperatives closed off to migrant labour, even more recent formations such as the women's trade union and cooperative are organized by gender and ethnicity, leaving out both male and female migrants who seek work in the fisheries. But what is especially critical to note is how this question of migrants has catalysed the opinion on the demand for an Act to protect the rights of traditional fisher communities, demanding exclusive access to be granted to such communities. While the political positions around this demand will be detailed in Chapter 6, set against the context of the larger picture of capital accumulation at work, it is critical to note that when the Kolis, otherwise marginal in the political economy of Mumbai, throw their weight behind such a demand, they are most often doing so with an eye on the migrant, who is viewed as ever threatening and always the 'other'.

6

Competing Dispossessions

Identity and Class in Fisher Politics

Developments in the fisheries and the city, as detailed in the previous chapters, were initiated with the aim of 'improving the fisheries', but the improvements occurred only for a section of the Kolis and other capitalists in the fisheries. In this context, a focus on the NFF's demand for fishing rights to be retained exclusively by traditional fisher communities presents an opportunity to understand how dispossession that affected a large section of the Kolis is understood not only at a macro level, but also in the everyday life of the urban poor. In other words, the contesting motives behind the demands—of protection for small-scale fishers, restriction on large capital, and restriction on migrant entry—offer an insight into how dispossession has been conceived in fisher politics in the city. Unpacking the trajectory of the fisher movement specifically and examining the context of social movements and nature of the state 1980s onwards leads us to understand why and how the exclusive access demand emerges from and shapes the politics of Mumbai.

Reconfiguring the Community

The decisive focus on revenue generation which guided much of the policy on fisheries in India was especially evident through the state's move to allow the entry of foreign capital in the Indian fisheries. Liberalization of the Indian economy in 1991 and the clause in the 1982 Law of Sea (Subramanian 2009: 206; see also United Nations Convention on the Law of the Sea 1982), requiring states to liberalize access to territorial waters if they were unable to fully exploit their own marine resources, propelled the state's decision to introduce this change in the policy on deep-sea fishing. This new strategy was aimed at utilizing the resources of the deep-sea through joint ventures between Indian and foreign capital, encouraged by the state through a variety of means such as easing credit access, fuel supply, and regulatory mechanisms to enable a greater volume of exports. In return, the state was to receive 12 per cent of the foreign exchange earnings and Indian firms would benefit from a transfer of technology (Subramanian 2009: 206).

The deep-sea fishing policy was eventually abandoned in 1997 following vigorous protests from the NFF which organized coastal fisher communities against the move. The protests saw the coming together of export merchants and workers and owners of net-making, ice-producing, and fish-processing industries, all of whom united to establish the National Fisheries Action Committee Against Joint Ventures to protest against the entry of foreign capital (Subramanian 2009: 207). Similar protests were rekindled in 2015, when the government issued a call for 270 Indian firms to enter into a possible collaboration with foreign companies to operate in the Exclusive Economic Zone lying outside of India's territorial waters (that is, beyond 12 nautical miles) and at a depth of 500 meters. The NFF protested this move and, in doing so, reiterated their arguments from the time when the policy was first initiated in 1994. Arguing that local fishers were already moving in to exploit the fishing ground that lay between 200 and 500 meters (owing to the overexploitation of fishing ground below 200 meters), they pointed out that the move inviting new firms was arbitrary. But what was striking was that both protests pivoted the discussion towards ecological concern. The press note issued by the NFF read:

> The NFF has repeatedly mentioned that the idea of opening up Indian seas is dangerous and detrimental to the fishing of Indian traditional fishers, as the fish resource is already been heavily depleted due to the

non ecological fishing done by these vessels. Hence further opening up the sea for more vessels to fish will only be construed as part of the global ocean grabbing conspiracy. (*The Hindu* 2015)

A critique of the development pattern of the fisheries built on the foundation of ecological sustainability was introduced by the NFF during the 1990s agitation concerning the deep-sea fishing policy. The agitation had led to the development of a broad alliance, with domestic fishers (artisanal and mechanized trawlers alike) coming together against foreign capital. This move was to have a significant effect on the movement led by the NFF. According to Subramanian (2009), the NFF, which had championed the rights of small-scale fishers against trawlers during the agitations that took place through 1980s and early 1990s,[1] now reconfigured the notion of 'community', 'undifferentiated by sector, region, or class and extended to the national scale' (Subramanian 2009: 208). A shift from the local to the national, with the forging of a national community of traditional fishers, marked a resurrection of capitalist nationalism, according to Subramanian (2009: 208). Many of these movements spoke in the language not only of resource protection but also of 'national self-sufficiency'. These ecological movements of the 1990s held a positive view of the state and looked to the state to protect communities from the incursions of transnational capital (Subramanian 2009: 209).

The demand for exclusive access has been built on the grounds of the political reconfiguration of the 1990s movement because it created the grounds for the alliance of small-scale and large-scale fishers, united by their ecological concern, who turned to the state for protection against both large capital and migrants. These movements would now be characterized as *new* social movements, but this

---

[1] Subramanian (2009) argues that this was particularly evident when the NFF approached the Supreme Court over the decision of the Kerala High Court, declaring that the monsoon trawling ban introduced by Kerala was a violation of the rights of trawl-net boat operators. The Supreme Court, while reversing the decision of the High Court, declared that the government was justified in seeking to protect the interests of traditional fishers. This verdict, according to Subramanian (2009: 210), typified the stance assumed by the NFF against capitalist development in the fisheries.

term demands some consideration—what is really new about these movements?

Accumulation by Dispossession and the 'New' Social Movements

David Harvey (2003) had, in his work, taken a different approach to understanding the problem of accumulation, as noted in Chapter 1. While he concurred with Luxemburg (1913b) that primitive accumulation was not a stage of capitalism that was restricted to its early life but one that remained integral to its functioning at all points, he differed over how he conceptualized the inherent problem of capitalism which necessitated primitive accumulation.[2] For Harvey, the problem in capitalism was instead one of over-accumulation. A surplus of capital without an opportunity to invest this capital profitably was the chief motive in pursuing primitive accumulation. Therefore, the problem of surplus capital was resolved through geographical and social expansion of capital, or what he terms as 'spatial-temporal fixes' (Harvey 2003: 89–91).

Harvey's argument allows us to conceptualize neo-liberalism's drive to privatize natural resources and state-owned assets as being a form of such accumulation (Harvey 2003: 149). Much like the urban processes described in Chapter 1, the capitalist transformation initiated in the fisheries corresponds to the process of accumulation.

Similar moves at accumulation include usurpation of common resources that have often spurred ecological movements. The Chipko movement, the Narmada Bachao Andolan, and so on, all characterize a range of struggles which while questioning capitalist development began with a focus on environmental questions that had an immediate local resonance for affected communities.

---

[2] Luxemburg (1913a), as previously mentioned, asserted that underconsumption is a significant problem of capitalism, which makes it necessary for capitalism to have some economies remain non-capitalist and under the control of capitalist economies. Harvey indicates, however, that the problem is of seeking new outlets for accumulation and not one of underconsumption. This drive to accumulate brings more areas under capitalist control.

Harvey (2003: 162) argues that such movements recognized as anti-globalization movements are of a wide variety and are 'seemingly inchoate', but do have the common minimum of 'reclaiming the commons'.

But Hensman (1994) posed a pertinent question: What exactly was new about these movements? The usual assumption was that they were not driven by class formations but rooted in identity, while another set of these movements have focussed on environmental questions. Hensman (1994: 1270–71) and Harvey (2003: 168) point that what was new to such movements was that they were no longer concerned with the capture of state power. The agenda of new social movements could be understood as:

> Neither the nationalist 'people's revolution' that Samir Amin advocates, nor the establishment of a 'socialist' state, but a gradual extension of the democratic space in which ordinary working people can deliberate over, make decisions about, and take action on matters which intimately concern them. (Hensman 1994: 1271)

Harvey's (2003: 168) discussion of the Zapatista Rebellion in Mexico echoed this view, where he claimed that despite the Zapatistas never seeking to capture state power, they sought an 'inclusionary politics' by democratizing discussions on alternative forms of development that would satisfy different social groups.

Castells (2010) identified significant social movements that were reactive (identity-based movements including the Zapatistas that were looking to challenge globalization in its hegemonic, economic, and social form) and proactive, such as the environmental and feminist movements which have set new global agendas and have become prominent movements of the twenty-first century. What remains significant to the wide range of these movements is their response to the state. This remains a complex issue mired in dynamics between central and local governments, as well as rooted in a background of the changing role of the state in neoliberalism. However, significantly, there have also been calls by these movements for 'national protection' (similar to the fisher movement of the 1990s and the 2000s). In light of this, Hensman's call for attention to the nature of state power is important. What changed for these movements to turn to the state for the protection of rights, instead of a takeover of the state itself?

The onset of globalization and the centrality of the state in the regulation of transnational flows of capital and labour have contributed to a shift in social movements. What remains critical is that even as the state's abetment of capital accumulation resulting in dispossession continues, communities turn to the state for protection. Thus, even as the state was seen as an external agent (like migrants) who altered traditional fishing, the challenge by the fisher movement was not posed to the state.

The Nature of the State

In his examination of the social movements of the twenty-first century, Castells posed the question differently. He argued that fragmented social interests produced varied identity-based movements which often turned to the state in order to have their interests addressed, but the question was whether the state was in a position to respond (Castells 2010: 334). The threat of a crisis remained imminent here, precipitated by the redefined role of the state under globalization.

A contrasting view is that the state in fact changed the manner in which it responded to demands from social groups rendered marginal by the process of accumulation. Partha Chatterjee (2008a: 55) argued that the state's functioning is not restricted to aiding capitalists anymore, and that democratic states could not pursue a singular course and must confront the challenges that arise from the consequences of accumulation. States, thus, engage in a simultaneous process of driving accumulation and addressing the needs of those dispossessed through accumulation, evidenced through rehabilitation policies. This does not mean that accumulation would end or even register a decline because as a critical component of capitalism, it cannot do so. But while previously there were means available to early capitalist societies to relieve the pressure that built up with accumulation, the same no longer exists. Specifically, colonies absorbed large streams of migrants who constituted of the dispossessed individuals/surplus labour who could not be absorbed into the capitalist system and, in doing so, prevented capitalist societies from being flooded with a surfeit of labour. However, since captive colonies are no longer a political possibility, Chatterjee (2008a: 55) argued that the state must spend to reverse the effects of accumulation.

For Chatterjee (2008a), the post 1990s period in India was characterized by the strength of the capitalists vis-a-vis other dominant classes and the perception of the state was not one of an autonomous institution. He believes that India was different from the other capitalist democracies of the West because of the presence of distinct categories of civil and political society, even as the former comes to be 'properly constituted' and the latter are more 'contingent' in nature. While the former comprised the urban middle class, the latter section has large sections of the rural population and the urban poor as its constituent. Critical to Chatterjee's (2008a) argument is the assertion that political society is not under the sway of the capitalist class and, more importantly, engages with the state in a manner entirely distinct from civil society.

The distinction between civil and political society also overlap with the categories of corporate and non-corporate capital, where the former is defined by its motives of accumulation and profit generation while the latter is concerned with satisfying 'livelihood needs'. Civil and political society inform, therefore, the new structure of the state which marked by the passive revolution has a role of assuaging the effects of accumulation.

For Chatterjee, the state is forced to do so because of the activities of political society, which exert a pressure on the state to extend welfare measures. An indication of how the nature of the state is informed by this logic is evident, according to him, by the fact that ideological differences no longer define the Left and the Right substantially, but that distinction between them has to do with the quantum of welfare measures extended by them (Chatterjee 2008a: 62).

Chatterjee's (2008a) argument on the difference in how the state treats the question of accumulation is, however, difficult to sustain when examined in close detail. Baviskar and Sundar (2008) highlighted the problems in his analytical framework, such as in the binaries he draws between civil and political society, corporate and non-corporate capital, government versus capital and market, and so on. They argued that in light of events such as police firing on protestors, the government used all forms of state power to ensure compliance with it. More importantly, there was nothing new in the provision of welfare measures by the state, since from the hey days of the exercise of eminent domain by the colonial state, there had been an acknowledgement that losses suffered as a result of accumulation had to be compensated by the state (Baviskar and Sundar 2008: 88). For Baviskar and Sundar (2008), the main argument was that the distinction that Chatterjee (2008a) established between civil and political society did not hold, that is, civil society did not always work within legal and constitutional frameworks. Chatterjee's (2008a) argument, they assert, reverses the actions of political and civil society, for it is usually the latter and not the former which could work outside the law and do so with some measure of impunity.

It is also vital to note that while the need for the state to address the dispossessed has always been present, this has not meant a blurring of the lines between the Left and the Right in India—the imagination of welfare can differ widely. The past five years have witnessed a drop in budgetary allocations towards welfare measures such as the National Rural Employment Guarantee Act (NREGA) and in education, and land has been speedily acquired for various projects. Welfare is no longer a simple and critical issue in electoral politics and, thus, Chatterjee's assessment of the role of the state seems to be misplaced. At a time when economic growth alone is seen as a measure of a nation's success, there is little doubt that the state will redouble its efforts towards capital accumulation. The concept of welfare itself has undergone shifts, the domain of rights no longer remains its only constituent, welfare activities can incorporate activities that enhance associational life—religious activities, political formations, and traditional forms of charity. For the dispossessed, welfare may also look very different from what is commonly imagined—work and associated identities could be found in new avenues—in vigilante groups for instance, or as wheelers and dealers in expanding technocratic regimes (Poonam 2018).[3] The Left and the Right, thus, may work on welfare but may imagine it entirely differently, such as the Sena and MNS's moves to invigorate the Koli and Hindu pride through Ganesh Mandal activities and Koli festivals, and the NFF and the MMKS members conception of it through the discourse of rights.

[3] Poonam's work is a fascinating study of the world of the rural and urban young of India, whose ambitions and aspirations of work must, for them, fit within the technologically driven economy and the religiously driven society.

Social Movements and the State

If the state continues to play a role in accumulation then we return yet again to the question of why movements have altered in form. Castells (2010) and Sassen (2006)[4] argued that it was globalization that produced a difference—there was a 'demise of statism' (Castells 2010: 2). There was, in other words, a twin process where, under global forms of capitalism, the state stands changed and the responses of people to these conditions too began to take new forms. Thus, it was the transformation of capitalism which led to *new* social movements that responded to a changed economic, social, and cultural regime by adopting defensive identity positions or through movements that seek to fundamentally alter social relationships. Castells included environmental movements, which from the 1980s, have played a significant role, in this latter form of movements. As the fisher movement and its demand for exclusive access demonstrate, environmental movements can also foreground defensive identity positions.

Environmental movements are both predominant and of a wide variety today. What is significant is that while these movements have built a certain global consciousness, particularly with respect to issues such as climate change, they have also reanimated the local as the site for struggle; it is here that defensive identity positions have often developed. What is new is precisely this move towards defensive identity positions as opposed to class formations, which informed earlier forms of environmental movements. Is the case, then, that there is little within Marxism to sustain ecological concern or that movements as such came to be led by diverse communities, wherein local factors such as discrimination against particular communities shaped the nature of the movement.

From the late 1990s, there has been an increasing amount of scholarship that coincided with the advent of environmental movements, which highlighted that Marx's work explored both the material world shaped through human production and the impact and constraints

---

[4] Sassen (2006), however, also argues that globalization is made possible and endures through institutional networks built originally around the nation state.

imposed by the natural world (Burkett 1999; Foster 2000). Indeed, as Foster (2000: viii) argued, Marx's ecological thinking was derived from materialism itself and was not secondary in his thinking. This scholarship has done much to illuminate the critical link that exists between capitalism and environmental damage. It has highlighted in the face of popular environmental movements, which focus on modifications of individual consumption and capitalism's own attempts to go green, that capitalist production threatens ecological sustainability. The early phase of the fisher movement was built precisely on this recognition of the environmental damage that capitalism produces.

Yet, just as surely, the fisher movement also distanced itself from a rejection of capitalism or a class analysis of the changes that had taken place. Outside of the environmental question, Harvey (2003: 169) pointed out that the Left did not always respond to the distress of those dispossessed. Was it perhaps the inevitability of dispossession and the necessity of this form of accumulation to capitalism that explained why the dispossessed were not a significant political subject for the Left?

For Marx, primitive accumulation was the severing of the link between the means of production and labour which leads to the breakdown of pre-capitalist relations and ushered in capitalism. Primitive accumulation is, thus, necessary for the advent of capitalism. Even as he focussed on the violence that defined the process, Marx also acknowledged capitalism as a stage that both dehumanises but contrarily also offers the potential for the development of the free individual to a much greater extent than any previous stage of development (Hobsbawm 1964: 15–16; Marx 1964: 84–5).

By and large, for movements on the Left, therefore, it was the contradiction between capital and labour which was to remain significant: 'The focus was, therefore, on class relations and class struggles within the field of capital accumulation understood as expanded reproduction. All other forms of struggle were viewed as subsidiary, secondary, or even dismissed as peripheral or irrelevant' (Harvey 2003: 169–170).

But this has not always been the case, of course, and there have been several instances of livelihood-based movements that have been led by the Left. Most notable in the Indian context is the struggle among the Warlis led by Godavari Parulekar in Thane, Maharashtra. As a member of the Communist Party of India, she organized the Warlis who were struggling against the administrative usurpation of their lands by the colonial state exercising control through a class of landlords.

Yet clearly through the 1980s and 1990s, as accumulation by dispossession expanded globally, class did not become a part of the foundation of the struggles. Movements from the 1980s in particular were likelier to come together on the basis of defensive identity positions (Castells 2010) as opposed to class. In addition, with the rise of global flows of capital and flexibility of accumulation, the Left faced a severe challenge and remained on the back foot. Post 1973, class-based movements were increasingly facing repression and with the expansion of production to East and South East Asia, such movements became harder to sustain (Harvey 2003: 171).

Labour organizations in this period continued to focus on the manufacturing sector and agriculture. Much of this continues even today, where the absence of the organized Left in social movements around resource dispossession has been conspicuous. As a member of the Centre of Indian Trade Unions (CITU) discussed,[5] their involvement with the movement of fishers and their struggle has been minimal owing to their focus on industrial labour and especially the problems of contract labour therein.[6] Similar views were echoed by Nalini Nayak, an activist, who believed that trade unions did not ally with the NFF because they were not part of the industrial proletariat and were unable to understand how fishers with a tradition of private ownership fit in their scheme (Subramanian 2009: 214).

Movements against dispossession have taken varied directions and have not always been progressive—often they made demands for a return to the older social relations of production which were equally if not more oppressive. Even though struggles have been waged at

---

[5] Personal interview conducted in June 2013 in South Mumbai.

[6] The exception to this would be in the case of the agitation against the Jaitapur nuclear plant, where the CITU has been working alongside the local fishing community 2010 onwards. He also noted that the CITU extended support to fisher unions in Kerala and Andhra Pradesh but that the organization unit in Maharashtra had its 'hands full'.

the global and/or local level,[7] increasingly, it was the local context that shaped the movement, and this came to be defined in terms of identity not class. And it was the state that could grant recognition to identities and guarantee rights.

'The More the World Becomes Global, People Feel Local'[8]

A globalized world was also increasingly local in character (Castells 2010: xxiii) and this spurred identity-based movements across the world. Defensive identities, as Castells (2010) terms them, have been adopted by communities in an effort to reaffirm their way of life. Not all of these movements are progressive, of course, including many of the fundamentalist religious movements that have spread over the last few years.

However, for Castells (2010), environmental movements do not fall into the category of such movements; instead they are classified as proactive movements that have managed to draw the attention of the world to the global nature of the environmental crisis we are currently faced with. Yet, many environmental movements have demonstrated defensive identities—seeking a restoration of earlier practices and not a complete rejection of global capital-driven development, but only a rejection of the form in which they encountered it. Described as a 'critical localism' by Dirlik, it was based on cognizance of the fact that localities were marked by 'processes of historical transformation but still need to be appropriated from the onslaught of new, even more pervasive forms of capitalist modernization' (Subramanian 2009: 211).

Environmental movements, it appears, either bear the burden of representing anti-capitalist politics or highly localized ones. Movements in India, such as the Chipko agitation, had been celebrated, by scholars such as Shiva for its resistance to a development discourse driven by commercial interest over conservation and

---

[7] For Harvey (2003) this was a response to the form of accumulation. Levien (2015: 149), however, argued that accumulation was not linked to the 'global imperatives of capital'—an argument that is hard to sustain in the global nature of advanced capitalism.

[8] Castells (2010: xxiii).

for women's participation in it (Shiva and Bandyopadhyay 1968). However, if one were to examine the local more closely here, it is not immediately apparent that the movement was a rejection of the politics of development that characterized the 1970s or that accumulation was driven by local factors alone. Local concerns regarding access to resources and benefits of the state policy relating to the use of timber, all played a significant role in shaping the Chipko agitation (Mawdsley 1998). Writing on the politics of the hills, Kumar and Vasan (1997) highlight that even resource-dependent communities do not possess an innate sense of environmental consciousness and like communities elsewhere, there are always local dynamics, economic calculations, and intra-community hierarchies which shape their responses.

It is this intra-community space which comes to be whitewashed in movements and discourses, particularly around the environment. The language of ecological sustainability may allow for a thrust towards broad consolidation (domestic fishers against transnational firms, traditional fishers against migrants, big capital against small-scale fishers) but the fissures within these consolidations constantly threaten to tear apart. Members of the fisher movement are alert to these concerns, but in Colachel (Tamil Nadu), just like in Mumbai, activists believe that it was ecological consciousness and threats to the environment that could consolidate the community. Subramanian (2009) asserts that such a politics allowed for fishers in Kanyakumari to assert their locality against a form of national capitalism.

The politics of 'locality', in other words, can take different forms. The struggle of artisanal fishers of Kanyakumari initially excluded trawler owners, who belonged to similar caste and faith as them. However, a later variant brought together these groups against 'foreign trawlers'. In Mumbai, even as local contradictions—of small-scale fishers against trawler and purse-seine boat owners, and of fisherwomen against private developers and the BMC—loomed large, political assertion was primarily around a community that was defined not on the basis of its shared norms but on a defensive identity of both caste and indigenous link to the city. Yet this assertion continues in the language of ecological sustainability that has come to define the NFF's approach from the late 1980s.

Rambhau Patil, the chairperson of the MMKS and ex-chairperson of the NFF, noted that between 1960 and 2013, that is, in a span of 53 years, resources have been depleted, and coastal waters, creeks, and rivers have been polluted. Pointing to the inherent problems with such technology, he believed that it was impossible to expect good returns if the resources were exploited.[9] It was in response to the introduction of trawlers and purse-seine nets, he argued, that 'my people' began altering the mesh size of their nets, making them smaller (similar to those of trawl and purse-seine nets). This led to younger and smaller fish being caught and contributed to the problem of a declining catch. But he argued that the introduction of these techniques came primarily from 'outside', even as around 50 per cent of owners of purse-seine netters came from the fishing community itself. Putting an end to the use of this technology, he argued, was now a matter of survival. A smaller, sustainable scale of production was central to his vision of sustainable fisheries. The state itself was responsible for much of the damage, as the fisheries department bureaucracy acted only in the name of increased production, ignoring the concerns of the NFF and the MMKS. The most pertinent demand of fishers was that the produce of fisheries be distributed equally and not usurped by a few. Maintaining biodiversity especially because of ecological problems was also important and therefore the demand was for a small group of fishers acting responsibly and sustainably.

The problem for Rambhau, however, was not specific to Maharashtra alone. The experience of Karnataka, for instance, was similar and he believed they had been more exploitative, leading to the fish stock of the area depleting, causing fishers from Karnataka to 'encroach on others fishing grounds'. Discussions with other fisheries activists highlighted the same, where fishers from neighbouring regions (Goa and Gujarat) were reported to have frequently used purse-seine and trawl nets in the waters of Maharashtra, having overfished from the waters closer to their state.[10] Such antagonism,

---

[9] All quotes from Rambhau Patil in this chapter are from a personal interview conducted on 9 June 2013 in Mumbai.

[10] The issue was one discussed at the MMKS meetings as well (held on 2 July 2013 at Sagar Park), where tackling the problem at a regional and international level was considered imperative.

it was claimed, had led to violent outbursts between the fishers. Rambhau notes that the responsibility for following sustainable fishing, therefore, does lie with the fishing community. But this community that he refers to would necessarily be one that is active not only at the local or regional level but also at the national level. The political subjects of the movement were all members of the fisher community. Looking to engage wider constituents in this environmental movement, however, meant a reconstitution of the community. Adopters of new technology were to be educated about its pitfalls. For Rambhau Patil, even though traditional fishers were complicit in the ecological problem, first those from outside the community needed to be stopped, and then, those who owned more than one vessel within the community needed to be restricted to single vessel ownership to tackle the problem.

Rambhau and other activists of the NFF and the MMKS are not absolving traditional communities. But they attributed a disruption to the environmentally conscious local practices of the Kolis to state policy, which encouraged new technology that spurred overfishing and enabled the entry of outsiders with capital to invest in the fisheries. Even as the demand on access was framed by them through restricting the entry of large capital (on the grounds that Kolis did not possess it); in the grassroots of the movement, this position came to settle close to the politics of nativism, which both valourized the local community and derided the outsider.

I will argue that this *unintended* consequence of collapsing the state of the fisheries into the politics of nativism has occurred in Mumbai, both because of the fertile ground available to nativist politics and because of the decisive shift in how the NFF articulates the problem of the fisheries. Beginning from 1989, the NFF consciously moved away from a class question on the fisheries to a movement that came together to engender ecological sustainability—'NFF ideologues now pointed to the inadequacy of class as a category for analyzing the dynamics of an economy characterised by natural resource harvest, common property, and private ownership of the means of production' (Subramanian 2009: 214). No longer were class-based mobilizations significant to the movement; rather, the effort was to limit and eliminate such technology. And if technology was seen as entering from 'outside' the community—either the state or private players—then this was where the dividing line came to be drawn.

This has come to significantly shape the political consciousness of fishers in Mumbai, where it has prevented a hard look at the intra-community hierarchy at work as well as led to the assumption that the migrant can only be a secondary political subject within the fisheries.

The Blunting of Class and Its Implications

Disrupting the narrative of the external entry of capital in the fisheries are accounts of the Kolis who have entered fishing as a business and not through the use of state subsidies. The invocation of the community of traditional fishers has led to some Kolis, such as Dheeraj (pseudonym), finding their way back into 'traditional work of [the] community'.[11] Dheeraj, who runs a popular bar and eatery in Mumbai (inherited from his father), had taken to fishing, not in the traditional forms imagined but rather through an investment in new trawlers. Just like Dheeraj, there are other Koli fishers who, even as they engage in trawling, see themselves and their work as constituting 'tradition'.

With the shift away from class, the community has consolidated, but the hierarchies within it are dulled from view. This has meant that conservation has taken precedence without being rooted in an understanding of unequal access to resources through technology, or what Subramanian (2009) terms as 'distributive justice'. Further, the blunting of the class question and the focus on conservation have led to two other critical problems—of users of capital-intensive technology inscribing themselves within the larger community and a neglect of the plight of workers in the fisheries. Both of these hold serious consequences for how the movement against the use of technology developed.

One such way in which class is rendered marginal, is through the continuing reliance on the category of owner-worker. As highlighted in the previous chapters, this has been a social relation that has seen a fundamental change with the onset of capitalism. Owners

---

[11] Personal interview conducted on August 2013 at Sagar Park.

of trawlers and purse-seine boats rarely work on their boats, hiring instead locals and migrants to work. The more damaging consequence of continuing with the owner-worker category has been seen in the inability of even the MMKS to register itself as a trade union. As discussed in previous chapters, several members cited continuity from the past and harmonious relations between the owners and workers, to argue against a trade union which they believed would champion the cause of workers alone. Even though the MMKS is affiliated to the NFF (registered as a union), it continues to face a challenge in doing so itself.

The notion of a moral economy (see Chapter 3) was grounded in the notion of distributive justice. The opposition to new technology was, therefore, in the inequality it perpetuated. But while many Kolis continued to use a framework of shared norms to indict users of technology, such as purse-seine nets, the language of ecological sustainability had allowed these users to re-inscribe themselves within an older moral economy, by identifying as victims of trying circumstances in the fisheries. Owners of trawlers and purse-seine boats agreed with the NFF view that such technology led to an exhaustion of resources.[12] The problem, they claimed, was that this technology was introduced with only short-term gains in mind. However, in spite of the seemingly grave confessions, they absolved themselves of responsibility. Kritish and Mohan (pseudonyms), owners of separate trawlers and purse-seine net boats declared: 'If the people around me do it, why not me.' Versions of this argument abounded. A trawler owner and the chairperson of a cooperative, Tejas (pseudonym)[13] remarked that the cooperative he headed was affiliated to the MMKS and had even participated in agitations, some of which concerned the use of purse-seine nets. But in spite of knowing that these methods of fishing were harmful and that scientists have advised that periods of ban were good for breeding, fishing could not be stopped because it was linked to livelihoods—'paapi pet ka sawaal' (compulsion of surviving), he clarified. Increasingly, thus, trawler and purse-seine owners were

[12] All quotes from Kritish and Mohan in this chapter are from the personal interview conducted on 8 June 2013 at Sagar Park.

[13] All quotes from Tejas are from a personal interview conducted on 18 June 2013 at Sagar Park.

using the language of survival and compulsion to link themselves to a moral economy from which they would be otherwise ousted. And by doing so, they re-inscribed themselves within a larger community identity of traditional fishers without any reference to their class and the technology they employed.

Through this they were able to fluidly move between describing themselves as engaged in a business or livelihood practice. Tejas frequently engaged with the discourse around livelihood and business, smoothly charting the turbulent waters that lay between categories of small-scale fishers (those engaged in livelihood practices), trawler owners, and purse-seine net owners, whom he collapsed into the former category. This particularly emerged in his discussion on the ban of technology, such as trawlers and purse-seine nets. The community, according to him, was torn on the question of survival, with both small-scale and artisanal fishers, and trawler and purse-seine net owners struggling to survive. In the context of 'survival' and the vanishing sustainability of the sea, thus, the capitalist class of fishers were construed to be similarly vulnerable to the small-scale fisher.

One of the factors that enabled such a comparison for them is the continued practice of a share system and not a fully developed wage system (see Chapter 3). In real terms, the practice was somewhere between a share and a wage system. Despite the transition to a capital system, increased production and most significantly where owners no longer work alongside labour, the system is transitioning from shares to wages. Although Subramanian's (2009) study documents workers as being in favour of the share system, arguing that it enabled them to amass savings which could be invested in boat ownership, workers in Mumbai had a different opinion, believing that ownership would not be a path available to them.

The share system was more vital to owners who could represent themselves as being as affected by the vicissitudes of the sea. They would frequently bring up the damaging losses they incurred in the trawling and purse-seine 'business'. Kritish (pseudonym) discussed how he would purchase diesel worth 2.5 lakhs for an 18-day trip of his trawler. Additional expenses incurred would include 14 tonnes of ice and other expenses such as food for and payment to the workers, engine maintenance, and so on, which would come to another few lakhs. His earnings, however, were much lower and he was unable to break even, adding that he had suffered losses on the purse-seine netter for the last two years. On the trawler, he earned up to 4 lakhs a year, but the entire amount was sometimes spent in repaying loans. Increasing expenses meant that the fishing business was now like a lottery—not everyone, he added, could win at it. Losses of this kind forced Tejas (pseudonym), to eventually give up his trawler. Such losses and the share system led the owners to believe that they suffered just as much as the workers and that the effects of overfishing were endured equally by both, irrespective of class.

Furthermore, the ecological discourse had meant that owners, in spite of their own culpability, were able to participate in the conversation on suffering because of destructive technology. But it was regulation, not elimination, that was seen as the favourable response by the owner class. Trawler owners and members of the local cooperative of the Sagar Nagar koliwada believed that declining catches were a result of weak regulation by the state. Particular kinds of boats and nets must operate in separate zones, they argued. 'This distinction is not maintained and as a result the catch declines', they stated.[14] Overfishing was not acknowledged, though a cooperative member recognized that the bans were violated by trawlers. But they believed that responsibility for this could lay elsewhere. Roshan (pseudonym), the chairperson, noted that the monsoon rains led to polluted run-off water from the land entering the sea; this pollution led to problems for those fishing closer to the coast (small-scale fishers) and also for people like them (trawler owners) who sent boats into the deep sea. The discourse of ecology and the cry for conservation had, thus, united the 'community' where every fisher suffered—the trawler owner, the boat worker, and even Koli women who faced rising prices owing to declining catches. The demand, therefore, by restricting entry into fishing, was seen as enabling better regulation.

[14] Conversation with a group of cooperative members on 17 July 2013 at Sagar Nagar.

The Fisher Working Class

The disavowal of class in the fisher movement has particularly affected workers in the fisheries—those labouring on boats as well as workers in allied industries of fish processing that emerged around the export market that capitalist production catered to. With the low share of income in fishing, combined with the rising levels of education,[15] young Koli men and women were increasingly choosing to pursue better-paying work outside the fisheries. However, with the change to capitalist production, there was also a need for labour in the fisheries. The use of new technology on the boats—engines, mandatory GPS systems, mechanized nets, technology that locates fish, and so on—have meant that customary knowledge and skills for fishing have been rendered redundant. This has enabled the entry of migrant labour, many of whom come with no prior experience of fishing. Rambhau Patil recalled:

> This (work on artisanal crafts) was a job that required hard labour, how-ever, after mechanization and the introduction of ready-made nylon nets and floats, and even boats made of fiber glass—it has become much easier. Gradually, more people bought vessels and tribal com-munities were brought in as labour, paid low wages, and taught skills required for fishing.

Migrant worker, thus, became a regular feature in the fisheries of Mumbai. With young Koli men aspiring for skilled and formal employment, migrant workers took over much of the manual work. There were no fixed contracts and migrant workers would seek work at the docks or in different koliwadas as labourers on boats. Those working on smaller mechanized boats at Sagar Nagar koliwada pre-ferred to work on trawlers because work on smaller crafts was often more physically demanding: nets, for instance, on trawlers were drawn in mechanically and not by hand, unlike the smaller boats.

---

[15] See Tables 4.2 and 4.3 in Chapter 4 of this book for the increase in the number of people leaving fishing between the prime working age of 18–30, divided by sex.

Trawler workers operating from Sassoon Docks[16] also seemed to have a union. However, workers on smaller boats, who migrated every season and moved between docks and koliwadas in search of work had no fixed location and, therefore, found it hard to organize.

Another worker who has become a regular feature of the fisheries is the worker in fish processing. This work has come to be performed largely by women and, much like other work in the fisheries, attracts a large number of migrants (see Chapter 3). Warrier (2001) analyses the fish-processing industry in Mumbai, marking the preponderance of migrant labour. As an industry built around the export market where competition was fierce, producers remained competitive by hiring contract labour who were typically migrants—their increased exploitation allowing for higher profits (Warrier 2001: 3554). Citing from an earlier study on processing units in Kerala, Warrier observed that the share of contract workers in processing industries has steadily risen.

Most of these workers happen to be migrant labour hailing from poor economic backgrounds. Her work on the migrating workers—women from Kerala—analyses how, despite oppressive conditions of work, there was still an intense desire to migrate, highlighting the conditions that compel women to migrate in search of work. As documented in Chapter 4, the conditions of work for women in such industries can be dismal. Long hours of work, low wages determined by the amount of fish processed, and no benefits had left such workers vulnerable. Bargaining power remained weak in the absence of any worker collectives and because of surfeit of labour in the informal economy, which allowed easy replacements. The capitalist transformation of the fisheries had, thus, led to the clear emergence of a class of workers, who were distinct from the owners of the new means of production. While activists from the NFF and the MMKS recognized the problems with capitalist development, the shift away from a class analysis had impeded their ability to engage with and mobilize the new ranks of workers emerging in the fisheries. The MMKS, for instance,

[16] Sassoon Docks in Mumbai is a large dockyard used by larger crafts, such as trawlers and purse-seine net boats. It also houses the offices of those with interests in the export of fish.

had not yet organized women in processing industries, unlike their work with Koli fish vendors; there had also been no collective of labour on boats as workers. Engaging with cooperatives was the strategy of the MMKS to penetrate deeper and wider in the political landscape of the fisheries. However, in doing so, its ability to take on certain issues had been blocked. The MMKS activists, however, did not believe that their links and membership drawn from cooperatives informed their political position. Rambhau Patil noted that even though the members of the MMKS comprised owners of purse-seine netters, their position on it was clear—an elimination of such technology.

But whether through elimination or regulation, the notion of equitable and sustainable fisheries was now reliant on restricting participants in the fisheries, and with the shift away from class, the MMKS adopted the defensive identity of 'traditional fishers', inadvertently rendering working-class migrants vulnerable.

The Demand for Exclusive Access in a Polarized City

The history of the NFF's change in name alerts us to the significance that fisher working class hold in their political programme. The NFF began as the National Forum for Kattumaram and Country Boat Fishermen's Rights and Marine Wealth, and following the inclusion of fisher unions, it became the National Fishermen's Forum and registered as a union in 1985. In 1989, after a walk-out by women members protesting against gender exclusivity of the name and the neglect faced at the hands of the Left movements in organizing fishers, the name transitioned into the National Fishworkers' Forum (Subramanian 2009: 214). The fishworker was, therefore, to be a critical part of the vision for an equitable sustainable fisheries. However, with a shift away from class, they have been unable to foreground the issues of workers within the movement, despite the best of intensions.

Purnima,[17] an activist with the NFF and the MMKS, acknowledges these problems.

> Cooperatives address issues regarding the business of fishing and may
> address certain other pertinent issues, but not very often. Issues regarding

[17] Conversations with author between April 2013 and January 2014.

people who work, their problems, questions regarding their safety and security, are not addressed. In my own observation, these issues are handled more by trade unions.

She believed, however, that the MMKS has been grappling with this issue for the last 20–25 years. Even their own registration as a union was blocked because almost 90 per cent of their members believed that it would cause a rift between the owner and the labouring class. This was even the case when the larger share of members of the MMKS were small boat owners and not trawler owners, who she believed paid migrant workers minimum wages and took care of their healthcare expenses. Clearly, the class line was becoming firmer and as workers at Sagar Nagar highlighted, even small-scale owners were no longer a labouring class.

The chilling effect of the inattention to class has led to a silence on a whole section of fishworkers who were part of the fisheries and its allied industries. In such a configuration, the morality of the Koli community was emphasized over the actual material conditions in the fisheries. Thus, the problem was seen as the capitalist system and its central participants were identified as those from outside the community. The MMKS activists stated that the capital needed to participate in the capitalist fisheries could only come from those who were richer, and a history of economic backwardness prevented the Kolis from participating in the same way.

But since conservation was now the main agenda, reverting to an older regime of use was seen as critical to the preservation of the sea and the fisheries. This older regime was one where access to the commons was restricted by means of knowledge, skill, and its linked caste identity. The discourse of conservation indicated that traditional fisher communities were best suited to the sustainable community management of the resource; this is what lay at the heart of the exclusive access demand. The recognition of rights of traditional fishing communities was central to the activists who invoked the Forest Rights Act (FRA) 2006. The FRA 2006 was introduced with the aim to protect the interests and livelihoods of 'traditional forest dwelling communities' and to concurrently address the need for conservation and protection of forest resources by securing the rights of such communities whose customary practices were considered as imbued with ecological consciousness. It, therefore, held much promise for activists in the fisheries who, in demanding access for traditional fishing communities, were seeking much the same.

The FRA 2006, however, was built on the foundation of a binary established between the traditional resource-dependent community on the one hand and the state and market on the other hand, or as Kumar and Vasan (1997: 3294) argue, a 'non-dynamic, binary model that merely juxtaposes a pre-capitalist, subsistence oriented local community to a bureaucratic state and commercial industrial-urban complex'. This understanding holds relevance to fisheries as well. For instance, internal differentiation within the community—even if acknowledged—is relegated to the margins, where the highlight is between external forces (state and capital, and migrants) which have introduced a new mode of production. This has been similar to the case of both the forests and the fisheries. Such an analysis has immediate limitations—it erroneously attributes changes as arising out of the state's intervention alone, instead of analysing how state intervention engenders a new basis for old inequalities. In the fisheries, only a certain class of fishers could avail of mechanization subsidies and loans, in spite of the purported aim of cooperatives to prevent this from occurring. More significantly, it presumes that this interaction between the state, market, and fisher communities is one-directional. Kumar and Vasan stress that this is not the case:

> market relations are two-way transactions, with equal values flowing in opposite directions. Thus the local community not only loses forest produce to the national market, it also receives back commodities whose social impact on small communities is much larger than is generally believed. (Kumar and Vasan 1997: 3295)

Similarly, small-scale fishers at the Sagar Nagar koliwada, who are left vulnerable through the operations of trawlers and purse-seine boats, blame the state and market for the destructive technology, but also see their links with the new markets as beneficial. Recollecting the earlier value for prawns, they noted that with the increasing international demand for prawns, its price rose significantly even in the domestic market to which they supplied. The price of most fish was similarly high because it commanded high prices in the export market. Members of traditional fisher communities, therefore, much like individuals from 'outside', established their own complex relationships with both the state and the market.

The more critical problem with the binary comes from how it envisions a traditional fisher community that continues to follow artisanal practices. It places on them an undue burden of connection with customary practices, one which it presumes they will continue to follow in spite of their economic and social location in a capitalist society. Even though the rights and protection of artisanal fishers may have been guaranteed to some degree with the passage of the Maharashtra Marine Fishing Regulation Act, 1981 (which secures coastal waters for their use), it does not consider how capitalism can exert a pressure and make it extremely difficult for smaller scales of production to sustain. There is also the assumption that artisanal fishers would continue customary fishing practices and would not adopt new technology even if it was likely to grant them better outcomes in terms of catch and income.

This binary model came to be epitomized in the Draft of the Traditional Coastal and Marine Fisherfolk (Protection of Rights) Act, 2009 Draft Act. The Draft Act modelled on the FRA 2006 recognizes the rights of the traditional fishing communities to pursue fishing through traditional means. Much like the FRA 2006, the 2009 draft based the need for rights on sustainable resource use—'conservation and maintaining of an ecological balance'—and invoked the role of the community to achieve this. The Draft Act envisaged securing rights to community-held lands, included provisions for the development of fisheries cooperatives which would purchase fish sourced through traditional means, established markets with fair prices determined for procuring fish caught using traditional means, and provided aid to purchase traditional gear required for such fishing. For ensuring much of this, as well as to regulate and register traditional vessels, the Act vested authority in the local panchayat which, however, had limited territorial purview.

The draft was, however, unsuited to the fisheries; the NFF pointed out, for instance, how local panchayats flouted the rules of the Maharashtra Marine Fishing Regulation Act, 1981, under local pressure. Mathany Saldhana, the chairperson of the NFF at the time, urged the state to not mimic other acts and to recognize that ownership of coastal land was privately held and not held as common land or under the state (*Times of India* 2011), as was the case with forests. Despite the NFF's rejection of the Draft Act, they saw in it a means to secure the rights of traditional fisher communities. However, the NFF's consultation was vital for this. Even as support for this came from the aim to promote small-scale and traditional fisheries, theirs was an indictment of capitalist development, argued, however, on the grounds of ecology and conservation alone. The first step toward this, however, as mentioned before, was reverting to an older regime of use, by limiting the use of the commons to those from traditional fisher communities and pursuing fishing through traditional means alone. But this aim always had the potential to be lost in translation in an ethnically polarized city.

Although the NFF and the MMKS activists argued that the provisions of the Draft Act were to safeguard the interests of small-scale and artisanal fishers, the community it configured for doing so did not explicitly include fishers who did not belong to fisher communities. While the Draft Act had also faced criticism from the NFF for seeking to 'ghettoize' traditional fishers and for not paying attention to the contribution of other communities who lived on the coast, the NFF made no mention of the migrant labour who were by now an integral part of small-scale fishing as well. These were migrants who, despite having worked in the fisheries for over two decades, were not recognized as traditional fishers and could not access any work other than as labourers. Expressing an interest in buying boats, one migrant, Vikas (pseudonym),[18] claimed that control rested with the Kolis alone, even though they (migrants) would consider themselves as fishers since this was the work they pursued for the majority of the year. Koli boat owners agreed that migrants could only work in fishing as labour. This argument was justified on the grounds that migrant workers did not possess the documents testifying their domicile in the area, which was vital for securing membership in the cooperative and state aid. Thus, though the stated aim of the Draft Act was to secure the interests of fishers using traditional means, this may very well come at the cost of disregarding the role of migrants in it.

[18] Personal interview conducted on 4 June 2013 at Sagar Nagar.

Troublingly, for many Koli women, the demand for exclusive access and the Draft Act was not just a means to reassert their hold over the livelihood, but also a decisive way to oust migrants. The hostility between migrants and Koli fisherwomen, as described in the previous two chapters, led the latter to believe that migrants were responsible for the perceived losses experienced in fish vending. A local MMKS activist, Omkar (pseudonym),[19] whose wife was a fish vendor, argued that the passage of the Act guaranteeing exclusive rights to the Kolis would benefit Koli women the most, who have suffered because of migrant entry.

Senior activists of the MMKS indicated that the demand, if agreed to, would not affect the ability of migrants to secure work in the fisheries. There are two consequences, however, of this iteration. First, while the demand may not inhibit migrant entry, it made no effort to engage with the precarious work migrants were confined to. By making a clear demand to limit the commons' access to traditional fisher communities alone, especially in small-scale fishing (which may be more affordable to poor migrants), it inhibited the ability of the migrant to be self-employed in the fisheries. Even in cases of small-scale fishers, there has been a tendency on the part of boat owners to retreat from the work of fishing and to primarily hire workers for it. This, coupled with the inability of migrant workers to effectively organize, has left them particularly vulnerable.[20]

Second, in the case of fishworkers engaged in fish retail, as most Koli women are, the demand legitimizes their call to end migrant work in fish retail, guaranteeing the right to Koli women alone. Migrant labour, which is present both in larger industries of fish processing and packaging as well as in fish retail (but is more heavily contested in the latter), will therefore be threatened with eviction. The Draft Act, which comes with its attendant definitions of fisherfolk and entitlements, makes this a strong likelihood.

'Fisherfolk' means the *traditional members or community of fisherfolk who primarily reside in and who depend on sea fishing for their bona fide livelihood needs; ... 'other traditional fisherfolk' means any member or*

---

[19] Personal interview conducted on 24 April 2013 at Sagar Nagar.
[20] This was observed in Sagar Nagar koliwada.

community who has for at least three generations prior to the 13th day
of December, 2009 primarily resided in and who depend on the ocean
for bona fide livelihood needs and employ traditional fishing practices.
Explanation—For the purpose of this clause, 'generation' means a
period comprising twenty-five years.... 'Traditional' refers to the use of
traditional mechanism for catching fish by traditional boats and gears
which are not mechanized. It will also include the fisherfolk who are
involved in traditional fish processing like curing, salting, drying,
marketing and other related processes [*sic*]. (Draft of the Traditional
Coastal and Marine Fisherfolk [Protection of Rights] Act 2009: 3;
emphasis added)

The definitions used above would include fisherwomen whose livelihood was dependent on sea fishing but who could also fall under
the definitional purview of the term 'other traditional fisherfolk'. The
rights stipulated also include 'any other traditional right customarily
enjoyed by the traditional fisherfolk', which could enable the inclusion of the customary right of women to engage in fish retail, given
the sex-based division of labour.

Bonacich (1972) discussed the outcomes of a split labour market
in which higher-priced labour is successful in preventing the entry
of lower-priced labour through exclusion of new entrants or higher-
priced labour operating as a 'caste'. Exclusion occurs when cheaper
labour enters from another territory. In cases where such exclusionary
moves did not yield results, the preferred policy was one of exclusiveness
or 'to operate as a caste'. Bonacich (1972: 555) defines caste as follows:

Caste is essentially an aristocracy of labor (a term borrowed from
Lenin, e.g. 1964), in which higher paid labor deals with the undercut-
ting potential of cheaper labor by excluding them from certain types
of work. The higher paid group controls certain jobs exclusively and
gets paid at one scale of wages, while the cheaper group is restricted to
another set of jobs and is paid at a lower scale. The labor market split
is submerged because the differentially priced workers ideally never
occupy the same position.

There are three ways in which such measures of establishing a 'caste'
status with an occupation was achieved by higher-priced labour. The
first was the monopolization of certain skills by the higher-wage class
so as to corner such jobs for themselves. The second was to limit the

education of lower-priced labour so as to restrict their ability to operate as strike breakers. The third, was minimizing the political resources that lower-priced labour can control, rendering them vulnerable. 'In other words, the solution to the devastating potential of weak, cheap labor is, paradoxically, to weaken them further, until it is no longer in business' immediate interest to use them as replacements' (Bonacich 1972: 556).

In Mumbai, the Kolis are of course a caste in more than the sense in which Bonacich considers. The occupational link with the caste hierarchy did give them a monopoly over the work and restricted knowledge of skills, but also marked them as 'backward' and prevented them from accessing education. But in the current context, it also forced them, particularly Koli fisherwomen, to reinforce their links with the livelihood. And, thus, as migrants and members of other castes enter fishing, it is not surprising to see the Kolis demanding a reaffirmation of their link to the livelihood, both in terms of caste as tradition as well as in the form that Bonacich (1972) describes. Entry for others has, thus, been contested, and even though there have been no measures to limit skill or education for migrants, Koli fisherwomen have at times worked alongside nativist parties to limit political resources of migrant fishers. Another point of difference that must be considered between Bonacich's (1972) study of the U.S. labour market and Mumbai is that migrants in Mumbai are not an immigrant population, but rather they come from the interior districts of Maharashtra or other states; migrants, therefore, have citizenship rights. Another difference is that while Bonacich (1972) argued that indigenous groups were likely to constitute the bulk of cheap labour, in the case of Mumbai, it is the local Kolis who can assert that claim.

Despite these differences, this framework remains useful. This is because, as examined through previous chapters, a history of nativist politics in Mumbai rendered migrants vulnerable, as local labour exercised a greater control over political resources. This is critical, since it limited the ability of migrants, even as citizens, to expect the regional government and its agents to act in the interest of protecting their rights. This was exemplified through the case where the Bhaiyaa Hatao Andolan turned violent and where migrant labour claimed the police did little to stop the Koli women from physically preventing them from working. Even if legal strictures ultimately protected them, such forceful eviction from work and other informal pressures continued to limit their ability to challenge the authority of higher-priced labour—the Kolis. Strategies of limiting skills and education have not been as significant to check migrants because they in fact have altered the mode of fish retail and, thus, arguably employ a skill set different from the one used by Koli fisherwomen. In fact, it can be argued that it was precisely the condition of deprivation which led to migrants selling fish differently, that is, only by pricing their labour for less could they survive.

The Draft Act, thus, can further secure the rights over livelihood and resource for the traditional fishers, such as the Kolis, but at the cost of weakening the position of migrants. This is a point that the MMKS are cognizant of, and it is especially true for activists who were engaged in mobilizing Koli fisherwomen; they acknowledged that the ethnic divide between migrant labour and Koli women was not one that could be bridged easily. Even though the MMKS had taken a clear stance to not extend any support to nativist mobilization that had previously occurred under the Shiv Sena, it highlighted that the issue was a 'touchy' one for fisherwomen (see Chapter 5). The MMKS activists made their own attempts to rectify this—they explained to Koli fishers that several migrants, including those from the north were also fishers. By doing so, they included migrant labour in the constituency of 'traditional fishers' and thus redefined the relation of migrants to the city. But while there was a section of migrant labour who hailed from fisher communities, there were also a significant number of those who were agriculturalists. This is not a pedantic concern alone. Given how the Act defined traditional fisherfolk (those who have resided and practiced fishing for at least three generations), many migrants may find no inclusion in the category of the traditional fisher.

However, the issue posed a deeper problem. Bonacich (1975: 601) established that, what emerged as an ethnic conflict was actually grounded in class and rooted in capitalism's need for a cheaper labour force.[21] Therefore, she stressed that the mere instance of an ethnically varied labour market did not lead to a split labour market.

---

[21] She clarifies that the working class that is ethnically divided does not constitute only people selling their labour power, but also includes

It arose specifically out of capitalism's need as well the notion of competition between groups in the labour market, both real and perceived. Thus, while capitalism may not create such ethnic divisions, it can abet them. In the polarized city, the capitalist class in the fisheries is, therefore, invested in maintaining ethnic differences that would render the migrant working class weak.

The disavowal of a class analysis, therefore, by the NFF with a focus on ecological conservation and the definition of traditional fishers did not equip the NFF and the MMKS to take on the challenge posed in the fisheries. What appeared as an ethnic divide in other words could not be addressed on ethnic terms alone. The term 'traditional fisher' prevented the formation of a broader alliance that could potentially be forged between dispossessed classes—the Kolis and migrant labour. Working through categories of traditional fishers, as the proposed Draft Act does, enabled the Kolis to reassert their hold over the livelihood of fishing by relegating migrants to the worst forms of work available in the capitalist fish industry. This includes work on trawlers and in fish processing and packaging industries—work that is unregulated and with no standards of minimum wage. Thus, in spite of the NFF and the MMKS's continued aim to challenge capitalist development in the fisheries, they were in a weak position to assert the unity of dispossessed classes if all members of the working classes could not be categorized as traditional fishers. Articulated as a question of priorities, this has led to the MMKS's decision to focus on the mobilization of traditional fishers first and migrant fishers later. An instance of this is the women's cooperative and trade union which did not include migrants in fish retail. Even if the argument was made that the union was for fisherwomen and migrant fish retailers were predominantly men, the exclusion of migrant women (who vend

---

'persons who use or exchange the products of their labor for the purposes of consumption rather than the accumulation of capital (Marx [1867] 1906, pp 163–73). By this definition, subsistence farmers, independent artisans, and small businessmen are all working-class people even if they hire a few helpers.... Small entrepreneurs are often driven into the ranks of the proletariat in their competition with capitalists, while members of the proletariat often aspire to small businesses or farms of their own. This leads to common personnel and interests' (Bonacich 1975: 606).

from markets) from these organizations points to how the hostility towards migrants had bled into new political formations under the MMKS.

It is in this context of an affirmation of identity and practice that the movement has turned to the state. But appealing to the state, which has championed capitalist development in the fisheries, could lead to the state enabling accumulation while simultaneously assuaging the dispossessed communities of traditional fishers. This is because the Draft Act only secured a livelihood for small-scale and artisanal fishers but did not disrupt capitalist production in the fisheries, which could continue through a continuance of the deep sea-fishing policy based on transnational capital and a restricted ability of panchayats to enforce regulation. In fact, the passage of the Draft Act would prevent migrant fishers from enjoying self-employment in the fisheries and restrict them into working as wage labour in both small-scale and large-scale fisheries, to the benefit of both the protesting Kolis and capitalists.

The path taken by the NFF and the MMKS was therefore fraught with contradictions, as they sought to balance the contradictory impulses of demands for exclusive access as well as focus on those impoverished by the capitalist turn. Both the NFF's and the MMKS's attempts at reviving small-scale and artisanal fisheries have focused on the ·inequalities of gender that plague the community, but the MMKS has yet to adequately address the question of class which has prevented it from staking a claim over all of the fisheries and for all of those who have been dispossessed.

Conclusion

In June 2019, the Government of India decided to establish an independent ministry for the fisheries (Ministry of Animal Husbandry, Dairy and Fisheries). The need for a ministry distinct from the Ministry of Agriculture had been a long-standing demand of the fisher movements that believed that while agriculture features prominently in the national imagination, fisheries have not been granted a similar position. This step was an indication of the state's commitment to developing the fisheries, but this is likelier a development motivated by economic concerns alone. Whether the creation of the ministry will lead to furthering the representation of fishers and whether the process will be an exercise in deliberative democracy, with fishers playing a role in determining the direction of state policy, remains to be seen.

It is this tricky question of determining the ways in which democratization in the fisheries will unfold that concerns fishers. The distinction between how the NFF articulates the demand for access and its local iteration among fishers in Mumbai is rooted in the question of who can participate in the fisheries. This question, even as it is manifestly about the particularities of the fisheries and their economic and social arrangements, is also instructive for a broader understanding of capitalism, urbanization, and social movements. Democratic participation, after all, is not just sought in the fisheries alone but also in the city. In the last five years, the existence of the Kolis has been in fact rendered even more vulnerable, as the capital driven city of Mumbai seems keen to run them out. Projects such as the Coastal Road, the Shivaji Statue, and the recent attempt of converting the Aarey forests in to a Metro shed are demonstrative of the fact that there is no room for the commons. Many of these initiatives have been resisted by the Kolis, but it is only in the case of Aarey where middle-class citizens were prominent in the resistance that the state has yielded—there is little room then for true democratic deliberation within such processes of urbanization. What, then, is the way out and what insight does the trajectory of the fisher movement in Mumbai and the politics of the Kolis offer?

The first clear indication would be that precisely because of the ways in which the commons and associated livelihoods are rendered marginal in cities, they demand hyper visibility. Scholarship on the urban, labour, and commons will benefit from looking at the ways in which the MMKS and the Kolis have drawn the attention of the city to its ecology and to themselves as lying not distinct but embedded in the dominant economy of the city. That even the work of the small-scale fishers is part of the global fishing economy or that artisanal fishers are urban citizens points us in this direction. This is not to simplistically celebrate integration in a global economy or 'economic contribution' to the city, but rather, it offers us a way to think about how even those who seek distance from a regime of accumulation, and are often considered as anachronistic, are subjects of a capitalist society.

It is precisely within such an understanding, then, that we can locate the call of the MMKS for preventing the entry of large capital in the fisheries. What they are contesting is the manner in which large capital can determine the course of production (causing ecological damage) as well as the development of the city. The right to livelihood and work cannot be imagined in abstraction after all. For fishers in the city, urbanization is as critical an issue as the transformation of the fisheries itself. This right to the city as it emerges in the work of the MMKS is, Harvey (2008) argues, a collective right based on the democratization of the process of urbanization. Such a right would have to reconstitute the relation between capitalism and urbaniza-tion, just as the fisheries would have to evaluate their own relation with capitalism if it seeks to promote equality. But collective rights can also be conceived in exclusionist terms, and these have unfortunately been the grounds on which the Koli struggle in Mumbai, at times, finding themselves on the same side as nativist politics.

The question of identity that this throws up goes to the heart of critical debates in the contemporary world. In the context of Mumbai, this is also a troubling case of a progressive and regressive notion of identity coming together. By no means am I suggesting here that a politics built around identity inevitably finds itself in this quandary, but the messy politics of Mumbai and the Kolis and the interventions by the MMKS and the NFF allow us to think of how collective identities can be reframed towards expanding democracy without negating the role of identities in this struggle.

This is especially significant when identity is also tied to resource and livelihood protection. The political implications of this are far reaching, as is evident through the manner in which the discourse of identity protection informed the court ruling demanding a National Register of Citizens for Assam. In the political turmoil that has followed the list, it is increasingly evident that the legitimate concerns of marginal communities regarding resource and livelihood protection have been whipped up and weaponized to demonize and disregard the basic rights of 'others'—Muslims, working classes, and migrants. It would be a mistake, however, to assume that there is always a necessary trade-off involved between securing community rights and securing rights to movement and livelihood for all. The NFF position on the Draft of the Traditional Coastal and Marine Fisherfolk (Protection of Rights) Act, 2009, is most instructive of this, where they have sought to dismiss the state's view of the community as isolated and ghettoized and emphasize the shared space of the coast. It is clearly not the case, then, that expulsion and exclusion are the only basis through which a restoration of rights is imagined. Yet, as this work highlights, in Mumbai, these have been the lines on which the struggle has unfolded.

This book has highlighted the many factors that have contributed to the view that expulsion and exclusion are the paths through which restoration of rights and/or preservation of the commons can be established. Outside of the particularity of Mumbai, the Kolis, and the seas, literature on the commons has contended with the question of community roles in resource management. Hardin's position was at one end of this, and the responses to it sought a place of primacy for communities, whether from the point of efficiency, sustainability, or social equity (Menon and Lele n.d.). However, as Menon and Lele argue, both questions of intra-community inequalities and the relationship with newer participants in the commons had not always found their way into mainstream scholarship. This is a position not only to be found in academia but also in the movements themselves. The NFF's stance on ecological sustainability that is built on the assumption that the Kolis and other traditional fisher communities alone are inherently deeply committed to sustainability demonstrates this. It looked beyond the material practices (often unequal), which underscored sustainability and tied communities to an assumed morality of sustainability rather than a moral economy of it.

What, then, is the path ahead? The global context on social movements, urban questions, and the commons all point to the ascendance of exclusivist politics, even though it may stem from—in some cases—genuine concern for securing rights for marginalized communities. There are no easy answers here. But perhaps as a first step, the effort must be to rethink responses, move away from assumptions of trade offs, and delve deep into the complex politics of building solidarities. In Mumbai, this would necessitate that instead of a zero-sum game of one dispossessed community being pitted against another or pitting sustainability against equality, a more fundamental change is imagined. One such imagination would be where the fisheries move away from capitalism, for the capitalist turn in the fisheries is precisely what introduced the accumulative drives that led to overfishing, threatening the environment, and with work undertaken by a low waged and politically weak labouring class.

Yet, it is also not quite possible to simply turn back the clock as the NFF imagines. New technology, links with global markets, and, most critically, entrants from other castes into the fisheries is a reality that will be hard to turn away from. Far more interesting possibilities lie in inhabiting this reality but severing its links with capitalism. It is true that alternative arrangements of common management would necessitate control being shared by very different institutions than what we have or has been imagined (such as panchayats in the Draft of the Traditional Coastal and Marine Fisherfolk [Protection of Rights] Act, 2009). It is imperative for meeting the objectives of social equity, addressing hierarchies, and maintaining sustainability that these be local institutions, but perhaps what could be critically different here is that these institutions not be defined by 'traditional' communities but by participants in the fish economy.

The means for this, in many ways, already exist in the form of the structure of the cooperative. But for it to be unmoored from the past requires that existing cooperatives operate as worker cooperatives, unlike the current form of owner cooperatives, where membership is not restricted by community or sex. These democratic cooperatives can also emerge in all forms of work in the fisheries—fishing, processing, and fish sale. These cooperatives should not be confused with their earlier avatars, particularly because those were introduced and popularized as cooperatives not of workers but owners—their links to capitalism were explicit. Such democratization of the fisheries can, thus, build a real stake in creating ecological sustainability and prioritizing questions of workers and participants in the fish economy. The nature of the fisheries, which includes boundaries of national and international waters, will necessitate that institutions are not limited in their jurisdiction and roles. Multiple institutions can be at the helm, but what can be foregrounded in their functioning is a concern for the environment and participation of local communities.

The effects of this reimagined cooperative can extend beyond the fisheries as well. Already with Koli fisherwomen cooperatives and unions, it was evident that foregrounding participation in work was enabling the fisherwomen to rethink questions of identity and rights to the city. Given that livelihood and the city are interlinked, it would be critical for fishers to force a change in how urbanization unfolds as well. Capitalism-driven urbanization, as this book has argued, directly threatens sites of work and living for fishers. Of course, this capital-driven urbanization poses a challenge to the urban poor as a whole and not just to fishers; it should not be the concern of the fishers alone that a Coastal Road project or the Shivaji Statue will unleash irreversible damage to livelihoods and ecology. The projects should also be seen for what they are—a fundamental re-imagination of who the city belongs to. But this is precisely where a reconfigured community of fishers stands to gain, through building solidarities with other sections; the potential of its expanded sense of community and its solidarities lie unexplored and untapped.

In the contemporary moment we find ourselves in, the world of work and livelihood has undergone a significant transformation and conditions of material insecurities are fuelling populist politics across the world. We need to understand the social dynamics of our time. How do we explain why in the moment of neoliberal crisis we are witnessing more exclusionary movements against immigrants, minorities, and working classes than we are seeing upsurges against the system? We need to consider how social identities which have often been linked to what we do are now changing, and its resulting political articulation demands closer study. These are all directions for promising future research.

This book was a modest attempt at exploring some elements of these questions. The transformation of livelihoods and a fight for the right over it demonstrated the interrelation between the city, the commons, and the community. If there is a simple answer to a rather messy politics that exists, it is that the struggles for the city and livelihood rights by marginalized communities such as the Kolis, while distinct, are also related to the concerns of many other urban poor communities. The Mumbai fishers' vision of building sustainable fisheries must evoke the particularity of their struggle, without entering into the zero sum game of pitting dispossessed against the dispossessed.

Bibliography

Agarwal, Bina. 2008. 'Environmental Management, Equity and Ecofeminism: Debating India's Experience.' *Journal of Peasant Studies* 25(4): 55–95.

Agrawal, Arun. 2003. *CPR Forum Response: Considering the Woods and the Trees.* Available at http://eprints.atree.org/143/; last accessed on 4 November 2017.

———. 2008. 'Sustainable Governance of Common-Pool Resources: Context, Method, and Politics.' In *The Contested Commons: Conversations between Economists and Anthropologists*, edited by Pranab Bardhan and Isha Ray. Oxford: Wiley Blackwell.

Agrawal, Arun and K. Sivaramkrishnan (eds). 2000. *Agrarian Environments: Resources, Representations and Rules in India*. Durham, NC: Duke University Press.

Albuquerque, Olay. 1995. 'Rise in Trawlers and Pollution Cause 50% Drop in Fish Catch.' *The Times of India*, 9 May.

Arnason, Ragnar. 2007. 'Advances in Property Rights Based Fisheries Mangement: An Introduction.' *Marine Resource Economics* 22(4): 335–46.

Banerjee, Sikata. 1996. 'Feminization of Violence in India, Women in the Politics of the Shiv Sena.' *Asian Survey* 36(12): 1213–25.

Banerjee-Guha, Swapna (ed.). 2010. *Accumulation by Dispossesion: Transformative Cities in the New Global Order*. New Delhi: Sage Publications India.

———. 2002. Shifting Cities: Urban Restructuring in Bombay.' *Economic and Political Weekly*. 37(2): 121–8.

Bardhan, Pranab. 2009. 'Notes on the Political Economy of India's Torturous Transition.' *Economic and Political Weekly* 44(49): 31–6.

Bardhan, Pranab and Isha Ray (eds). 2008. *The Contested Commons*. New Delhi: Oxford University Press.

Basu, Radha. 1996. 'Fishermen All Set to Strike Work Today.' *The Times of India*, 18 January, p. 5.

Baviskar, Amita. 1994. 'Fate of the Forest: Conservation and Tribal Rights.' *Economic and Political Weekly* 29(38): 2493–501.

——— (ed.). 2008. 'Introduction.' In *Contested Grounds: Essays on Nature, Culture and Power*, pp. 1–12. New Delhi: Oxford University Press.

Baviskar, Amita and Nandini Sundar. 2008. 'Democracy versus Economic Transformation?' *Economic and Political Weekly* 43(46): 87–9.

Bay of Bengal Programme. 1982. *Marine Small-Scale Fisheries in India: A General Description*. Madras: Development of Small-Scale Fisheries in the Bay of Bengal, Food and Agriculture Organisation of the United Nations.

Bayly, Susan. 2008. *Caste, Society and Politics in India from the Eighteenth Century to the Modern Age*. Cambridge: Cambridge University Press.

Beteille, Andre and T.N. Madan. 1975. *Encounter and Experience*. New Delhi: Vikas Publishing House.

Bhatta, Ramchandra. 2003. 'SEZ's and the Environment.' *Economic and Political Weekly* 37(20): 1928–30.

Bhatta, Ramachandra, K. Aruna Rao, and Suguna K. Nayak. 2003. 'Marine Fish Production in Karnataka: Trends and Composition.' *Economic and Political Weekly* 38(44): 4685–93.

Bhattacharya, S. 1981. 'Capital and Labour in Bombay City, 1928–1929.' *Economic and Political Weekly* 16(42/43): 36–44.

Bhowmik, Sharit, K. 2010. 'Urban Public Space and the Urban Poor.' In *Accumulation by Dispossession, Transformative Cities in a new Global Order*, edited by Swapna Benrjee-Guha. New Delhi: Sage Publications India.

Bombay High Court. n.d. 'Marine Fishing Regulation Act 1981.'Available at http://bombayhighcourt.nic.in/libweb/acts/1981.54.pdf; last accessed on 12 March 2015.

Bonacich, Edna. 1972. 'A Theory of Ethnic Antgonism: The Split Labour Market.' *American Sociological Review* 37(5): 547–59.

———. 1973. 'A Theory of Middlemen Minorities.' *American Sociological Review* 38(5): 583–94.

———. 1975. 'Abolition, the Extension of Slavery and the Position of Free Blacks: A Study of Split Labor Markets in the United States, 1830–1863.' *American Journal of Sociology* 81(3): 601–28.

———. 1976. 'Advanced Capitalism and Black/White Race Relations in the United States: A Split Labor Market Interpretation.' *American Sociological Review* 41(1): 34–51.

Bose, Sutapa. 1988. 'The Problem of Primitive Accumulation.' *Economic and Political Weekly* 23(23): 1169–74.

Bottomore, Tom (ed.). 1991. *A Dictionary of Marxist Thought*. Oxford: Blackwell Publishers Ltd.

Brara, Rita. 2006. *Shifting Landscapes: The Making and Remaking of Village Commons in India*. New Delhi: Oxford University Press.

Breman, Jan. 2010. *Outcast Labour in Asia*. New Delhi: Oxford University Press.

Bruce, Steve and Steven Yearley. 2006. *Sage Dictionary of Sociology*. London: Sage Publications.

Burgess, Ernest. 1925. 'The Growth of the City: An Introduction to a Research Project.' In *The City*, edited by R. Park, E. Burgess, and R. McKenzie, pp. 47–62. Chicago: University of Chicago Press.

Burkett, Paul. 1999. *Marx and Nature: A Red and Green Perspective*. St. Martin's Press: New York.

Castells, Manuel. 2010. 'The Information Age: Economy, Society and Culture.' In *The Power of Identity*, Volume II. Wiley Blackwell: West Sussex.

Cederlof, Gunnel and K. Sivaramakrishnan (eds). 2006. *Ecological Nationalisms: Nature, Livelihoods, and Identities in South Asia*. Seattle: University of Washington Press.

Census of India. 1901. *Caste, Tribe and Race*, Volume XI. Mumbai: Directorate of Archives, Elphinstone College.

Central Marine Fisheries Research Institute. n.d. 'Marine Fisheries Census 2010 Maharashtra.' *Central Marine Fisheries Research Institute*. Available at http://eprints.cmfri.org.in/9007/; last accessed on 13 April 2013.

Chandavarkar, Rajnarayan. 1981. 'Workers Politics and the Mill Districts in Bombay between the Wars.' *Modern Asian Studies* 15(3): 603–47.

———. 1994. *The Origins of Industrial Capitalism in India: Business Strategies and the Working Classes in Bombay, 1900–1940*. Cambridge: Cambridge University Press.

———. 2009. *History, Culture and the Indian City: Essays by Rajnarayan Chandavarkar*. Cambridge: Cambridge University Press.

Chatterjee, Partha. 2008a. 'Democracy and Economic Transformation in India.' *Economic and Political Weekly* 43(16): 53–62.

———.2008b. 'Classes, Capital and Indian Democracy.' *Economic and Political Weekly* 43(46): 89–93.

Chaware, Dilip. 1994. 'Versova Kolis in Troubled Waters.' *The Times of India*, 17 February, p. 5.

Chopra, Preeti. 2007. 'Reconfiguring the Colonial City: Recovering the Role of Local Inhabitants in the Construction of Colonial Bombay 1854–1918.' *Buildings and Landscape: Journal of Vernancular Architecture Forum* 14: 109–25.

Choudhury, Arundhuti Roy. 2000. 'Amusement Parks versus People's Livelihood.' *Economic and Political Weekly* 35(37): 3286–8.

Chouhan, Hemantkumar A., D. Parthasarathy, and Sarmistha Pattnaik. 2016. 'Coastal Ecology and Fishing Community in Mumbai: CRZ Policy, Sustainability and Livelihoods.' *Economic and Political Weekly* 51(39): 48–57.

Chowdhry, Prem. 1993. 'High Participation and Low Evaluation: Women and Work in Rural Harayana.' *Economic and Political Weekly* 28(52): 135–148.

Clark, Alice W. (ed.). 1993. *Gender and Political Economy: Explorations of South Asian Systems.* Delhi: Oxford University Press.

Date, Vidyadhar. 1995. 'Fishermen Resent Open Sea Policy.' *The Times of India,* 6 May, p. 8.

Davidge, W.R. 1924. 'The Development of Bombay.' *The Town Planning Review* 10(4): 275–9.

D'Cruz, Sharon and Avinash Raikar. 2004. 'Ramponkars in Goa: Between Modernisation, the Government and the Deep Blue Sea.' *Economic and Political Weekly* 39(20): 2048–54.

Denis, Eric, Partha Mukhopadhyay, and Marie-Hélène Zérah. 2012. 'Subaltern Urbanisation in India.' *Economic and Political Weekly* XLVII(30): 52–62.

Dietrich, Gabriele. 1995. 'Women's Struggle for Production of Life: Public Hearings of Women in Informal Sector.' *Economic and Political Weekly* 30(26): 1551–4.

Dobbin, Christine. 1970. 'The Parsi Panchayat in Bombay City in the Nineteeth Century.' *Modern Asian Studies* 4(2): 149–64.

———. 1972. *Urban Leadership in Western India, Politics and Communities in Bombay City 1840–1885.* London: Oxford University Press.

Dossal, Mariam. 1989. 'Limits of Colonial Urban Planning: A Study of Mid-Nineteenth Century Bombay.' *International Journal of Urban and Regional Research* 13(1): 19–30.

———. 2005. 'A Master Plan for the City: Looking at the Past.' *Economic and Political Weekly* 40(36): 3897–900.

Draft of the Traditional Coastal and Marine Fisherfolk (Protection Of Rights) Act. 2009. Available at https://indianlegal.icsf.net/en/indian-legal-instruments.html?static=2&nation=2&fisheries=1&start=40; last accessed on 1 October 2020.

Dsouza, Lajwanti. 1996. 'Coastline Construction Is on Despite Supreme Court Ban.' *The Times of India,* 23 April.

Durrenberger, Paul E. and Gisli Pálsson. 1987. 'Ownership at Sea: Fishing Territories and Access to Sea Resources.' *American Ethnologist* 14(3): 508–22.

Falzon, Mark-Anthony (ed.). 2009. *Multi-Sited Ethnography: Theory, Praxis and Locality in Contemporary Research.* Surrey: Ashgate Publishing Ltd.

Farooqui, Amar. 1996. 'Urban Development in a Colonial Situation, Early Nineteenth Century Bombay.' *Economic and Political Weekly* 31(40): 2746–59.

Food and Agriculture Organisation (FAO). 1982. *Marine Small-Scale Fisheries of India: A General Description.* Available at http://www.fao.org/3/a-ae481e.pdf; last accessed on 20 September 2020.

Foster, John Bellamy. 2000. *Marx's Ecology: Materialism and Nature*. Monthly Review Press: New York.

Fox-Genovese, Elizabeth and Eugene D. Genovese. 1976. 'The Political Crisis of Social History: A Marxian Perspective.' *Journal of Social History* 10(2): 205–20.

Frank, Andre Gunder. 1977. 'On So-Called Primitive Accumulation.' *Dialectical Anthropoolgy* 2(2): 87–106.

Ghurye, G.S. 1963. *The Mahadev Kolis*. Bombay: Popular Prakashan.

Gordon, Scott H. 1954. 'The Economic Theory.' *Journal of Political Economy* 62(2): 124–42.

Gotham, Kevin Fox. 2001. 'Urban Sociology and the Postmodern Challenge.' *Humboldt Journal of Social Relations* 26(1/2): 57–79.

Government of India (GoI). 1901. *Census of India*, Volume I. Mumbai: The Directorate of Archives, Elphinston College.

———. 1909. *The Gazetteer of Bombay City and Island*, Volume 1. File no. N 29086, 29087. Mumbai: The Directorate of Archives, Elphinston College.

———. 2011. *Animal Husbandry: Fisheries*. Available at http://www.archive.india.gov.in/sectors/agriculture/index.php?id=20; last accessed on 10 January 2014.

———. 2014. 'Census of India 2011.' In *District Census Handbook*, Series 28, Part XII A, p. 14. Maharashtra: Directorate of Census Operation.

Gumprez, Ellen McDonald. 1974. 'City–Hinterland Relations and the Development of a Regional Elite in Nineteenth Century Bombay.' *Journal of Asian Studies* 33(4): 581–601.

Gupta, Dipankar. 1982. *Nativism in a Metropolis: The Shiv Sena in Bombay*. Bombay: Manohar.

Hansen, Thomas Blom. 2001. *Violence in Urban India: Identity Politics, 'Mumbai', and the Postcolonial City*. Delhi: Princeton University Press.

Hardin, Garett. 1968. 'Tragedy of the Commons.' *Science* 162(3859): 1243–8.

Hart, Hencry C. 1961. 'Bombay Politics: Pluralism or Polarization?' *Journal of Asian Studies* (20)3: 267–74.

Harvey, David. 1985. *The Urbanization of Capital*. Oxford: Basil Blackwell.

———. 2003. *The New Imperialism*. Oxford: Oxford University Press.

———. 2008. 'Right to the City.' *New Left Review* 50. Available at https://newleftreview.org/issues/II53/articles/david-harvey-the-right-to-the-city; last accessed on 1 January 2011.

———. 2010. 'The Right to the City: From Capital Surplus to Accumulation by Dispossession.' In *Accumulation by Dispossession: Transformative Cities in the New Global Order*, edited by Swapna Banerjee-Guha, pp. 17–32. New Delhi: Sage Publications India.

Hensman, Rohini. 1994. 'Social Movements: What's New?' *Economic and Political Weekly* 29(21): 1270–2.

Heuzé, Gerard. 1996. 'Cultural Populism: The Appeal of the Shiv Sena.' In *Bombay Metaphor for Modern India*, edited by Alice Thorner and Sujata Patel. New Delhi: Oxford University Press.

Hindu, The. 2015. 'NFF Slams Deep Sea Policy.' 9 February 2015. Available at https://www.thehindu.com/news/cities/puducherry/nff-slams-deep-sea-policy/article6873420.ece; last accessed on 20 October 2020.

Hobsbawm, Eric. 1964. 'Introduction.' In *Pre-capitalist Economic Formations*, translated by Jack Cohen, pp. 1–65. New York: International Publishers.

Indo-Asian News Service (IANS). 2008. 'MNS Men Attack North Indians.' *India Today*, 19 October. Available at https://www.indiatoday.in/latest-headlines/story/mns-men-attack-north-indians-31885-2008-10-19; last accessed on 5 August 2018.

———. 2011. 'Raj Thackeray Attacks North Indian Migrants.' *New Indian Express*, 19 July. Available at http://www.newindianexpress.com/nation/article421264.ece?service=print; last accessed on 12 March 2013.

Iyengar, Vishwapriya L. 1985. 'Fisherpeople of Kerala: A Plea for Rational Growth.' *Economic and Political Weekly* 20(49): 2149–54.

Jean-Platteau, Phillipe. 2008. 'Managing the Commons: The Role of Social Norms and Beliefs.' In *The Contested Commons: Conversations between Economists and Anthropologists*, edited by Pranab Bardhan and Isha Ray, pp. 25–45. New Delhi: Oxford University Press.

Jeffery, Roger and Nandini Sundar (eds). 1999. *A New Moral Economy for India's Forests? Discourses on Communities and Participation*. New Delhi: Sage Publications.

Johari, Aarefa. 2015. 'Deserted and Barren: What the Promenades along Mumbai's Planned Coastal Road Could Look Like.' *Scroll.* Available at http://eprints.atree.org/143/; last accessed on 22 June 2015.

John, Mary E. and Satish Deshpande. 2008. 'Theorising the Present: Problems and Possibilities.' *Economic and Political Weekly* 43(46): 83–6.

Johnson, Craig. 2000. 'Common Property, Political Economy, and Local Resource Management: Reflections on "Rights Based" Fishing in southern Thailand.' *South East Asia Research* 8(1): 31–53.

Johnson, Gordon. 1973. *Provincial Politics and Indian Nationalism, Bombay and the Indian National Congress 1880–1915*. Cambridge: Cambridge University Press.

Joshi, R.H. 1991. 'Fisheries in Maharashtra State.' *Central Marine Fisheries Research Institute Bulletin* 44(3): 525–32.

Jha, Manish and Pushpendra Kumar. 2016. 'Homeless Migrants in Mumbai: Life and Labour in Urban Spaces.' *Economic and Political Weekly* 51(26–7): 69–77.

Kaiwar, Vasant. 1994. 'The Colonial State, Capital and the Peasantry in Bombay Presidency.' *Modern Asian Studies* 28(4): 793–832.

Kartikeya. 2005. 'Fishermen Want Waterfront Plot Back after Clean-Up Drive.' *The Times of India*, 11 October, p. 6.

Katzenstein, Mary. 1973. 'Origins of Nativism: The Emergence of Shiv Sena in Bombay.' *Asian Survey* 13(4): 386–99.

Khan, Sameera. 2007. 'Negotiating the Mohalla: Exclusion, Identity and Muslim Women in Mumbai.' *Economic and Political Weekly* 42(17): 1527–33.

Kidambi, Prashant. 2007a. 'Introduction.' In *The Making of an Indian Metropolis; Colonial Governance and Public Culture in Bombay, 1890–1920*, pp. 5–15. Hampshire: Ashgate Publishing.

———. 2007b. 'The Rise of Bombay.' In *The Making of an Indian Metropolis; Colonial Governance and Public Culture in Bombay, 1890–1920*, pp. 17–48. Hampshire: Ashgate Publishing.

Klein, Ira. 1986. 'Urban Development and Death: Bombay City, 1870–1914.' *Modern Asian Studies* 20(4): 725–54.

Kohli, Kanchi and Manju Menon. 2008. 'Re-engineering the Legal and Policy Regimes on Environment.' *Economic and Political Weekly* 43(23): 14–17.

Kollapan, B. 2014. 'Use of Trawlers Contentious Issue at Fishermen's Meet.' *The Hindu*, 28 January. Available at http://www.thehindu.com/news/national/tamil-nadu/use-of-trawlers-a-contentious-issue-at-fishermen-meet/article5622499.ece; last accessed on 16 April 2015 .

Kooiman, Dick. 1980. 'Bombay Communists and the 1924 Textile Strike.' *Economic and Political Weekly* 15(29): 1223–36.

———. 1981. 'Labour legislation and Working Class Movement, Case of Bombay Labour Office 1934–1937.' *Economic and Political Weekly* 16(44/46): 1807–22.

Korakandy, Ramakrishnan. 1984. 'Purse Seine Fishing in Kerala.' *Economic and Political Weekly* 19(13): 566–70.

Kosambi, Meera. 1985. 'Commerce, Conquest and the Colonial City.' *Economic and Political Weekly* 20(1): 32–7.

Kosambi, Meera and John E. Brush. 1988. 'Three Colonial Port Cities in India.' *Geographical Review* 78(1): 32–47.

Krishnan, B.J. 2000. *Customary Law*. Available at http://www.india-seminar. com/2000/492/492%20b.%20j.%20krishnan.htm; last accessed on 24 January 2014.

Kumar, K.G. 1988. 'Organising Fisherfolk Cooperatives in Kerala.' *Economic and Political Weekly* 23(12): 578–81.

Kumar, Mukul, K. Saravanan, and Nityanand Jayaraman. 2014. 'Mapping the Coastal Commons: Fisherfolk and the Politics of Coastal Urbanisation in Chennai.' *Economic and Political Weekly* 49(48): 46–53.

Kumar, Sanjay and Sudha Vasan. 1997. 'Models and Reality: Case of Forest Communities.' *Economic and Political Weekly* 32(51): 3294–6.

Kurien, John. 1984. 'The Marketing of Marine Fish in Kerala State: A Preliminary Study.' Trivandrum: Centre for Development Studies.

———. 1985. 'Credit and Indebtedness amongst Fishermen.' *Economic and Political Weekly* 20(40): 1689–90.

———. 1993. 'Ruining the Commons: Overfishing and Fishworkers' Actions in South India.' *Ecologist* 23(1): 5–12.

———. 2008. 'State, Modernisation and Conflict in Fisheries.' In *State, Natural Resource Conflicts and Challenges to Governance*, edited by N.C. Narayanan, pp. 59–90. New Delhi: Academic Foundation.

Kurien, John and A.J. Vijayan. 1998. 'Income Spreading Mechanisms in Common Property Resources: Karanila System in Kerala's Fisheries.' *Economic and Political Weekly* 30(28): 1780–5.

Kurien, John and T.R. Thankappan Achari. 1990. 'Overfishing along the Kerala Coast.' *Economic and Political Weekly* 25(35–6): 2011–18.

Lefebvre, Henri. 2003. *The Urban Revolution*, translated by Robert Bononno. Minneapolis: University of Minnesota Press.

Lele, Jayant. 1995. 'Saffronisation of Shiv Sena: Political Economy of City, State and Nation.' *Economic and Political Weekly* 30(25): 1520–8.

Levien, Michael. 2015. 'From Primitive Accumulation to Regimes of Dispossession: Six Theses on India's Land Question.' *Economic and Political Weekly* 50(22): 146–57.

Li, Tania Murray. 2008. 'Situating Resource Struggles: Concepts for Emperical Analysis.' In *Contested Grounds; Essays on Nature, Culture and Power*, edited by Amita Baviskar, pp. 193–216. New Delhi: Oxford University Press.

Libecap, Gary D. 2007. 'Assigning Property Rights in the Common Pool: Implications of the Prevalence of First-Possession Rules for ITQs in Fisheries.' *Marine Resource Economics* 22(4): 407–23.

Lucas, W.H. 1911. *Report on the Improvement of Fisheries in the Bombay Presidency*. Volume 8, 18 August 1910. Marine Department, Bombay Presidency. Mumbai: The Directorate of Archives, Elphinstone College.

Luxemburg, Rosa. 1913a. 'The Struggle against Natural Economy.' In *The Accumulation of Capital*. Available at http://www.marxists.org/archive/luxemburg/1913/accumulation-capital/ch27.htm; last accessed on 3 June 2012.

———. 1913b. 'The Reproduction of Capital and its Social Settings.' In *The Accumulation of Capital V*. Available at https://www.marxists.org/archive/luxemburg/1913/accumulation-capital/ch26.htm; last accessed on 1 December 2014.

Makabe, Tomoko. 1981. 'The Theory of the Split Labour Market: A Comparison of the Japanese Experience in Brazil and Canada.' *Social Forces* 59(3): 786–809.

Mansukhani, Bhisham. 2001. 'Fishermen Expulsion May Send Fish Prices Soaring.' *The Times of India*, 8 September, p. 4.

Marcus, George. 2011. 'Multi-Sited Ethnography, Five or Six Things I Know About It Now.' In *Multi-Sited Ethnography; Problemsand Possibilities iin Translocation of Research Methods*, edited by Simon Coleman and Pauline Von Hellermann, pp. 16–34. New York: Routledge.

Martyris, Nina. 1997. 'School Building for Kolis: An 18-Year-Old Dream Comes True.' *The Times of India*, 13 April, p. 5.

Marx, Karl. 2010a. *Capital: A Critical Analysis of Capitalist Production*, Volume I, pp. 667–70. New Delhi: LeftWord Books.

—————. 2010b. *Capital: Fixed Capital and Circulating Capital*, Volume II, pp. 160–72. New Delhi: LeftWord Publications.

—————. 2010c. *Capital: The Law of the Tendency of the Rate of Profit to Fall*, Volume III, pp. 211–60. New Delhi: LeftWord Publications.

—————. 1964. *Pre-capitalist Economic Formations*, translated by Jack Cohen. New York: International Publishers.

Mathew, Sebastian. 2008. 'Coastal Management Zones: Implications for Fishing Communities.' *Economic and Political Weekly* 43(25): 17–23.

Mawdsley, Emma. 1998. 'After Chipko: From Environment to Region in Uttaranchal.' *Journal of Peasant Studies* 25(4): 36–54.

Mazumdar, Ranjani. 2001. 'Figure of the "Tapori": Language, Gesture and Cinematic City.' *Economic and Political Weekly* 36(52): 4872–80.

McCay, Bonnie J. and James M. Acheson (eds). 1987. 'The Human Ecology of the Commons.' *The Question of the Commons: The Culture and Ecology of Communal Resources*, pp. 1–36. Tucson: University of Arizona Press.

Menon, Ajit and Sharachchandra Lele. n.d. *CPR Forum Commentary: Critiquing the Commons: Missing the Woods for the Trees*. Available at http://eprints.atree.org/143/; 4 November 2017.

Meuriot, Eric. 1995. 'The Common Fisheries Policy: Origin, Evaluation and Future by M.J. Holden.' *Marine Resource Economics* 10(3): 321–2.

Ministry of Agriculture. 2014. *Handbook on Fisheries Stastics*. New Delhi: Department of Animal Husbandry, Dairying and Fisheries, Government of India.

Ministry of Agriculture & Farmers' Welfare. 2016. *Annual Fisheries Survey of India 2016–17*. Mumbai: Department of Animal Husbandry, Dairying & Fisheries, Government of India.

Ministry of Statistics and Program Implementation. 1990. *NSSO, 43rd Round, 1989–90*. Government of India.

————. 2012. *NSSO, 68th Round, 2011–12.* Government of India.

Ministry of Environment and Forests. 2001. *Gazette of India S.O 329 (E),* 12 April. New Delhi: Department of Environment, Forests and Wildlife, Government of India. Available at http://environmentclearance.nic. in/writereaddata/SCZMADocument/Amendment%20CRZ%20 Notification,%201991%20dated%2012.04.2001.pdf; last accessed on 1 October 2009.

————. 2011. *Gazette of India S.O 19 (E),* 6 January. New Delhi: Department of Environment, Forests and Wildlife, Government of India. Available at http://www.environmentclearance.nic.in/writereaddata/ SCZMADocument/Coastal%20Regulation%20Zone%20Notfication,%20 2011.pdf; last accessed on 1 January 2012.

Mishra, Ambarish. 2004. 'North Indians Fishing for Trouble: Kolis.' *The Times of India,* 5 February, p. 2.

Mitter, Partha. 1986. 'The Early British Port Cities of India: Their Planning and Architecture Circa 1640–1757.' *Journal of the Society of Architectural Historians* 45(2): 95–114.

Morris, Morris David. 1965. *The Emergence of an Industrial Labour Force in India: A Study of Bombay Cotton Mills 1854–1947.* Bombay: Oxford University Press.

Nadai, Eva and Christoph Maeder. 2009. 'Contours of the Field(s): Multi-Sited Ethnography as a Theory-Driven Research Strategy in Sociology.' In *Multi-Sited Ethnography; Theory, Praxis and Locality in Contemporary Research,* edited by Mark-Anthony Falzon, pp. 233–50. Surrey: Ashgate Publishing Ltd.

Nandwani, Deepali. 2001. 'Fishing in Troubled Waters.' *The Times of India,* 22 April, p. 6.

National Fishworkers' Forum (NFF). n.d. MMKS. Available at http://www. nffindia.org/nffmaharashtra.php; last accessed on 3 March 2014.

————. 2015. *Press Statement.* 7 February. Available at http://www.nffindia. org/pdffiles/NFF_Press%20Note_5%20Feb%202015.pdf; last accessed on 7 March 2015.

Neera Adarkar and Meena Menon. 2004. *One Hundred Years, One Hundred Voices, The Millworkers of Girgaon: An Oral History.* Kolkata: Seagull Books.

Newman, Richard K. 1981. *Workers and Unions in Bombay 1918–1929: A Study of Organisation in the Cotton Mills.* Canberra: Australian National University.

Office of the Registrar General & Census Commissioner, India. n.d. *Census of India, 2001.* Available at https://censusindia.gov.in/2011-common/ census_data_2001.html; last accessed on 17 June 2012.

————. n.d. *Census of India, 2011.* Available at https://www.censusindia.gov. in/2011-Common/CensusData2011.html; last accessed on 2 March 2014.

Olzak, Susan. 1989. 'Labour Unrest, Immigration and Ethnic Conflict in Urban America, 1800–1914.' *American Journal of Sociology* 94(6): 1303–33.

Ostrom, Elinor. 1990. *Governing the Commons: The Evolution of Institutions for Collective Action.* Cambridge: Cambridge University Press.

Parthasarathy, D. 2011. 'Hunters, Gatherers and Foragers in a Metropolis: Commonising the Private and Public in Mumbai.' *Economic and Political Weekly* 46(50): 54–63.

Patel, Sujata. 1998. 'Work and Workers in Mumbai 1930s: 1990, Changing Profile, Enduring Problem.' *Economic and Political Weekly* 33(46): 2904–8.

Peled, Yoav and Gershon Shafir. 1987. 'Split Labor Market and the State: The Effect of Modernization on Jewish Industrial Workers.' *American Journal of Sociology* 92(6): 1435–60.

Pinto, Ambrose, Berin Leekas, and Latha Radhakrishnan. 1995. 'No Fish to Eat: Impact of Liberalisation.' *Economic and Political Weekly* 30(4): 204–6.

Planning Commission. 2001. *Report of the Working Group on the Fisheries for the Tenth Five Year Plan.* New Delhi: Government of India.

Poonam, Snigdha. 2018. *Dreamers: How Young Indians are Changing Their World.* Penguin Random House India: New Delhi.

Prakash, Padma. 1993. 'The Making of Bombay, Social, Cultural and Political Dimensions.' *Economic and Political Weekly* 28(40): 2119–21.

Press Trust of India (PTI). 2008a. 'MNS Activists Attack 13 Railway Board Examination Centres.' *Economic Times,* 19 October. Available at https:// economictimes.indiatimes.com/news/politics-and-nation/mns-activists-attack-13-railway-board-examination-centres/articleshow/3615529.cms; last accessed on 5 August 2015.

————. 2008b. 'Raj Thackeray Arrested for MNS Attack on North Indians.' *LiveMint,* 21 October. Available at http://www.livemint.com/ Politics/1r1EOfvaK9ZdPIyq321kEL/Raj-Thackeray-arrested-for-MNS-attack-on-north-Indians.html; last accessed on 12 March 2013.

Punekar, Vijaya. 1959. *The Son Kolis of Bombay.* Bombay: Popular Book Depot.

Ram, Kalpana. 1991. *Mukkuvar Women: Gender, Hegemony and Capitalist Transformation in a South Indian Fishing Community.* London: Zed Books.

Ramachandran, P. 1974. *Some Aspects of Labour Mobility in Bombay City.* Bombay: Somaiya Publications Pvt Ltd.

Ramanna, Mridula. 1989. 'Social Background of the Educated in Bombay City: 1824–1858.' *Economic and Political Weekly* 24(4): 203–11.

————. 1992. 'Profile of English Educated Indians, Early Nineteenth Century Bombay City.' *Economic and Political Weekly* 27(14): 716–24.

Roy-Choudhury, Arundhati. 2000. 'Amusement Parks versus People's Livelihood.' *Economic and Political Weekly* 35(37): 3286–8.

Sangvai, Sanjay. 2006. 'Convention of People's Movements.' *Economic and Political Weekly* 41(33): 3563–5.

Sassen, Saskia. 2006. *Territory, Authority, Rights; From Medieval to Modern Assemblages.* Princeton: Princeton University Press.

————. 2010. 'The Global City: Strategic Site, New Frontier.' In *Accumulation by Dispossesion; Transformative Cities in the New Global Order,* edited by Swapna Banerjee-Guha, pp. 33–54. New Delhi: Sage Publications India.

Shah, Mihir. 2008. 'Structures of Power in Indian Society: A Response.' *Economic and Political Weekly* 43(46): 78–83.

Shaikh, Junaid. 2005. 'Worker Politics, Trade Unions and the Shiv Sena's Rise in Central Bombay.' *Economic and Political Weekly* 40(18): 1893–1900.

Shaikh, Zeeshan. 2019. 'Explained: Here's What Census Data Show about Migrations to Mumbai.' *The Indian Express,* 28 July. Available at https://indianexpress.com/article/explained/explained-heres-what-census-data-show-about-migrations-to-mumbai/; last accessed on 9 October 2020.

Shajahan, K.M. 1996. 'Deep Sea Fishing Policy: A Critique.' *Economic and Political Weekly* 31(5): 263–6.

Sharma, Chandrika. 2011. 'CRZ Notification 2011: Not the End of the Road.' *Economic and Political Weekly* 46(7): 31–5.

————. 2012. *Women Fish Vendors in Mumbai.* Chennai: International Collective in Support of Fishworkers.

Sharma, Kalpana. 2003. 'Can Mumbai become Shanghai?' *The Hindu,* 11 October. Available at http://www.thehindu.com/2003/10/11/stories/2003101100941000.htm; last accessed on 19 April 2015.

Shiva, Vandana and J. Bandyopadhyay. 1968. 'The Evolution of, Structure, and Impact of the Chipko Movement'. *Mountain Research and Development* 6(2): 133–42.

Sinha, Pravin. 2004. 'Representing Labour in India.' *Development in Practice* 14(1/2): 127–35.

Sivaramkrishnan, K. 1999. *Modern Forests: Statemaking and Environmental Change in Colonial Eastern India.* Stanford, CA: Stanford University Press.

South Asia Archive. n.d. 'Annual Report of the Department of Fisheries 1941–42; Marine Fisheries.' Available at http://www.southasiaarchive.com/Content/sarf.141630/203749/017; last accessed on 28 August 2014.

Spengler, Oswald. 1928. *The Decline of the West,* Volume 2. London: Allen and Unwin.

Spodek, Howard. 2013. 'City Planning in India under British Rule.' *Economic and Political Weekly* 48(4): 53–61.

Srinivas, M.N., A.M. Shah, and E.A. Ramaswamy. 2002. *The Fieldworker and the Field: Problems and Challenges in Sociological Investigations.* New Delhi: Oxford University Press.

Steelman, Toddi A. and Richard L. Wallace. 2001. 'Property Rights and Property Wrongs: Why Context Matters in Fisheries Management.' *Policy Sciences* 34(3/4): 357–79.

Subramanian, Ajantha. 2009. *Shorelines: Space and Rights in South India.* Stanford: Stanford University Press.

Sujata Patel and Alice Thorner. 1996. *Bombay: Metaphor for Modern India.* Oxford University Press.

Susser, Ida (ed.). 2002. *The Castells Reader on Cities and Social Theory.* Massachusetts: Blackwell Publishers.

Times of India, The. 1871. 'Editorial Article 2.' 26 January, p. 2.

———. 1902. 'The Fishermen of Bombay: A Petition to the Governor.' 12 March, p. 3.

———.1905. 'Mandvi Kolis and the Port Trust.' 10 May, p. 6.

———. 1910. 'Fish Supply.' 30 November, p. 4.

———. 1914. 'Conference of Kolis: A Fishermen's Meeting.' 19 May, p. 8.

———. 1919. 'Bombay Corporation: Sewri–Koliwada Scheme.' 5 September, p. 10.

———. 1926. 'Bombay Industries No 36: Fishing: The Kolis Harvest of the Sea.' 23 December 23, p. 16.

———. 1927. 'Current Topics: More Old Women Professor Pimpledinck Adds His Remarks.' 7 January, p. 8.

———. 1932. 'Education of Koli Children: Benefits Explained to Parents.' 5 February, p. 13.

———. 1933a. 'Bombay's Fishery Resources.' 14 July, p. 8.

———. 1933b. 'Revolution in Fishing: Use of Motor Boats Danda's Red Letter Day: Governor's Our Special Correspondent.' 11 November, p. 13.

———. 1935. 'Bombay's Fish Supply Not Adequate: Kolis Becoming Steadily Poorer.' 15 October, p. 7.

———. 1939a. 'Koli Education Conference: Raja Jawhar's Plea.' 1 April, p. 18.

———. 1939b. 'Kolis' Needs.' 25 May, p. 13.

———. 1954. 'Merger of Bombay City in Maharashtra: Communist Assurance to Gujeratis.' 18 April, p. 14.

———. 1956. 'Inclusion of Bombay City in Maharashtra Inevitable: Pt. Kunzru on Alternative to Bilingual.' 2 May, p. 8.

———. 1994a. 'Fisherfolk Rally at Raj Bhavan Today.' 23 November, p. 3.

———. 1994b. 'Fishermen's Blockade on November 23.' 30 October, p. 3.

———. 1994c. 'Fisherfolk Up in Arms against Sewage Project.' 3 October, p. 5.

———. 1994d. 'Versova Kolis in Troubled Waters.' 16 February, p. 5.

————. 1995a. 'Fishermen Hit Out at Foreign Trawlers.' 1 October 1, p. 5.

————. 1995b. 'Straight Answers: President, Maharashtra Machimar Kriti Samiti.' 9 June, p. A1.

————. 1995c. 'Primeval Existence in a Sea of Modernity.' 10 January, p. A2.

————. 1996. 'Prices Go up as Fish Markets Down Shutters.' 23 February, p. 4.

————. 2000a. 'Caught in the Net: Curbs on Kolis May Dampen Fish Trade.' 18 February.

————. 2000b. 'A Fishy Tale.' 12 August, p. B1.

————. 2001. 'Fishing in Troubled Waters.' 22 April, p. 6.

————. 2003a. 'Now, the Sena Fishes for Kolis.' 24 October, p. 3.

————. 2003b. 'Mumbaidevi Temple was Earlier at Boribunder.' 3 December, p. 2.

————. 2004a. 'HC Sets Aside Notification on Trawlers.' 19 March, p. 5.

————. 2004b. 'Kolis Swim Out of Troubled Waters: Tell HC They Never Objected to North Indians Doing Business.' 25 March, p. 3.

————. 2004c. 'North Indians Fishing for Trouble: Kolis.' 5 February, p. 2.

————. 2005a. 'Fishermen Want Waterfront Plot Back after Clean-Up Drive.' 11 October, p. 6.

————. 2005b. 'Water Way to Live.' 21 October, p. B4.

————. 2011. 'MoEF Set to Make VPs Protect Fisherfolk.' 11 January. Available at http://timesofindia.indiatimes.com/city/goa/MoEF-seeks-to-make-VPs-protect-fisherfolk/articleshow/7256516.cms; last accessed on 19 April 2013.

Thevar, Krishna. 2015. 'MNS Attacks North Indian Hawkers at Jogeshwari in Mumbai.' *Economic Times*, 29 April. Available at https://economictimes.indiatimes.com/news/politics-and-nation/mns-attacks-north-indian-hawkers-at-jogeshwari-in-mumbai/articleshow/47093201.cms?from=mdr; last accessed on 1 September 2019.

Thompson, E.P. 1971. 'The Moral Economy of the English Crowd in the Eighteenth Century.' *Past and Present* 50(1): 76–136.

Tulupe, Bagaram. 1982. 'Bombay Textile Worker's Strike, A Different View.' *Economic and Political Weekly* 17(17/18): 719–21.

Ujimoto, Victor K. 1982. 'The Economic Basis of Ethnic Solidarity by Edna Bonacich: John Modell.' *Pacific Affairs* 55(1): 169–71.

United Nations Convention on the Law of the Sea. 1982. 'Article 62: Utilization of the Living Resources.' Available at https://www.un.org/Depts/los/convention_agreements/texts/unclos/UNCLOS-TOC.htm; last accessed on 10 October 2020.

Upadhyay, Shashi Bhushan. 1989. 'Communalism and Working Class Riot of 1893 in Bombay City.' *Economic and Political Weekly* 24(30): 69–75.

———. 1990. 'Cotton Mill Workers in Bombay 1875 to 1918, Conditions of Work and Life.' *Economic and Political Weekly* 25(30): 87–99.

Vidyathil, Trina and Gayatri Singh. 2012. 'Spaces of Discrimination: Residential Segregation in Indian Cities.' *Economic and Political Weekly* XLVII(37): 60–6.

Vikas. 2001. 'State and People's Intitatives: Experience of Tawa Matsya Sangh.' *Economic and Political Weekly* 36(49): 4527–30.

Visvanathan, Susan (ed.). 2001. *Structure and Transformation: Theory and Society in India.* New Delhi: Oxford University Press.

Vivek, P.S. 2000. 'Scavengers Mumbai's Neglected Workers.' *Economic and Political Weekly* 35(42): 3722–4.

Vohra, Gautam S.G. 1980. 'Overfishing by Trawlers Reduces Catch.' *Times of India*, 5 July, p. 11.

Warrier, M.V. Shobhana. 2001. 'Women at Work: Migrant Women in Fish Processing Industry.' *Economic and Political Weekly* 36(37): 3554–62.

Weber, Max. 1958. *The City*, translated by Dan Martindale and Gertrud Neuwirth. New York: The Free Press

West, E.G. 1969. 'The Political Economy of Alienation: Karl Maex and Adam Smith.' *Oxford Economic Papers, New Series* 21(1): 1–23.

Windmiller, Marshall. 1956. 'The Politics of State Reorganisation in India: The Case of Bombay.' *Far Easten Survey* 25(9): 129–43.

Wirth, Louis. 1938. 'Urbanism as a Way of Life.' *American Journal of Sociology* XLVI(1): 1–24.

Whitehead, Judy and Nitin More. 2007. 'Revanchism in Mumbai? Political Economy of Rent Gaps and Urban Restructuring in a Global City.' *Economic and Political Weekly* 42(25): 2428–34.

Xaxa, Virginius. 1999. 'Tribes as Indigenous People of India.' *Economic and Political Weekly* 34(51): 3589–95.

———. 2005. 'Politics of Language, Religion and Identity: Tribes in India.' *Economic and Political Weekly* 40(13): 1363–70.

Index

About the Author

Gayatri Nair teaches sociology at the Department of Social Sciences and Humanities, Indraprastha Institute of Information Technology, New Delhi, India. She is an urban sociologist interested in questions of labour and its intersections with gender, caste, and technology; and popular culture. She completed her PhD from Jawaharlal Nehru University, New Delhi, India, in 2016 and has previously taught at the University of Delhi, India; Symbiosis School for Liberal Arts, Pune, India; and the Tata Institute for Social Sciences, Hyderabad, India.